Sue Dengate is a psy[...] became interested in [...] iour as a result of her own children's experiences. Since then, Sue has published five best-selling books and a DVD, spoken to thousands of people all over the world and has been twice nominated as Australian of the Year. For the last 15 years, Sue and her food scientist husband, Dr Howard Dengate, have run the Food Intolerance Network through the website www.fedup.com.au.

Also by Sue Dengate

Different Kids
The Failsafe Cookbook
Fed Up with Asthma
Fed Up with ADHD

Fed Up

Sue Dengate

Understanding how food affects your
child and what you can do about it

RANDOM HOUSE AUSTRALIA

A Random House book
Published by Random House Australia Pty Ltd
Level 3, 100 Pacific Highway, North Sydney, NSW 2060
http://www.randomhouse.com.au

First published by Random House Australia in 1998
This revised and updated edition published by Random House Australia in 2008

Addresses for companies within the Random House Group can be found at
www.randomhouse.com.au/offices.

National Library of Australia
Cataloguing-in-Publication Data

> Dengate, Sue.
> Fed up.
>
> Fully updated.
> ISBN 978 1 74166 725 7 (pbk.).
>
> 1. Children – Nutrition – Psychological aspects. 2. Human
> behaviour – Nutritional aspects. 3. Food allergy in
> children. 4. Food additives – Health aspects. I. Title.
>
> 613.2083

Illustrations by Joanne van Os
Design by Luisa Laino
Typeset by Midland Typesetters, Australia
Printed by Griffin Press, South Australia

Random House Australia uses papers that are natural, renewable and recyclable
products and made from wood grown in sustainable forests. The logging and
manufacturing processes are expected to conform to the environmental regulations
of the country of origin.

10 9 8 7 6 5 4

Acknowledgements

A huge number of people have contributed to this book in the original and revised versions. My thanks in particular go to the people listed here. My husband, Howard, for everything – advice, shopping, cooking, testing recipes, insisting on walks when I needed a break, reading the manuscript, discussing scientific method and, most of all, for encouragement and love. Rebecca, Arran, Emma and Matthew for turning out so well and permitting their story to be told. Margie Turner and Jane Moore for their invaluable help with developing and reading the manuscript.

Doctors Anne Swain, Velencia Soutter and Robert Loblay at the Royal Prince Alfred Allergy Unit in Sydney, Australia, whose elimination diet based on their research changed our lives. Dietitians Liz Beavis, Jan Branch, Joan Breakey, Marion Leggo, and Melanie Reid; nutritionist Leonie Pullinger; doctors Ross Diplock, Ken Rowe and Alan Ruben.

The hard-working local contacts and group leaders of the Food Intolerance Network, above all Kathleen Daalmeyer and Jenny Ravlic in Melbourne, Brenda Hunting, Katrina Rooke and Anne Hurman in Brisbane, Bronwyn Pollnitz in Adelaide, Jennifer Berthold in Sydney, Bernard and Marie Trudgett in Wollongong, Jan Cafearo in the UK, and Robin Fisher and Linda Beck in New Zealand; Sally Bunday from the Hyper-active Children's Support Group (UK) and Jane Hersey from the Feingold Association (USA).

The many thousands of readers who have been willing to share their triumphs, laughter and tears, especially the following people who contributed recipes or ideas to the original: Sue Armstrong, Meg Boyd, Duncan Cross (UK), Jane Figg, Robin Fisher (NZ), Linda Glasson, Chris Griffiths, Deborah Harding, Judy Horner, John Humphries, Kayleen Jenner, Lesley Joiner, Peta Jones, Kerry, Leanne McGill, Ros Mitchell, Tracy Percival, Fiona Shanahan, Gwen Sculley, Birgit Setiawan, Arlene Schar (USA), Gloria Vorenkamp;

Julia Cain, John Cody, Caro Llewellyn, Katie Stackhouse, Louise Stirling, Margaret Sullivan at Random House Australia; cartoonist Joanne van Os; librarian Christine Turner; the Australian Consumers' Association for permission to quote from *Choice*; and to the revised version – Helen Ampt, Helen Barrett, Maurean Brand, Lodzia Celeban, Stacey Cunningham, Kylie Dallow, Karen Franks, Megan Jesser, Jill Joy, Nicole Judge, Michelle Jurgens, Deanne Langford, Janelle Morrow, Michelle Page, Catherine Short, Wenzel Sinclair, Sheryl Sibley, Andra Somerville, Janelle Spicer and Susie and members of all the failsafe email groups. If your name isn't here, my apologies and please let me know.

Finally, my sincere thanks to Roberta Ivers at Random House Australia for never losing faith that this book would one day be back in your hands.

Sue Dengate
Woolgoolga, 2008

Contents

Fed Up

Introduction

When two committed adults marry, they reasonably expect to have happy and successful children. My husband and I were therefore surprised when our children encountered difficulties right from the start. Both struggled to learn skills we had found easy, and by the time our daughter was seven we were especially perplexed by her behaviour, which was sometimes charming and creative, at other times restless and defiant. We were assured by their teachers that they would 'grow out of it', but they didn't.

The mystery deepened when we considered my husband Howard's older children. By 15 his daughter was failing in half her school subjects, while his son, at 13, could not read well enough to keep up with his class. Yet their mother had a postgraduate degree, Howard was a research scientist with a doctorate, and I was a former English teacher with a degree in psychology. We had all done well at school, so I kept thinking 'Why are our children worse?'

After years of searching, we discovered a remarkable reason for their difficulties. Most of their troubles were caused by the foods they ate every day. All six members of our family experienced unexpected improvements in mood or health when we changed what we ate, based on new research. Behaviour, mood swings, intelligence and health improved. In the most dramatic case, our daughter's defiant behaviour vanished and her school marks, like her measured IQ, jumped from average to well above.

'Kids have changed,' says one primary-school principal with 34 years of teaching experience. 'You see them arriving at school angry or unhappy. They stay like that all day. I used to think it was television, or a problem with the parents. But you have to look at food. They come to school eating junk, and when you ask, "Why are you eating that?" they answer, "It's my breakfast".' In a society where rages and depression are on the increase it is worth taking seriously this observation about angry and unhappy children.

Foods can explain the irritable, restless or inattentive behaviours in much greater numbers of children than those with attention deficit hyperactivity disorders (ADHD). When an entire class of six-year-olds avoided additives for two weeks, nearly 60 per cent of their parents reported improvements in behaviour, cooperation and sleeping.

I am disappointed that most health and teaching professionals dismiss the role of food in disruptive behaviours, especially since studies have been unable to demonstrate long-term benefits of medication. By comparison, families using dietary management in the long term report significant changes. Possibly the most important improvement is self-control, which is thought to be the single biggest predictor of success in adult life.

Our magic answer

The diet that turned out to be such a miracle for us is the Elimination Diet developed by doctors Swain, Soutter and Loblay at the Royal Prince Alfred Hospital Allergy Unit in Sydney, Australia.

This book is intended as a support for families on the RPAH diet, as well as an introduction for families who don't want to do an elimination diet but would like to reduce their intake of food additives and troublesome natural food chemicals.

General information about food intolerances, along with comprehensive charts showing the content of natural salicylates, amines and glutamate in most common foods is available in *Friendly Food* by Anne Swain, Velencia Soutter & Robert Loblay, published by Murdoch Books Australia, 2004. *Friendly Food* and additional information about the RPAH Elimination Diet and challenge protocols can be obtained online via the Royal Prince Alfred Hospital (RPAH) Allergy Unit website (www.cs.nsw.gov.au/rpa/allergy).

The RPAH diet is free of additives and low in three natural chemicals called salicylates, amines and glutamates (naturally occurring flavour enhancers). Most parents are happy to avoid additives but reluctant to cut down on salicylates, which are natural pesticides in many fruits and vegetables such as tomatoes, oranges, strawberries and broccoli. However, when they see such massive improvements they are convinced. As one mother wrote:

> I cut back my five-year-old daughter's intake of fruit to about ¼ of what she normally had. Within days we saw dramatic changes. Her behaviour evened out . . . she was more sensible and obliging, less aggressive and defiant – altogether much more pleasant to live with.

Over the years I have talked to many thousands of families whose children have food-related behaviour, health or learning problems. They start off in one of three groups:
- know that foods are a problem but not sure which ones
- haven't seen a food connection
- haven't realised there is a behaviour problem.

As a mother from Italy said: 'He used to be so unbearable that I would make myself scarce; we were often at different ends of the house to get away from each other. Yet I wouldn't have said he was abnormal. Now the real, nice, intelligent person has come out. It is worth a few sacrifices, even for me!'

People have to be desperate before they will change their lifestyle, and difficult children make parents desperate.

This book is full of their stories.

Many spoke of seeking help from health professionals, only to be discouraged by comments such as 'food has nothing to do with children's behaviour', 'foods only affect a few, so it's not worth trying', 'it's too difficult, I wouldn't bother'. Some were given the wrong information, such as an out-of-date diet, or the wrong advice, such as 'don't worry about sticking to it too strictly'. Most needed more information and support. Fortunately this is changing as doctors see what diet can do, and an increasing number of experienced and supportive dietitians are available to supervise the RPAH diet – you can write to request our list at confoodnet@ozemail.com.au.

Overwhelmingly, people were amazed to find that fruits which were perceived as healthy could be the worst offenders. The mother of a nine-year-old reported: 'I had my son on a diet free of junk food and high in fruits and vegetables for four years and it turned out I was doing all the wrong things for him. Some natural foods are just as bad for him as the lollies and soft drinks.'

Parents were also surprised to find it's not the sugar in the lollies and soft drinks that cause the problems, but the additives.

Most health professionals tell us that only a small subgroup of children is affected by foods, but I do not agree. In theory, anyone can react to food chemicals if the dose is high enough, and because of the over-consumption of processed foods, these doses are increasing every year.

People assume that they will know if they react to foods because they will see an immediate reaction. This is wrong. Most food reactions are delayed. They are not a quick allergic response, but are actually the side effects of food chemicals. Everyone knows that drugs can have side effects, but few people are aware that both artificial and natural chemicals in foods can cause the same sort of reactions. And, like the side effects of drugs, the side effects of food chemicals are often misinterpreted.

Thirty years of change

Food scientists estimate that it takes 30 years to notice the effects of a national change in diet. There have been enormous changes in Australia in the last 30 years and these changes are continuing ever more rapidly due to globalisation. Today, party foods have become everyday foods and additives that did not even exist thirty years ago are eaten frequently. The use of additives has crept up on us. In 2007, a British survey found that people consumed up to 50 additives per day but underestimated their additive intake. The average was 20 additives per day overall and 19 additives per day for people who ate home-cooked foods. Whereas people living in subsistence villages don't eat *any* additives.

Children and adults are affected in varying degrees by the changes in our diet, but these effects are mostly unrecognised or ignored. Hyperactive children are just the tip of the iceberg. Irritability has increased in our society as a whole. Considering irritability and restlessness have been found to be the main behavioural effects of foods, it seems likely that far more people are affected by these major changes in diet than is recognised.

Since the 1960s, humans have been exposed to unprecedented quantities of industrial and agricultural chemicals that can provoke sensitivity to food chemicals. It is even possible that behavioural changes and learning disabilities due to chemical exposure can be passed on to the next generation. Changes in behaviour and learning ability are the early signs of chemical toxicity (see Notes), yet food chemicals are not tested for their effects on children's behaviour or learning before approval. In fact, although it is hard to believe, such chemicals are not systematically tested for their effects on children at all before approval.

To protect our children and ourselves, and to prevent a national decline in behaviour and learning standards, it makes sense to avoid the chemicals that are affecting us. Irritable, restless or inattentive behaviour, sleep disturbance, anxiety, depression, eczema, other itchy skin rashes, migraines, recurrent headaches, stomach discomfort, bloating, diarrhoea, reflux, colic, urinary urgency and asthma are some of the symptoms that can be caused or aggravated by common foods. If you have any of the above problems or if you have ever seen, even once, a reaction to foods such as cordial, cola, alcoholic drinks, chocolate, savoury snack foods or takeaways, then it is worth taking food chemicals seriously. Many people who are affected have never noticed a food reaction.

Since the first edition of *Fed Up* was published in 1998, every day I have heard from grateful parents whose lives have been transformed like ours. One of the first ever *Fed Up* readers, whose 'badly behaved, sullen, hyperactive and hot-tempered' daughter improved on failsafe, wrote with an update: 'nearly a decade on I am happy to say that the young lady who interviewed you by phone for her radio program is the very same child who used to sit under a table snarling and spitting after eating a packet of chips.'

To find out how foods affect people, why food reactions are so difficult to identify, which foods are likely to cause problems, and how to manage the side effects of foods, please read on . . .

Q. What does *failsafe* mean?

A. It's a kind of dyslexic acronym meaning **f**ree of **a**dditives, and **l**ow **i**n **s**alicylates, **a**nimes and **f**lavour **e**nhancers.

1

Sleeping Beauty

My first baby, Rebecca, was not a good sleeper and her sleep-lessness dominated our lives. Unless she fell asleep at the breast, she had to be rocked, walked in a stroller or taken for a drive. Daytime naps were brief, night-time waking was frequent. The first time Rebecca ever fell asleep by herself, at the age of ten months, we were so alarmed by the sight of her lying motionless, eyes closed, that we called a doctor.

'This child is asleep,' he said, after a quick look, no doubt thinking we were very strange. We can laugh about it now, but living with a child who couldn't go to sleep was no joke. Before our marriage I had spent seven months trekking in the mountains of Nepal, unthinkingly observing the mothers breastfeeding, carrying and sleeping with their babies. These were the role models I remembered, so that's what I did, but it seemed to me their babies had been much more settled than mine.

There were other problems, too. As she grew older, Rebecca became very difficult. She grew into the terrible twos and never came out again. There were episodes of charm and sunshine, but these were interspersed with a child whose favourite word was 'no', who was irritable and defiant, who struggled at school despite glimpses of intelligence, and did not do well socially. Rebecca had what is now described as oppositional defiance. Symptoms include frequent temper outbursts, arguing, refusing requests or defying rules, deliberately annoying others, blaming others, being touchy and easily annoyed, angry and resentful.

For 11 distressing years we discussed our daughter with doctors, teachers, psychologists, dietitians and alternative practitioners. Altogether we tried nearly 30 different treatments including counselling, behaviour management, herbal and homeopathic remedies, megavitamins, motor sensory programs, educational kinesiology, tutoring, stimulant medication and various diets.

Nearly everything we tried helped, but it wasn't enough. The only treatment that made Rebecca *worse* was the 'healthy' diet with heaps of extra fruit and vegetables, as recommended by a dietitian. Finally, we discovered a truly effective solution. It was a low salicylate elimination diet. The symptoms of Rebecca's so-called disorder were actually the side effects of foods she ate every day.

When we changed what Rebecca ate, her oppositional defiance stopped. Of course, there were established patterns of behaviour too, and we had to change those by using principles of behaviour management such as positivity and consistency. Oppositional defiance can occur alone or together with attention deficit hyperactivity disorder, another diagnosis of Rebecca's. This too improved dramatically with a change in foods.

The Prickly Princess

We are not the only family to experience a dramatic change in a child's behaviour due to foods. Over the years I have heard the same story many times. One mother sent me this entertaining description of similar problems with her own daughter:

> When she was good she could only be described as an angel, but when she was bad she was unbelievably impossible. Tantrums that made everyone sit up and take notice had the desired effect of making sure that no one crossed her intentionally. Hence our pet name for her was 'The Prickly Princess'. We really believed that we had a major problem on our hands, and suddenly the clever parents were looking anything but clever in bringing up good children.
>
> When we changed what we ate we really did see dramatic changes in behaviour, not angels, but manageable. My husband actually enjoyed coming home before the kids were in bed, as there was peace and harmony in the house and not a tense, electrified atmosphere that we had all but accepted as our lot in life.
>
> After a few months we were also delighted to learn of remarkable changes in behaviour and school performance of our nephews, and my brother-in-law had discovered a new non-moody non-abrasive self, as a result of the elimination diet in their family.

Our changing food

During the first 11 years of Rebecca's life, our ideas about foods had evolved against the backdrop of a rapidly changing food supply. When she was born in New Zealand in the 1980s, people still ate mostly traditional foods in their own homes, processed food was just starting to become popular and McDonald's was years away. I had noticed Rebecca's restlessness when I ate fruit while breastfeeding, but didn't realise I was also eating an artificial colour nearly every day in a common food I perceived as healthy.

Moving to Australia when Rebecca was two, we were surprised to find commercial sweets, ice-creams and takeaways that we had regarded as party foods in New Zealand were everyday foods for Australian children. Two years later we noticed that she had a reaction to orange food colouring after a particularly garish preschool birthday cake. Gradually we started reducing artificial colours, and by the time we moved to tropical Darwin in the Northern Territory when she was six, we were avoiding most additives and sugar as well.

Rebecca would crave junk food, especially sugar. She was like an addict and her strongest memories were all related to food, such as where she had eaten a particular lolly or doughnut. In cafés she ate sugar straight from the packet and saved some to hoard at home. We thought that Rebecca seemed to react to sugar with a range of symptoms: sugar-craving or refusal to eat, defiance, anxiety, panic attacks and occasional exercise-induced 'hypos' of lethargy and confusion to the point of collapse, similar to a diabetic condition. On a few occasions she became irrational and incoherent. We followed recommendations for hypoglycemics, avoiding sugar and eating small, frequent, balanced meals. When she did experience a hypo, we found that, like a diabetic, she improved quickly with a spoonful of sugar.

Eventually I convinced our paediatrician that we had a real problem. Rebecca's suspected hypoglycemia was investigated during a 24-hour, water-only fast with regular blood tests in hospital. At first she was exceptionally rude and defiant, needing several nurses to hold her down while inserting a cannula for taking blood. The hospital doctor obviously thought it was my fault as a mother and infuriated me by giving me a patronising lecture about behaviour management.

However, Rebecca's blood sugar readings were found to be perfectly normal. By the end of the 24 hours, so was Rebecca. She had become a calm, cooperative, agreeable and focused child. Soon after finishing the pizza we had promised as a reward for going to hospital, she was back to her old self again.

Only half-joking, I told our paediatrician, 'We've discovered the right diet for her – water only!'

The big answer

The remarkable change in Rebecca encouraged the paediatrician to take her food reactions seriously and our whole family began the RPAH elimination diet, supervised by a dietitian. Within days, Rebecca started improving and after a few weeks she was the settled, respectful, happy child we had seen on the water-only diet. Each night she fell asleep soon after going to bed. 'I wish we'd done this earlier!' I thought. We could have saved ourselves so much anguish.

The next step of the elimination diet is to find out exactly which foods and food chemicals have been causing the problems. So we started reintroducing one group of foods at a time for about a week each, according to a schedule from our dietitian. These food challenges showed whether Rebecca was affected or not.

We discovered that Rebecca reacted, as we already thought, to food additives and dairy foods. She wasn't affected by natural chemicals called amines, so we could add foods such as bananas, tinned fish and chocolate back into her diet. The big surprise was her reaction to salicylates. Salicylates occur naturally in varying amounts in most fruit and some vegetables. This explained many of Rebecca's problems because all her favourite foods had high levels of salicylates – strawberries, kiwifruit, grapes, mandarins, oranges, canned pineapple, olives, broccoli, pizza and tomato-based spaghetti sauce.

'Sugar highs' – NOT!

On the other hand, after all those years of thinking sugar was a problem, reintroduction of sugar produced no reaction at all. As it turns out, salicylates and/or additives can cause all the symptoms we had been blaming on sugar, from overactivity, defiance and insomnia to the white-faced weak and shaky feeling of low blood sugar. There is even a medical condition known as salicylate-induced hypoglycemia. We now know that if Rebecca avoids additives and salicylates, she can eat unlimited amounts of sugar with no effect. It is common for parents to wrongly blame sugar for children's behaviour, as this failsafe mother reported: 'I recently went to a failsafe kids' party. The other parents commented how well-behaved all the children were, without the 'sugar high' normally seen at parties. They were very surprised when told the foods did contain sugar but were additive-free and low in salicylates.'

How do you know if you're affected by salicylates?

People have so much trouble believing that fruit might be bad for them that the usual response to Rebecca's story is 'I'm glad I don't react to salicylates.' How do you know? That's what I said when I first heard about salicylates, and it took me six years to take them seriously, yet when we did our elimination diet, everyone in the family reacted to salicylates in different ways. We had never made the connection before because salicylates are eaten many times every day. Yet salicylates are a common cause of food reactions. The only way to find out whether you are affected by salicylates in daily foods, drinks, medications and perfumed products is by reducing your exposure for a few weeks to see if there are any positive changes in your health, mood, energy levels or ability to think clearly.

Changes vary from person to person. Over the years I have heard of many, many improvements in people's lives.

Remember the mother from Italy described in the introduction, who wouldn't have said her son was 'abnormal'? Readers of *Different Kids* will remember this same mother saying: 'What is all this talk about hyperactivity? My sister talks about it too. She says her son has it. That's ridiculous. They can't all have it. None of the children in Italy have it. I've never heard of it.'

Seven years later, concerned about her 14-year-old son's lack of concentration at school, this mother and her son tried the elimination diet and were amazed to observe the effects of salicylates. Like me, she had taken many years to accept that 'healthy' foods like fruit and vegetables could cause as many problems as artificial additives.

The two Rebeccas

When we started our elimination diet, our idea was to get through it as soon as possible. 'When can we have pizzas again?' asked the children.

At first we thought we could get away with staying failsafe during the week and breaking out on the weekends, but when we did that we found Rebecca changed back to the way she used to be. So we tried cooking our own pizzas and stuck strictly to failsafe during the school term. After about 18 months, Rebecca chose not to break her diet at all. She preferred to be happy and in control of her life.

By that time, I had learned that I really had two daughters: Rebecca-before-diet and Rebecca-after-diet. I would have liked Rebecca-after-diet to have been my daughter from birth.

As a result of failsafe eating, all Rebecca's symptoms of oppositional defiant disorder melted away. Symptoms of attention deficit disorder such as restlessness, impulsiveness and inattention improved so much that they were rarely a problem and could be managed by various strategies such as checklists to overcome short-term memory problems. After we changed our foods, we started to receive comments like this one from a waitress: 'I remember you, you've been here before. Your children drink water and they are so well-behaved. Most kids demand cola and their behaviour is dreadful.'

Rebecca's lifelong struggle to get to sleep was over, and her intelligence improved too. Tests showed that her measured IQ rose an extraordinary 24 points when we got the diet right.

In a UK study, Professor Jim Stevenson tested the IQs of identical twins before and after eating an additive-free diet or their usual diet. After two weeks, the additive-free twin's IQ had risen by 15 per cent (see Notes).

In the past, we had spent large amounts of time, effort and money on tutoring, particularly in maths, the subject in which Rebecca had appeared to be most learning disabled, unteachable in fact. At one after-school maths coaching center, a tutor gently suggested we were wasting our money when Rebecca failed to improve at all after an entire year of classes. She could recite a multiplication table after a solid coaching session, only to have no memory of it the next day. Within six months of starting her diet she caught up to grade level with very little help.

'How did you do that?' I asked, when I realised she had learned her multiplication tables.

'I knew I needed them. I found them written on the back of the textbook, so I memorised them,' she replied.

Another major area of concern was Rebecca's poor co-ordination. When I told a physiotherapist I was enrolling her in a ballet class at age 6, he exclaimed, 'Your daughter will never do ballet!' After diet, the improvement in her coordination enabled her to learn the skills she had missed before, and ultimately led to her dancing major roles in a regional ballet company. It was the same with music lessons. Rebecca-before-diet had dropped piano lessons at the age of seven as she had seemed to have little aptitude and simply could not learn to read music. When Rebecca-after-diet started again, she taught herself to read music and enjoyed the piano.

Self-control

One of the benefits of failsafe eating we noticed was the marked improvement in Rebecca's self-control. This too had been reported by mothers of children on elimination diets since the 1970s. There is an interesting study about self-control in which four-year-olds were left alone with a marsh-mallow after being told they could eat the marshmallow immediately, or have two marshmallows if they waited 20 minutes. Years later, when the children turned 18, researchers found that those who waited for their two marshmallows at age four were more socially competent, personally effective and academically successful than the immediate marshmallow eaters. As a predictor of success, the marshmallow test was found to be twice as useful as IQ test scores. Researchers concluded that for success in life it is more important to teach children self-control than academic subjects. 'I would have eaten the marshmallow straight away, because I wasn't on the diet then,' said Rebecca. 'But if I had been on the diet when I was four, I would have waited.'

Dark times

When Rebecca started high school, we felt the worst was behind us and were – undeservedly, as it turned out – optimistic about the future. A few months into the school year, my mother died unexpectedly. This was a sad time for me as we had become especially close since my father had been killed in a car accident. Mum had been supportive of our diet, unlike the grandparental diet sabotage I've heard about from so many others.

Not long afterwards we set off as a family to hike what must be one of the world's best wilderness walks. Starting from the spectacular Katherine Gorge, we walked 70 kilometres in five days across stony desert to deep gorges, waterfalls, monsoonal rainforest and water holes with sandy beaches, camping at night under a sky full of stars. With us was a high-school teacher who has been bushwalking for over 30 years. 'I've been hiking with a lot of high-school students,' she commented, 'and Rebecca is one of the strongest walkers I've seen.' None of us could have foreseen what would happen next.

First, Rebecca caught mycoplasma pneumonia – so-called 'walking pneumonia' because it is not serious enough to cause hospitalisation. While she was struggling to recover from that, her appendix ruptured. She reacted badly to post-operative antibiotic medication and threw up constantly for four days, losing weight she didn't need to lose. When the antibiotics stopped, so did the nausea, but she was very tired. 'She looks like the sleeping beauty,' commented a nurse. With her long dark hair spread out on the pillow, she did indeed look like the sleeping princess. We did not know how prophetic these words were to be.

After a month at home, Rebecca returned to school only to come down a week later with what we thought was a bad flu. After another week off she struggled back to school but

was sent home again a few days later with a very high temperature and swollen glands. Instead of recovering, Rebecca's condition worsened. Soon she was sleeping 16 hours a day and feeling exhausted the rest of the time. Eventually she was diagnosed with chronic fatigue syndrome (CFS). In a bizarre twist of fate, the child whose early life was dominated by her inability to sleep had become a teenager who spent all her time either sleeping or feeling tired.

Researchers now suggest that mycoplasma pneumonia or other flu-like illnesses often precede chronic fatigue syndrome, which was probably aggravated by the illness, antibiotics and stress surrounding her appendectomy. There's also a question about previous chemical exposure. In early pregnancy I had been horrified to find an empty drum of the agricultural chemical Tordon in the river where we had been trout fishing and eating our catch – Tordon was one of the chemicals used as a defoliant during the Vietnam War and exposure to these chemical defoliants has been suggested as a cause of the high rates of illness among Vietnam veterans. In another incident, when Rebecca was four, we were caught for about 20 minutes in a cloud of herbicide from crop spraying while out walking in the countryside. We will never know if there is a link between Rebecca's chemical sensitivity and these experiences.

Although Rebecca was already eating failsafe, during the

time she had CFS she became more sensitive to chemicals like the smell of household cleaners. It became even more important for her to stick to her diet as her symptoms – debilitating fatigue, foggy brain, muscle aches and pains, headaches, unrefreshing sleep and depression – worsened with the smallest mistake. As well as diet, we tried management strategies, mostly rest, rest and more rest, but also sleep management, exercise, sunshine, and a protein powder supplement (see Notes).

Over the years, I have heard from many people with chronic fatigue whose condition has improved when they changed what they ate. A woman whose husband had CFS for 12 years wrote after one month of failsafe eating:

He sleeps better and is generally having more good days than bad. When he cheated – not on purpose – by having 'junk' food, he suffered for it the next few days, not sleeping properly, and with the usual general aching and unwellness.

Seven months later, she wrote again:

I just wanted to let you know that we are still following the diet, although not as rigidly. After having tried so many doctors, remedies, medicines and alternatives – at high cost emotionally and financially, when nothing worked – I can't believe how a simple diet change has made a huge difference to his and our quality of life.

The wasted years

Rebecca recovered from chronic fatigue syndrome in two and a half years. Having missed most of junior high school, she went to senior college and finished the final two years of school at the same time as her former classmates. It was the first time we had had a chance to see exactly what the diet could do for her at high school. Despite missing so much schooling, she achieved her best grades ever, including an A in advanced maths – the very subject she had been totally unable to grasp previously. She gained a tertiary entrance rank that opened many doors for her, an outcome that would have been unthinkable before failsafe eating.

Obviously we would have preferred Rebecca not to have chronic fatigue, but it is one of those unfortunate events that do occur in life. However, the effects of food are different – they *are* avoidable. Rebecca has described her life before diet as 'all those wasted years'.

2
Landing on their feet

Our son Arran was born when Rebecca was three. He turned out to be at least as food sensitive as Rebecca, although Arran reacted to food chemicals with health rather than behavioural problems. Mothers who come to my talks often say, 'I came because of my hyperactive son but now I realise my other child is sensitive too.' Food intolerance in quiet children can be overlooked because they are so easy to live with.

Looking back, I can see there were many missed signs of food intolerance with Arran. Breastfed babies can have nappy rash, hives, other rashes, reflux, colic, sleep disturbance or restlessness due to food chemicals in the mother's diet passing through her milk. Arran was a fussy feeder, pulling away and throwing up frequently during feeding. With help from breast-feeding counsellors I learned to manage, but it would have been better if they had told me about food intolerance. More than twenty years later, food sensitivity is still not common knowledge, yet it would have been so much easier for us to do the full elimination diet right at the start.

Symptoms change with age, so just when we thought Arran had grown out of one problem, another would arise – from rashes and ear infections to stomach aches, headaches, asthma and, later on, foggy brain. I'm sure Arran's life would have been more difficult if we hadn't cut out additives so early. I am convinced that there are many more children like him who do not have behaviour problems but whose quality of life is diminished by the effects of foods.

Intolerance is often triggered by illness or medical interventions. Arran's sensitivity worsened after his three-month vaccinations (see my position on immunisation on p. 146) and a gastric bug at ten months. After that, constant low-grade diarrhoea and slow weight gain became a problem serious enough for a doctor to suspect coeliac disease. This is an intolerance to gluten in wheat and other grains that can result in malabsorption of food and consequent malnutrition. Tests showed that he wasn't coeliac, but we didn't discover exactly which foods affected him until we did our elimination diet for Rebecca.

Other failsafe mothers have similar stories of children tested for coeliac disease. If the result is negative, the doctor has no more suggestions to offer. One mother explained:

> He's so small for his age that some people comment on it. You can see him cringe. We went to a dietitian once about his weight but she recommended lots of milkshakes and milk-based multi-vitamin powder to build him up, and his diarrhoea got much worse. He can't concentrate in class, jumps around all the time, can't sit still and he's having problems with schoolwork. He drinks a lot of cola and eats a lot of lollies.

Everything in this family's history – migraines, asthma, problems with milk as a baby – pointed to the side effects of foods. Yet this mother had to contact me to hear about an elimination diet that worked. By then her son was 14, which is the worst age to try a restricted diet. However, if given a chance to see how foods affect them, children with stomach aches and other uncomfortable symptoms will often take full responsibility for their own foods because they like to feel well.

Nose and throat problems

Arran was eight when we embarked on the RPAH elimination diet (see p. 162) and it turned out to be as much of a miracle for him as it was for Rebecca.

One of the first benefits we noticed was that his frequent nosebleeds stopped. Nosebleeds or a stuffy or runny nose, also known as rhinitis – even if related to pollen and other environmental allergies – can be aggravated by foods, and Arran and I both discovered ours was related to dairy products. Similarly, an attention deficit classmate of Arran's was taking medication for his rhinitis, which was so bad that he couldn't breathe or talk properly. When this boy eliminated milk as the last stage of going failsafe, both his behaviour and rhinitis improved dramatically. His mother explained: 'Our paediatrician was really surprised. He said he could tell the rhinitis was better, because the hairs in his nose have grown back.'

Chronic throat-clearing, caused by a build-up of mucus in the back of the throat, can also be related to diet. This can be very aggravating for listeners, as this mother describes: 'My husband used to clear his throat all the time. I thought it was a habit. It used to drive me mad, and I felt like telling him to shut up. Then when the kids went on this diet we did too, and I realised the other day I haven't heard him do it for a while.'

Hating school

Before we started our elimination diet, Arran hated school and did little schoolwork. He often complained of headaches and stomach aches and one doctor suggested his complaints were an attempt to avoid school. However, anyone who has regular headaches knows that you might be able to get through work or a social occasion and even forget the headache for a while if you are enjoying yourself, but ultimately it is there, making you tired, irritable and miserable. Experts now realise that even babies and young children can have migraines but are unable to explain their symptoms. Food challenges showed Arran's symptoms were related to amines, salicylates, additives, dairy foods and, to a lesser extent, wheat. We had seen a few episodes of colouring-related hyperactivity when he was young. If Arran had ever eaten the average Australian diet, including colours and fast food, he might possibly have displayed enough symptoms to be mistakenly diagnosed with the inattentive-type attention deficit hyperactivity disorder.

Halfway through his first year at school, we moved Arran and then Rebecca to a private parent-run primary school with a guaranteed maximum of 20 children per class, where discipline was based on respect and self-esteem was emphasised. Although this school wasn't ideal – we really needed a school that supported failsafe eating – it worked better than any of the state schools we had tried because our children were treated as individuals.

Giftedness

Parents often complain to me that their children are behaving badly because they are gifted children who are too bored to achieve. Like the father whose 12-year-old son had thrown a chair at his teacher during a temper outburst: 'There's nothing

wrong with my son. He's very bright, and he's bored. If the teacher made the lessons more interesting he'd be all right.'

While this is a possibility, having investigated all that ourselves I would recommend looking at foods first, before blaming boring teachers for your child's behaviour.

One mother wrote:

> Although our son is a bright boy, often selected for gifted programs at school, his behaviour was atrocious (severe temper, disruptive, tearful, moody, silly noises, etc.). Since starting failsafe he has had a huge turnaround. He is very proud of his new self and is just starting to believe in his own potential – potential we, as his parents, always knew he had.

In our case, Arran started enjoying school soon after going failsafe, although handwriting problems related to low muscle tone in his hands held him back. It wasn't until he did home-schooling distance-education lessons at age 14 – when he reached the end of the private school – that he discovered he could achieve high marks.

Foggy brain

It is much more difficult to see the effect of foods on learning than on health or behaviour. You need to score similar types of homework or a short reading exercise every night during the food challenges to see any change in the way your children manage the exercise. Children themselves have no idea how they are affected. Arran would say 'school was hard this week' or 'school was easier this week', depending on what he was eating, but it wasn't until the end-of-semester report cards that we could really see a difference.

It was easy for us to accept we had to avoid salicylates, amines and additives that caused stomach aches, headaches or sleep disturbance, but it took us years to realise that avoiding milk for the obvious symptom of nasal congestion was not enough to prevent the more subtle effects of inattention. Unless Arran avoided all dairy products – even small amounts of yoghurt and ice-cream – learning delays we couldn't see would build up during the term and he would get Cs instead of As. We were discovering that some food reactions would be obvious almost immediately. Others, however – and just enough to make life difficult – would build up over time.

One mother wrote about her son: 'There was no reaction to the salicylate challenge except that he couldn't do his homework', implying this was too trivial a reason to avoid salicylates. But ability to do schoolwork is important because your final school mark accompanies you through life and can determine the opportunities that will be available to you. Thus 'foggy brain' must be the ultimate irony: people eating food chemicals that make them foggy-brained are too foggy-brained to understand they shouldn't be eating them.

Could-do-better-if-they-tried

Mothers are most likely to try the elimination diet for difficult children, but quiet children failing to reach their potential are just as handicapped. Like this six-year-old whose mother originally complained that he was dreamy, inattentive, not thinking well, slow with putting words into actions, easily distracted, had to be told things many times, and was failing to achieve at school:

After about two weeks [on the elimination diet], we suddenly noticed – James was a different child. He was interested, inter-active, motivated, talking more, spontaneous, happy to do things, had received a good note home from school, his writing and drawings improved markedly and his teacher was very pleased with his behaviour and school work. James was more loving towards us and less emotional over silly little things. In fact, the whole family felt better – we were sleeping more soundly and woke up brighter and a little earlier. When we challenged salicy-lates, after four days James came home, had a note of how he had been inattentive in class again and just sat down and cried. 'I don't want to be on these salicylates any more – I just want to be back on the good food.' Thus we abandoned salicylates forever . . . James is very good at saying the word 'salicylates' – they are his number one enemy!! It took about a week to clean him out again and now he is back to being a happy, attentive, thinking child again.

Fights between siblings

Parents frequently complain that their children fight, dismissing it as 'but that's normal, isn't it?' When they try an elimination diet, they are surprised to find their children play cooperatively together. I noticed early on that raised voices and the sounds of a fight usually indicated a food mistake by Rebecca, so for Arran a benefit of our family going failsafe was that due to the improvement in his sister, they became good friends.

Managing the diet

At primary school Arran had a failsafe friend, and it was good to see them together because they were so matter-of-fact about what they had to avoid. I asked the friend how he felt about being failsafe.

'It's okay,' he said.

'Have you noticed any difference?'

'Oh yes!' he replied. 'Before I started on it, I was bottom of the class in maths. Now I'm top.'

On outings and holidays, we preferred to camp, cater for ourselves or travel to nearby Indonesia, where at that time traditional unprocessed foods were still available. Most of the time, Arran was highly motivated to stick to his diet, but sometimes, especially in junior high school, he would decide to eat whatever he wanted at a party. The next day the dark circles under his eyes would be back and he would be very quiet. We had noticed that these circles appeared when he was not failsafe.

While my children lived at home as teenagers I made them a standing offer. If they were visiting friends and needed a failsafe takeaway, I would deliver a lamb stew on rice (see Irish stew – p. 238) or similar, hot, ready to eat and packaged with a spoon in a takeaway foil container, direct to the door with no questions asked – just like a pizza delivery person. All they had to do was phone. Though they rarely took advantage of this offer – more often they would take it with them and heat it up in the microwave – I think knowing it was available helped them to manage.

Another trick that Arran liked in senior college was to take home-cooked muffins (p. 216) in his lunchbox to share with his friends. I was amazed to find I had a reputation as a great cook – I'm not, I hate cooking and always choose easy recipes. Sometimes he would even request home-cooked double choc muffins (p. 217) that his friends loved, even though he couldn't eat them himself due to the amines in the chocolate. While he was at university we would send occasional cakes (Fete, p. 285, or sticky gingerbread, p. 297), especially at exam time. Arran's view: 'I'm not worried about food intolerance. I can live with it.'

The older children

Howard's older children were the result of a secret arrangement between Howard and a childless couple in New Zealand, where Howard and I had lived until Rebecca was two. As agreed, they were growing up unknown to us. But the couple split up and – in an emotional meeting for all of us – the children met Howard as their biological donor father for the first time when Matthew was 12 and Emma was 14.

We were amazed to find that Matthew and Emma were experiencing similar kinds of health, learning and behaviour problems as our children, despite growing up in a different country with a completely different environment.

Matthew's year

Right from our first meeting it seemed to us that Matthew wanted to be with us, so we asked him if he would like to live with us for a year and he jumped at the chance. At that time we had no idea what we were taking on, and when Matthew came to live with us in Darwin he was a virtual stranger.

Although he was in his final year of primary school, Matthew had reading difficulties that made his chance of success in high school very small. This problem has turned out to be much more common than I would have thought – by definition, people who have problems with printed materials encountered in everyday life are regarded as 'functionally illiterate', with a NSW survey showing an extraordinary 35 per cent of 14-year-old boys in this category.

As it is not socially acceptable to be a poor reader, Matthew had found a number of ways of covering up his difficulty. In class and at home he used endless delaying tactics. If those failed, he gave me a polite smile and asked nicely, 'I don't understand this question. Can you help me?' He seemed unable to finish anything, and was lacking in ambition or motivation.

It was only when I started a literacy program with Matthew that I fully realised the extent of his problems. Tutoring him every night of the week, I found it easier to evaluate his performance.

On joining our family, Matthew adopted our eating habits. Although at that time we were not yet sticking strictly to failsafe, Matthew's results surprised everyone. If he ate take-aways, he was unable to concentrate and generally had some kind of accident. If he stuck to failsafe, he progressed. Throughout the year, Matthew became more and more determined to succeed, working harder and learning more. He also worked hard at martial arts, enjoyed trips to the bush and learned social skills. By the end of the year, he had overcome delays of nearly four years in spelling and more than two years in reading to catch up to his grade level – an improvement that had previously been considered impossible by the school counsellor – and was awarded one of the two class prizes for his year, an extraordinary achievement.

Emma

The eldest of Howard's children, Emma was 14 when we first met her. It didn't take us long to realise that Emma shared Rebecca's oppositional defiance. While the rest of us drank soda water, Emma ordered colas, insisting that 'food doesn't affect me'.

Although she was obviously bright, Emma was just failing in half her subjects and just passing the others. She was living with her father in New Zealand, and if she wanted to go to a late party and turn up at school the next day with a hangover, she did. At the time, we felt we must accept Emma uncritically. She was angry about our invitation to Matthew, feeling we had 'stolen her brother', but after a few months she wrote to say it was obviously the right decision because he seemed so much happier.

Emma's change in attitude did not prepare us for what happened on Matthew's return when she saw the huge changes in his confidence and personal development. As she said, 'He went away being so unintelligent and came back being rather above average.' As a result, she made her own decision to try failsafe. The change was as remarkable in her as it had been in the others. In fifth form she had been averaging 50 per cent. After changing foods at the beginning of sixth form, her marks leapt to between 60 and 96 per cent. 'I didn't even know I had the potential to do well at school,' she commented. Moving back in with her mother meant accepting boundaries about late nights and being supported in her efforts to eat differently.

Emma noticed her handwriting became neater, that she slept much better and her relationships improved, particularly with Matthew. They stopped their frequent fighting. As a vegetarian, Emma initially refused to give up salicylates, but eighteen months later, when her mother suggested a few weeks' trial of low salicylates, the results were so dramatic that Emma was convinced.

Where are they now?

All four children are grown up now, so to protect their privacy the story stops here. It's enough to say that they all did well at university and are happy and productive. As one of my friends commented, 'Matthew has landed on his feet'. They all have.

They all continue to watch what they eat, and since women are generally more sensitive than men, it makes sense that Emma and Rebecca are particularly strict. Vegetarians have the hardest time adapting to failsafe, so Emma initially had a more difficult task than the rest of us, although after a while she added chicken to her diet for variety, especially when eating out. She has developed a cooking style that she seems to be able to use wherever she is, even travelling.

While at university, Rebecca and Arran chose residential halls with cooking facilities rather than catered meals. They seem to have worked out how to break their diets occasionally when they can control the consequences, for instance during holidays, but have a repertoire of alternatives – such as cooking an omelette for themselves while their friends order in pizza.

The increase in the numbers of people with known allergies, food sensitivities, coeliac disease, diabetes and obesity is making it easier for our children all the time. 'We're not the only ones,' they say. 'In any group there are always other people who want to avoid certain foods for different reasons.' And they all add: 'I know it's food "intolerance", not "allergy" – but people are much more understanding if you say it's allergy . . .'

Children – and adults – like to do well, and they like to be liked. They deserve the opportunity to see what failsafe eating can do for them. When you give children a choice – as we have seen in our and other failsafe families – they generally continue to eat foods that allowed them to do well. Which group is deprived: children who choose to avoid certain foods, or children whose potential is slowly eroded by the effects of what they eat on their health, intelligence and behaviour?

3

Adults too

Adults can be affected by food chemicals too, although they usually don't see it. Symptoms vary and adults who try diet for their children's behaviour generally take time to realise that they themselves can be affected. The mother of an aggressive two-year-old wrote 'since learning about his diet, I have started to investigate mine' and eventually discovered that the irritable bowel symptoms she had suffered for years were related to the very same foods that affected her son's behaviour.

Real men go failsafe

The cattlemen and women of northern Australia must be some of the toughest people in the world as they live for extended periods in isolated stock camps, battling extremes of heat, dust, flies and wild cattle. One cattleman followed the elimination diet for problems caused by exposure to chemicals used in poisoning tree-stumps. 'The dietitian told me it would cure me, as long as I stuck to it. She said that most people couldn't stick to it,' he said. 'I told her, I'm used to living for months at a time on beef and bread in stock camps. Hell, I can stick to it!' And he did. After six months, his problems were gone.

This is unusual. Most of the women I meet stick to the diet well, but it is the opposite with men. I always suggest that the whole family does the elimination diet, both to support the child and because other family members usually improve too in different ways. Fathers generally refuse to do this, although the most supportive of them will agree to eat failsafe at home and whatever they like when out.

Howard

We made the decision to avoid all artificial colours and some preservatives in our diet when Rebecca was five. Most consumers don't realise they are affected by additives until they reduce their intake and that is what happened to Howard. Thinking that we were avoiding additives only for Rebecca, he ate a bun with pink icing at work and was surprised how fidgety he felt during the next meeting. After that, he was motivated to avoid additives for himself too. He also noticed on our lower-additive diet that his legs no longer twitched while he was trying to go to sleep. This condition is called restless legs syndrome (RLS) and many of the adults in our network have described what it feels like: 'sort of itchy', 'crawly', 'jumpy', 'I can't keep still, I have to keep moving my legs'. I wonder how long it will take medical experts to realise that this new syndrome, like many others, is aggravated by chemicals in foods and medications.

Years later, when we started our strict elimination diet, Howard refused to do it with us. He was supportive, but insisted, 'It's too hard for me to do it because of work. I'll wait until I see what Rebecca reacts to. I know I'll be the same.' He was right, although he had a greater tolerance to salicylates, which is what you would expect. The dose of salicylates in an apple, for example, will obviously have a greater effect on a person with a lower body weight.

At first Howard ate failsafe during the week and splurged

on the weekend. After a while, I made a request: 'Weekends are the times we spend together. I would prefer to be sharing the good quality time that you are having during the week too.' I was surprised at the difference from small changes, such as switching from wine to whisky, and other adults have reported the same. Eventually Howard settled into a routine of staying failsafe at home and making the safest choices he could while on business trips.

As happens with many adults, Howard had been identified with attention deficit as a result of his child's diagnosis. However, he refuses to regard attention deficit as a disorder, and considers that any negative symptoms are due to food intolerance. He has observed that in situations requiring lateral thinking, creativity, or in times of crisis, people with so-called attention deficit come into their own. Howard says the people who consider attention deficit a disorder have got it wrong: 'All you non-attention-deficit people are so boringly focused.' He is sceptical of the claim that attention deficit is due to an inborn lack of brain chemicals requiring medication, as suggested by many doctors.

Our own experience with stimulant medication was less than impressive. Doctors were recommending medication for Rebecca, but we thought we'd rather try it out on an adult first. So, during a particularly stressful period at work, Howard started a month's trial of a stimulant drug commonly pre-scribed for ADHD. At first he enjoyed the benefits of being able to concentrate in boring meetings but the trial came to an abrupt end during a business trip to Indonesia. When he opened his mouth to talk to a taxi driver, he was horrified to find he couldn't remember any Indonesian. As soon as he stopped the medication his previous fluency returned. We later found it was due to a condition called state-dependent learning, which means that whatever is learned in a certain state – while either medication-free or on medication – is better remembered in the same state. So the language he had learned without medication could only be remembered without medication. The reverse can also be true. One family spent a year having their son tutored in maths, only to find that when he stopped medication due to growth problems he seemed to lose all he had learned.

Food, behaviour and the brain

Researchers measured brain electrical activity in ADHD children. They found that when the children ate foods known to trigger their behaviour problems, there was a significant increase in brainwave activity in certain areas of the brain. These areas are associated with control of behaviour, language and emotion (see Notes).

I have found that most people with ADHD will benefit from a change of diet. I have also seen families benefit from medication but I would prefer families to be offered a trial of diet first. Medication can seem to be a miracle in the short term, but after twelve months, or in high school – when it is more difficult to change diet – users often begin to notice that not all their problems have been solved. There are also side effects that can lock the users into what one psychologist called 'the medication merry-go-round', where people think the only answer to their problems will be more or a different medication.

I understand that many children are unable to change their diet due to lack of support. In one sad call, a young girl phoned about her little brother who wanted to use diet instead of medication because the medication made him feel sick – but without the support of his mother and doctor, what could he do? We felt lucky that failsafe eating enabled Howard and Rebecca to avoid medication and its side effects.

The main benefits of failsafe eating for Howard turned out to be ease of falling asleep, thinking more clearly, the ability to concentrate better and more confidence. Another benefit became obvious during a trip to New Zealand, where he and Arran met up with Emma and Matthew on the snowfields. As a former ski-field manager, Howard had been a fast skier able to keep his balance on steep slopes in bad conditions, although curiously lacking in style. This time, despite misgivings about his ability to ski after a ten-year break, he found himself more coordinated and skiing better than ever before.

As a frequent traveller, Howard is scathing about the lack of plain foods in restaurants, dismissing over-complicated concoctions on menus as 'pickled larks' tongues' and choosing to prepare his own meals wherever possible.

Families who cook together stay together

Desperate fathers sometimes contact me, wondering what they can do to help their out-of-control families. Most are reluctant to have anything to do with food, or to get involved in the cooking, yet this is the most practical help they can give their partners. Within a few years of our family going failsafe, Howard took over the weekly supermarket shopping, cooked evening meals on the weekend, and did more when he stopped travelling so much for work. This is good solid support and the weekly frustration over lack of suitable food in the supermarket introduced him to the problems we were facing more than anything else could have.

Sue

Like most parents, I started off from the smug position of 'I'm not affected by foods, this is for my kids', but learned my lesson one night after eating all the glacé cherries on our restaurant desserts thinking I was the only one unaffected by artificial colours. While the others slept, I spent a sleepless night with racing mind and jumpy legs. Anyone who even once experiences a big reaction like this is probably experiencing many smaller and less noticeable reactions to a variety of foods every day – but I didn't know that then. People can be born food-sensitive, and their symptoms can change throughout their lives, triggered by illness or medication. Women frequently become more food sensitive after the birth of a baby, and this is what happened to me. Looking back over my life, I can see that previously unrelated episodes all fit together.

Hives as a toddler and my first migraine while celebrating school finals were some of the obvious signs of food intolerance. At university I developed a long-lasting itchy rash over my body after taking over-the-counter cold medication. A skin specialist recommended avoidance of 'foodstuffs coloured brown – coffee, tea, chocolate, Vegemite, cola'. It would be twenty years before I learned that all those foods contained salicylates and/or amines.

After the birth of my first child I became more sensitive to food chemicals, although I didn't realise it at the time. After a bout of giardia in Bali resulted in permanent stomach aches and bloating, I eventually discovered that these symptoms were related to salicylates, and, after several more bouts of giardia over the years, to gluten as well. Bloating is a common complaint among the women who contact me. One nurse described her problems graphically: 'I wake up in the morning with a flat stomach. During the day my stomach blows up, then I spend all night passing wind. About every three days I have this big, runny, explosive bowel motion that gets rid of it all for a while, then the whole cycle starts again.'

For years I dismissed my frequent mild headaches as eyestrain or dehydration, and my occasional migraines as 'not often enough to see a doctor'. Within days of starting the elimination diet, my head felt noticeably clear and free from headaches and the amine challenge showed me where my headaches and migraines had come from. A small quantity of amines from broccoli, bananas or pawpaw resulted in a mild headache and fatigue. A large quantity, like a main course of previously frozen fish, mushroom and cheese sauce, a chocolate dessert, orange juice, wine, and I could expect a migraine in the next day or two.

Migraines are interesting because many doctors are determined that they are not related to food, yet when you know how many foods can contribute you realise that all but the most careful of diets are doomed to failure. The famous neurologist Dr Oliver Sacks, who dismissed dietary causes in his book *Migraine*, quoted the case study of a 38-year-old woman with migraine who had a family background of migraine, hay fever, asthma, urticaria, Ménière's disease, peptic ulcer, ulcerative colitis, and Crohn's disease. Although this is a classic history of a very food-intolerant family, Dr Sacks put the blame on the family: 'It was difficult to avoid the feeling that this stricken family was, in effect, committing physiological suicide.'

How unhelpful. I know many families with similar backgrounds, including mine. Most people are only too pleased to find they can feel well again by avoiding some foods – but it would be so much easier for us if there was more understanding. As one man in his mid-twenties commented, 'I am sick to death of explaining to people that I can't have a beer with them because I will get a headache next Tuesday.'

British researchers found over 90 per cent of children with severe frequent migraines recovered after being placed on an elimination diet, as did seven of their parents who decided to try the diet after seeing the success in their children (see Notes).

'Don't you want to hear about this?'

A mother from Melbourne and I were surprised to find we had similar experiences with earlier chronic illness, which appeared to be related to food. In my case I had suffered repeated attacks of cystitis and infections that damaged my kidneys. 'If you don't take these antibiotics, you won't live to be forty,' my doctor had warned me, and talked about kidney transplants. The antibiotics made me feel sick all the time, didn't prevent the attacks and probably set me up for irritable bowel symptoms later on. I stopped taking the medication, changed my diet and never had another attack. I had noticed that red wine and citrus seemed to cause my attacks, although my doctors ignored this observation. 'Your condition resembles analgesic abuse,' commented one specialist. I had rarely taken painkillers but I did eat a diet very high in salicylates, which are part of the same family as aspirin.

The Melbourne mother's story is strangely similar:

> I had ulcerative colitis, with associated liver problems and spontaneous bruising. I was a mess. The doctors were talking about a possible liver transplant in ten years. My job meant I travelled and ate out frequently. I kept telling the doctors I thought it was something to do with food but I couldn't pinpoint what it was. Then I quit my job, stopped eating out, ate very simple food and got better. My last liver function test was quite good. I asked my doctors, 'Don't you want to hear about this because it could help someone else?' They weren't interested.

When this mother tried a low-fat 'healthy' diet high in fresh fruit and vegetables, she spent three weeks in bed, feeling dreadful because she was sensitive to the salicylates and amines that are so high in those foods.

Powerhouse brain

I would never have chosen to do the elimination diet if it wasn't for Rebecca, but once I understood food intolerance my life started to make sense. Another clue came from an 18-year-old reader of the first edition of *Fed Up*:

> The diet has been immeasurably useful. I can now think better, clearer, and I can reason logically where before an idea would

just revolve around in my head . . . Thanks to the diet, I am going to try again to pass Year 12 next year, so I can go to university. It's quite interesting to trace the time in my life when I started doing badly in school. It was the exact time that I moved to the city, started eating more junk food like meat pies, ham, etc. I continued to do worse and worse in school until I dropped out last semester. Now, I can be confident of having my old power-house brain back again.

My own story was like that. I had been a straight-A student eating old-fashioned food until we moved to the city when I was 14. I now understand my deteriorating school marks were due to city food, in particular an artificially coloured product that I ate every day. Food's effect on high-school performance is at least as important as its role in preschooler behaviour because how you perform in your final year at school can determine the rest of your life.

It's now over 15 years since we became failsafe and they have been some of the best years of my life. Failsafe for me means being healthier, happier, calmer, having more energy and thinking more clearly. A surprising bonus was the disappearance of premenstrual symptoms that had plagued me for years – failsafe women often joke that the disadvantage of failsafe is you never know when your period is coming, because you don't get PMS to warn you.

In our family, everyone is easier to live with when failsafe, including me. Our children say my example has inspired them to stick to their own diets, and they are happy and achieving. We have a close, harmonious family that would have previously been inconceivable. For us, failsafe eating is a way of life, and every day I hear from families with similar reports.

How are we meant to know?
The hardest part of eating failsafe is the difficulty obtaining plain, additive-free foods and being sure of the ingredients. Every year, plain foods become a little harder to buy. As one mother commented, 'So many commercially made foods that

we couldn't use – you don't realise until you start looking.' People who care for young children, usually mothers, grand-mothers and childcare workers, are the ones most likely to be concerned about this problem. 'How are we meant to know about these additives?' they ask me, and 'Why are they allowed when they affect our children so badly?'

When I saw how much help parents needed, I founded the Food Intolerance Network through our website. It's a voluntary organisation funded by the sale of my books and DVD. Lobby-ing the government food regulators is an important role of this organisation. The regulators have been through three name changes since Howard and I started lobbying and are currently called FSANZ (Food Standards Australia New Zealand). They say that informing the public about the effects of food additives is not their job. Bizarrely, they have complimented the Food Intolerance Network for what we do in this area.

Most parents think that food regulators wouldn't permit additives if they were harmful. But regulators don't require food additives to be tested for their effects on children's behaviour or learning ability; don't require food additives to be tested on children at all; don't monitor effects after they have been approved; see effects as only 'minor' problems; and say that people who are affected by food additives can choose to avoid them by reading labels – even though a lot of food is not labelled and there is no requirement to tell consumers what's in it.

When my children were little I believed the authors of childcare books who claimed that the Feingold diet had been discredited and food additives had no effect on children. So I fed my children the yellow colouring called tartrazine nearly every day, either inadvertently through my breastmilk due to a popular spread in New Zealand, or later on in a Vitamin C enriched orange-flavoured breakfast drink powder. As a result my children were restless, irritable and poor sleepers. These are known effects of tartrazine, although I wasn't aware of that then. I would have appreciated an informative label, similar to the warning on cigarettes, on foods that contained such additives. When I suggested this to our food regulators, the response was, 'We couldn't do that. Consumers may not want to buy the product.' Precisely. The list of troublesome additives they don't want you to see is on p. 166.

Consumers need to understand that new additives are introduced and ingredients in products change constantly with no warning except a slight change in the fine print on the label – or no warning at all if you are buying an unlabelled product. The bread preservative calcium propionate is one such example.

The preservative in bread

In 1989, Howard was offered a new job in charge of horticulture industry development in the far north of Australia, famous for its crocodiles, cyclones, steamy heat and tropical sunsets. At that time we were living in a regional city west of Sydney where Howard was director of an agricultural research institute. So we moved thousands of kilometres to Darwin, unaware that the residents of Darwin at that time were being used as guinea pigs in a secret experiment for a national bread manufacturer. A new method of bread-making using maximum doses of preservative 282 (calcium propionate) was being trialled.

Soon after we arrived I noticed this new preservative in bread because I was already a label reader. I knew it was listed as 'possible adverse effects' in the Royal Prince Alfred Hospital Allergy Unit's book *Friendly Food* (p. 328), but we decided to try it on then six-year-old Rebecca and see what happened. She managed some sandwiches with no problems, so we started eating this new brand of bread.

After five days I was alarmed by Rebecca's increasingly vague behaviour and a report from her teacher: 'She's been lying on the floor at odd times during class and her handwriting has been getting bigger and messier every day.' She had also been eating increasing amounts of the preserved bread and appeared to be addicted to it, which is always a bad sign. She returned to her previous good behaviour within hours of withdrawing the bread from her diet.

It took two years for us to discover that there were other Darwin children badly affected by this new bread preservative. By then I was running the Darwin ADHD support group. The advice from FSANZ to avoid additives that affect you by reading labels didn't help because at that time there were no preservative-free breads available. In Darwin and most country towns we travelled through on our regular 6000-kilometre pilgrimage down south to see relatives, if you wanted to eat preservative-free bread you had to bake your own. We bought a breadmaker and travelled with it on the back seat of the car.

Contrary to popular belief, the bread preservative does not make your bread fresher or last longer. Enzymes and other new methods do that. Calcium propionate is there purely for the convenience of the manufacturer, to stop mould growth when they put hot loaves into plastic bags. Since there is no mould on a freshly baked loaf of bread, you can achieve the same effect by wiping slicer blades and work benches with vinegar, but when I suggested this to one bakery the manager exclaimed, 'We don't have time to do that.'

'There's no evidence'

Of all food additives, I regard calcium propionate as the worst because bread is a healthy food eaten every day. The effects build up so slowly that they are almost impossible to identify. When I contacted our food regulators – by phone, letter and in person, many times – about the effects on children, I was told 'there's no evidence'. My concerns were dismissed and I was assured that the regulators were interested only in the results of scientists, not the opinions of consumers.

It is hard to see what evidence they have that the propion-ate preservatives 280–283 are safe. Like other additives they were never tested for their effect on behaviour or learning in children, but when propionic acid (280) builds up naturally in the body – due to a malfunctioning enzyme in a condition called propionic acidemia – it can cause developmental delay and a range of neurological conditions. Parents of children with propionic acidemia regard propionic acid as a toxic chemical. Laboratory studies have shown that neurological effects in young rats can be caused by giving them doses of propionates similar to that which is eaten by a young child with a high bread intake (see Notes).

The bread preservative study

At that time, although RPAH researchers had reported adverse effects related to propionates, there were no published studies specifically looking at the effect of 282 on children's behav-iour. So I decided to do a study and a community paediatrician very kindly agreed to help me. Children were asked to complete two to three weeks of the RPAH elimination diet. They were then given two sets of coded bread samples in a row. Only one sample contained the bread preservative, although neither I nor they knew which one. When our study was published in a medical journal in 2002, I appeared on national television and thousands of Australian parents tried it for themselves. I was swamped with reports of how much children and adults had improved when they stopped eating the bread preservative.

For readers at home, it's worth a try. You avoid bread, rolls, wraps, crumpets, hamburger buns, cakes and other products with propionate preservatives (280–283) for two to three weeks and see what happens. It's best to find a bread free of vinegar and nasty additives such as antioxidants, see Shopping List. Not everyone reacts, but if you are affected and have been eating calcium propionate or other propionate preservatives every day for years, you could be in for a big surprise. Avoiding the bread preservative has been the first step for many failsafe families.

In our study we found that 282 contributed to irritability, restlessness, inattention and sleep disturbance in more than half the children. As well, there were other symptoms we hadn't been looking for, including migraines in a parent and extreme bedwetting and urinary urgency in some of the younger children. Since then, consumers have reported many other symptoms: speech delay, lethargy, depression, foggy brain, learning difficulties, eczema, irritable bowel symptoms, urinary incontinence in senior citizens, rapid heart beat and palpitations severe enough to require hospitalisation. Noteworthy reports included the following:

- A baby who cried for 18 hours a day every day for the first ten weeks of his life was found to be affected by food chemicals in his mother's breast milk – 282 was the worst.
- Parents of well-behaved children were surprised to notice an improvement in schoolwork when switching to unpreserved bread.
- The mother of a two-year-old who was eating the very large dose of ten slices of preserved bread per day reported dramatic improvements in her son's previously out-of-control behaviour, sleeping patterns and epileptic seizures when they switched to preservative-free bread.
- A mother from the USA described her reaction to eating bread with calcium propionate: 'After two days I got so incredibly tired and thought I was getting sick. All I wanted to do was sleep; I felt like a slug. I have excessive energy normally, so this was quite a change. When I stopped the challenge I felt better overnight.'
- The mother of a five-year-old contacted me because her son seemed 'addicted to bread' and was behaving badly.

When I suggested the preservative, she exclaimed: 'I don't believe this. I've read your book. I know about the bread preservative. It was right under my nose. My son was reacting to preserved bread and I didn't see it.'

- Some Australians had been diagnosed with chronic fatigue syndrome when their main problem was the bread preservative.

Within two years, all of the major bread manufacturers in Australia had withdrawn calcium propionate from their best-selling loaves due to 'consumer concerns'. But this is no reason for complacency: our food regulators have actually increased the level of calcium propionate permitted in bread, so Australia now has the highest maximum permitted level in the world, and propionate preservative 282 is appearing in specialty breads such as wraps and flat breads that people assume are healthy.

Diet works

I learned some valuable lessons from the bread preservative study. After years of listening to reports about the remarkable effects of foods on children, I saw behaviour rated on a scale out of 100 and was surprised at the size of the improvements when children were failsafe. In our study, during two or three weeks of elimination diet before the bread challenges, all of the children improved significantly and some of the children went from being in the top five per cent for *bad* behaviour to the top five per cent for *good* behaviour within three weeks. The mother of one of these big responders, a six-year-old, initially remarked, 'She'll be a street kid by the time she's 11 if we don't do something.' After the study she wrote: 'The changes have been amazing. It is wonderful to wake up each day to a little girl who is so helpful, loving, funny, cuddly, quiet and happy (at home and school) – life is a joy.'

Nearly all of the mothers noticed remarkable improvements in their children's concentration and reading ability, with comments such as: 'he could sit and concentrate on homework and other tasks for a long time and actually seemed to enjoy it'. These are important observations considering that if a child hasn't learned to read well by the age of nine, they are likely to remain poor readers for the rest of their lives and suffer life-long economic disadvantage (see Notes).

One of the biggest responders in this study was a part-Aboriginal child. In a report on Aboriginal nutrition for the Australian Medical Association, fears were expressed about the health effects on Aboriginal communities where high levels of junk food had replaced traditional bush tucker. The report said that in many areas, undrinkable water meant the Aboriginals drank cola or cordial, and I've seen this for myself in remote communities. While this is considered a possible factor in the high rate of diabetes among Aboriginals, health workers may also need to consider the behavioural and learning effects of a diet high in junk food.

What mothers need

In my experience, mothers need much more than just a written list of foods to eat and avoid. They need the right information about diet provided by a dietitian and/or doctor who will inspire rather than discourage them, access to suitable foods, easy recipes that kids will eat, and support from schools, family and community. The mothers most highly motivated to continue were the ones who saw the best results and recognised that the best results came from sticking strictly to the diet. When asked 'What helped you most to stick with this diet?' a typical reply was 'The change in my son's behaviour.' I also noticed it seemed quicker and easier to do the diet properly from the beginning, rather than cutting down gradually and getting confused the way many people do.

When we realised how important support was, Howard and I set up the website www.fedup.com.au, with email support groups and the Product Updates section for people to keep up-to-date with suitable foods. It would be so much easier for everyone if additives such as artificial colours were removed from the foods that children eat.

Beyond bread

After I finished the bread preservative study in 2001, we used Howard's long service leave to go travelling with our then teenage children. Our trip included Indonesia, Nepal and Egypt, all developing countries where traditional food was still available although processed food was becoming common. I was outraged to realise that we could eat traditional foods without problems, compared to the enormous struggle to buy safe food for our children in Australia.

I was surprised to find that additive use was different in every country. The colours used in Fanta soft drink seemed to be an indicator of how consumers felt about additives. Orange-flavoured Fanta was coloured with artificial colours in Australia, New Zealand and the USA, with a safe natural colour (betacarotene E160a) in most European countries, and with fruit juice in Italy. At that time, foods in European countries such as Germany, France and especially Italy contained far fewer additives than in Australia, although additive intake was obviously rising due to the increase in processed foods. As I would have expected, the USA was worst of all, so bad for both food additives and perfumed products that we ended up camping and cooking for ourselves (see 'Additives around the World' factsheet on www.fedup.com.au).

A few years after our return, we left Darwin and moved south. By then, Howard had become as angry as I was about the state of Australian food. He combined part-time work in agribusiness with running our website, lecture tours and additive lobbying. It was obvious to us that parents needed the chance to see what food chemicals were doing to their children, so we talked to parents and organised additive-free trials in schools. At our presentations we met so many people with remarkable stories that we produced the DVD *Fed Up with Children's Behaviour*. Although aimed at our usual audience – namely, mothers – surprisingly, it turned out to be remarkably effective at getting the message across to fathers, children, teachers and the wider community.

The good news

Thanks to a 2007 study by University of Southampton researchers, there has been a sudden turnaround in attitudes to food additives in the UK. Amid fears that parents will be able to sue food manufacturers in Big Tobacco style, as I write all major UK supermarket chains and confectionery manufacturers are removing artificial colours from their products and considering other artificial additives.

In Australia the rate of change is slower, but at least some manufacturers are phasing out the use of artificial colours and a few preservatives. It doesn't mean that all nasty additives will vanish from our foods, but it is a huge step in the right direction.

What you can do

- Do not rely on food regulators to protect you.
- Do not assume that you will know if your children are affected by food chemicals – you have to stop eating them to see if there is an effect (either a three-week additive-free trial avoiding all the nasty additives on p. 166, or a three-week supervised trial of the RPAH elimination diet, depending on the severity of symptoms).
- If you want nasty additives removed from foods, contact food manufacturers directly through their hotline number or website.

4

Lives half-lived

What happens if people fail to recognise the effects of food chemicals? Some of my readers have answered this question with stories from their own lives. Bianca was a teenager when she started on the elimination diet. She reported that she felt she had 'lost the first 15 years of her life', because her life really started when she began the diet. This is despite previously taking medication for ADHD for four years. Her mother wrote, 'The diet has been simply life-changing. If Bianca has any salicylates, her brain shuts down and that is that.'

Sixty-four-year-old Duncan had eliminated artificial food additives ten years previously and described his improvement: 'Most astonishing, though, was the effect upon my mental powers; clarity of thought, conceptual grasp and intellectual awareness. It was as if I had been reborn. I realised that my real persona had been denied me all my life, my brain fogged by chemical additives. I felt I had to let people know this, to alert them to what might well be true of whole swathes of the nation.'

A family undertook the elimination diet for their two-year-old. 'Her main problem is her stuffed-up nose. It's often so bad she can't talk properly. She's been like that most of her life.'

This little girl is now 'as clear as a bell' following her elimination diet. But that wasn't the only benefit. Unlike the others in this chapter, the two little girls in this family haven't had to struggle with their problems for long. It would seem that their lives now have a greater potential for happiness as a result of their mother's early discovery of the effects of foods. Their mother explained:

> My children have always been bad-tempered in the morning. They used to fight a lot. I thought that was normal. It wasn't until we tried the diet that they started waking up happy and playing happily together . . . Even [the four-year-old] has changed. For the first time I've enjoyed being with her. She's become this gentle, loving little person . . . I wouldn't have said my children had behaviour problems before we started this, but now I realise that sometimes they were obnoxious little toads.

Bedwetting or soiling (also known as sneaky poos) can have serious effects on a child's self-esteem, often aggravated by the social problems associated with sleepovers and school camps. These are usually the first problems to improve on eating failsafe.

> My 13-year-old nephew was still wetting the bed. His family had tried behaviour modification, the electric pad and alarm system, and finally drugs. While taking medication he was better but not perfect. Then his mother changed their eating habits. They had been eating takeaways most nights. Returning to home-cooking and avoiding additives was enough to stop the bedwetting which had dominated my nephew's life.

Scientific studies confirm the benefits of diet. In a group of bedwetting children who also had either migraine or ADHD, more than 75 per cent improved on a strict elimination diet, with bedwetting stopping completely in more than half.

It's not just children. After reading the original *Fed Up*, a 60-year-old man wrote: 'we stopped eating 282 preservative in bread and within a week my wife was free of urinary incontinence'. Vulnerability to the adverse effects of chemicals is considered to be highest during early development and again later in life, which means that seniors need to know about the effects of food chemicals

Failsafe eating can make a difference with asthma too, as one mother reported with satisfaction: 'I only did this diet to help my son's behaviour, but I've had chronic asthma for years. Now I don't even need any medication. I got rid of it. Fifteen different kinds of medication.'

A long-distance cyclist in her thirties wrote her 'personal story of hell' about a two-year rash caused by new flavour enhancer 635: 'I thought I was dying. The itching was absolutely maddening.' (See the 'Ribo Rash' factsheet on www.fedup.com.au.)

Another mother describes her daughter's release from pain: 'My daughter was diagnosed with juvenile arthritis when she was three. By the time she went to school, at five, she was crippled with it. She's now 25. Three weeks after she started her elimination diet, she told me: "Mum, the pain's gone. For the first time in 23 years, I have no pain".'

Prison

Colin was a father of three who served time in prison for armed robbery. He spent ten years on street amphetamines, basically medicating himself because it felt better. 'It didn't affect me like all my friends,' he says. 'Instead, I felt relaxed and wanted to go to sleep.' His problems arose from buying bad batches, cut with toxic substances. 'One night I thought I was going to die, other times I felt bad and lashed out.'

After prison he learned about ADHD, started prescribed medication and felt wonderful. It turned his life around. 'Why don't they screen prisoners for ADHD? I reckon they could reduce the prison population by doing that.' But medication was not the whole story for him. 'Even while I'm taking Dex,

I can notice oranges affect me. I had no idea food could be so important. Why don't they change the food in prison? I bet there are lots like me in there.'

It seems Colin is right. In the USA a big study of juvenile offenders showed that changing their diet reduced more than half of their behaviour problems. Conducted in detention centers, using a diet which excluded processed foods but included many foods we would have avoided, the researcher found:

> . . . this diet policy, for unknown reasons, played a major role in reducing the antisocial behaviour in approximately 25 per cent of the confined juvenile population. Furthermore, the improvement in 25 per cent of the youths resulted in a long-term 61 per cent reduction in institution-wide behaviour problems at no cost and apparent risk to anyone. Dietary intervention is clearly a cost-efficient approach to reducing institutional behaviour problems.

Kerry

Of all my callers, the person who most touched my heart was 25-year-old autistic Kerry. Kerry first phoned me because she had heard about my book from a friend, she wanted to know about diet but she couldn't read. She was going from one health professional to another, as she had done all her life.

Autism is a disorder of social interaction, communication and imagination first described in the 1940s. Like Kerry, autistic children often have associated intellectual disability, seizures, spasms or tics, problems of coordination and balance, intense preoccupations or fixations, language delay or odd language disorders including verbosity. Asperger's Syndrome is regarded as high-functioning autism, often with high intellect and fewer neurological problems. People with Asperger's can explain their experiences and emotions whereas those with classical autism cannot.

Kerry seemed to have a combination of the two. As a child she was very slow to sit up, stand and walk, still falling over at the age of five. She had been variously diagnosed with cerebral palsy, autism, Asperger's Syndrome and epilepsy. Like Dustin Hoffman's character in the movie *Rain Man*, Kerry used to have the autistic's uncanny rote memory for large numbers, although this has decreased with her increasing 'normality'. She had taken numerous medications for her epilepsy and behaviour.

'I'm not sure whether you have ADHD, but you can try medication and see if it helps,' the latest specialist advised. She became a regular caller, and there were times when I would hang up and cry because life has been so hard for her, although she would remain determinedly optimistic. I admired Kerry's extraordinary persistence.

She couldn't read and couldn't find anyone to help her – 'The dietitian didn't seem to have any time for me. When I rang her up she made me feel as if I was a nuisance' – so Kerry decided to phone me from the other end of Australia. 'I don't like doctors. They won't listen to me, and they don't know everything, although they think they do,' she said. Unwilling to take yet more medication, she wanted to try the elimination diet. At first I was reluctant to talk her through an elimination and challenge diet. With a background as an intellectually disabled adult, Kerry had low credibility among her relatives. She was still living at home, and although her father and boyfriend were supportive, the women who made the decisions about the food were not. Family gatherings were often at fast-food restaurants or included takeaway food.

Kerry was clear that she would not be able to stick to the diet strictly, but equally insistent that she wanted to give it a go. The changes were quick and extraordinary. Her forgetfulness improved. She became a lot more fun to converse with. Her boyfriend rang me to say how much she had improved and asked me to help her stay on it. Kerry developed subterfuges like keeping tissues in her pocket for removing unsuitable food from her plate or swapping with her boyfriend. She had to squeeze challenges into times she thought she could maintain her diet, and use social occasions as challenges too.

I had a few desperate calls from Kerry. When she ate salicylates she had a low frustration tolerance and was likely to react in a negative situation with an emotional outburst. In Kerry's words, 'I get all angry and worked up and I can't cope with any frustration. I shout and I scream. Sometimes I throw things or hit my head and I can't control it. I hate being like that.' Taking an antidote (see p. 185) helped her to calm down, but she was likely to forget and had to be reminded.

Soon after she started the elimination diet, Kerry reported that her epileptic seizures had stopped. I was surprised and looked up the research. Sure enough, researchers had tried an elimination diet with epileptic children. Some of the children had epilepsy alone and some had epilepsy plus ADHD or 'allergic' symptoms such as migraine and stomach aches. None of the children with epilepsy alone improved, but the results for the other group were dramatic. Most of the children improved and, in more than half, the seizures stopped altogether except when provoked by food challenges.

In Kerry's case, her seizures were related to large amounts of salicylates or the yellow food colouring called tartrazine. The seizures could be triggered by flashing lights or sudden loud noises, but only when she had salicylates or tartrazine in her system.

After three months, Kerry's concentration had improved so much she could read my book. 'All my life I thought I was intellectually disabled,' she explained. 'Now I don't think

I am.' At school, Kerry had gained Es and Fs in her first exams at high school, although she always won As for effort. She was then placed in non-exam subjects that do not lead to a career. She wondered how her life would have been had the food reactions been identified when she was a baby. It was hard to comprehend what opportunities she might have missed.

Insisting that 'I'm just like Rebecca, I won't react to amines because Rebecca doesn't', Kerry did her amine challenge by eating amine-rich foods every day for a week. Each night she phoned me to report. We became more and more excited as the week progressed. When we finally decided there was no reaction, it was like a celebration. Kerry had passed a challenge!

Some food colourings had an immediate effect on Kerry, making her restless. 'I have all this energy in my brain, too much, and it doesn't know where to go.' The monosodium glutamate challenge was interesting. 'After a few hours, I was sitting on the couch and all of a sudden my brain went to sleep. I wanted to get up and go to the toilet but I couldn't remember how.'

Preservatives also made Kerry vague and forgetful, some causing muscle weakness and lethargy to the point of collapse. This feature had previously been attributed to her cerebral palsy, as well as shakiness. Kerry now realised the shaking was a classic hypoglycemic reaction, occurring when she had salicylates in her system and had gone too long between meals, 'just like Rebecca'.

One afternoon I received a frantic phone call after Kerry had eaten some chicken from a large supermarket and was experiencing a sudden out-of-control reaction. I could only guess that the chicken must have been flavoured. Although Kerry had the autistic's discomfort about socialising and dealing with people, she returned to the supermarket and asked them about the chicken, explaining that she had reacted badly. The staff were helpful and explained that the chicken skin had been sprinkled with 'ham seasoning'.

Another time I had a call while she was on the job delivering pizzas. Although Kerry had discovered by trial and error that the only pizza she could manage was a bacon, egg and cheese pizza with no tomato paste, on this occasion her boss had given her some ham and pineapple pizza before her shift. She phoned me, upset, between deliveries. She and her boyfriend were working as a team – he drove, she navigated. She had forgotten the first delivery and was now unable to make sense of the street directory. I reminded her of the antidote for food reactions (see p. 185).

After more than a year of failsafe eating, Kerry, a former junk food enthusiast, decided to lose weight. She learned about nutrition and started a walking program, losing 12 kilos in three months. Months later, following a particularly disastrous Easter eating the wrong foods, Kerry decided to reduce her infractions and avoid dairy foods as well. As soon as she started talking I could hear the difference. Her usual slow speech had speeded up and the nasal tone was gone as Kerry described her newfound social skills. 'I've always been uncomfortable socially, like most autistics. At parties, I would sit in a corner of the room with a sour look on my face and look at the floor. Now I find my social confidence is improving. I've been to several parties I really enjoyed and I've started taking the initiative when we deliver pizzas. That was something I would never do before. I used to think it would be really hard, sitting next to someone who was eating my favourite food and not being able to eat it myself. But it's not like that. Now I know how badly it affects me, there's no way I want to eat it,' Kerry explained. She was succeeding against extraordinary odds.

After two years, the changes in Kerry were astonishing. At her best she could hold brisk, businesslike, interactive conversations which she was just as likely to terminate as I, compared to previously rambling, obsessive monologues in which she seemed to have no sense of time and frequently forgot what she'd already said. She was working as a part-time volunteer at a day-training center for autistic and intellectually handicapped adults, welcoming the challenge of meeting new people and new experiences. Both of these can be difficult for people with autism. 'How am I going to get over my autism unless I confront it head-on?' she said. She and her boyfriend were sharing a flat and starting a business. By sticking to failsafe eating, Kerry had a chance of a productive and independent life. How much easier it would have been for her if she was believed and supported by friends, family, employers and the medical profession.

Not only did Kerry help herself, but through an autism newsgroup on the internet Kerry told the mother of a mildly autistic girl about her success with the diet. When this mother contacted me, she described her daughter as nearly four years old and 'only babbling like a one-year-old'. Within ten days of our first email, this mother phoned from another country to tell me about her daughter's progress. 'I was feeding her all the wrong things,' she cried. Within ten days of trying failsafe, the child had 'calmed right down', toilet trained herself, and, according to the special-needs teacher who visited the family twice a week, made 'fantastic' progress, including normal eye-contact. 'I just phoned to say thank you,' the mother said.

Another mother who saw a huge diet-related improvement in her son wrote about his deterioration after five days of reintroducing salicylates: 'My son's "weirdness" has come back. I spied on him at school the other day in the playground and he just walked around by himself looking lost. He actually stopped and stood by himself near groups of children, but didn't know how to join in. My heart broke. His hands have stiffened and he makes "autistic" type hand gestures, silly noises and is whingeing all the time.'

If autistics are offered any diet at all, it is usually the gluten-free casein-free (GFCF) diet, but a growing number are joining our network after finding that it is much more effective to go fully failsafe – that is, additive free, gluten and dairy free, low in salicylates, amines and natural flavour enhancers, and, for many, avoiding perfumes and other volatile organic compounds as well (see p. 156).

Hearing voices

Schizophrenia is a major psychiatric illness involving distorted perceptions of sound, sight, other people and sensations from the body. The age of greatest risk is late adolescence in men and mid-twenties in women. Thirty years ago mothers were blamed for causing this illness, which is now thought to be associated with a chemical imbalance in the brain. Although the exact cause is unknown, experts suggest that the condition has a hereditary element and that stress may be the trigger for the symptoms.

An aggressive near-teenage boy with a schizophrenic relative heard 'noises in my head' and 'voices – they tell me what to do' while taking prescription medication for his behaviour. During an elimination diet, this boy was found to be exceptionally food sensitive and improved dramatically. Some months later, when he took some over-the-counter cough medicine, the voices reappeared for several weeks. I have known adult schizophrenics with disordered eating patterns whose symptoms worsen during periods of binge eating or drinking. One of these people experienced a marked improvement on the elimination diet, but needed far more community support than was available to be able to stick to it.

Death by food

Food intolerance is dismissed as a minor inconvenience by officials, yet I have spoken to two women who nearly lost their lives because of it. Amy avoided additives because she knew they affected her, but in her thirties she adopted a raw fruit and vegetable diet on the advice of an alternative practitioner. All the fruit and vegetables she chose to eat were exceptionally high in salicylates. When she phoned me she was unable to sleep, her legs were twitching and she was extremely agitated.

'I feel much worse. I can't sleep no matter what I do, my legs feel itchy and crawly, I feel as if I'm going to explode.' She confessed she had contemplated suicide. Amy turned out to be sensitive to salicylates. When she changed her diet, she started feeling better within hours.

Julie is another who considered suicide as a result of 'healthy' food. She would often experience intense food cravings, on one occasion eating nothing but pineapple for several days. Pineapples are high in both salicylates and amines and Julie found herself in hospital after slashing her wrists, with no memory of what had happened. 'I get so impulsive, I don't know what I'm doing.'

After a few days of the elimination diet, staff in the psychiatric ward were amazed at the change in her. One nurse commented: 'I've known you for five years. This is the first time I've been able to sit down with you and have a conversation without you jumping around all over the place. There must be something in this diet.'

In the original edition of *Fed Up* I wrote that diet had come too late to turn Julie's sad life around, but I was wrong. Many years later I saw Julie again by chance. 'You don't know who I am, do you?' she asked with a smile. She had gone back to school, qualified in a profession and appeared so happy and confident that I could scarcely recognise her.

Depression, panic attacks and anxiety are just some of the many symptoms that started increasing in both adults and children with the introduction of the Western diet, and which are treated with medication. We have received numerous accounts of formerly anxious or depressed adults and children who, like Julie, have turned their lives around by avoiding certain foods. For some people it can be as simple as avoiding certain additives, like a 39-year-old man who spent a year attending an anxiety group only to find his anxiety attacks completely disappeared when he avoided the 600-number flavour enhancers. Others are relieved to find their life-long depression has been due to salicylates in fruit or amines in chocolate that they can now choose to avoid. You can read their stories in the 'Depression' factsheet on www.fedup.com.au.

The final word comes from a mother who spent six years with severe depression after the birth of her daughter. When she altered her diet due to her daughter's behaviour problems she discovered:

> My depression went away. I'm in control, I'm free of the symptoms of despair and irrationality. It was just the most amazing discovery. But even though I was suicidal quite often . . . in all that time no health professional suggested that I look at what I was eating, which totally amazes me now. I just can't comprehend why people have got to go through what I went through.

5

How many people are affected?

Some experts claim that only a small percentage of children react to food additives. However, reactions are related to dose. This means the more you eat, the more likely you will be affected. As formerly sceptical American toxicologist Professor Bernard Weiss says: 'Even though present studies have shown only a small subgroup of the population to be sensitive, practically any one of us may be [affected by additives] if we consume enough'.

Some people are more sensitive than others. Sensitivity can alter according to factors such as family history, age, stress, exposure to manmade chemicals and medications, illness, or hormonal changes. Babies, young children, women of child-bearing age and seniors are likely to be more sensitive than men in their prime. But, basically, the take-home message is that if we keep on eating more troublesome food chemicals, we can expect to see more food-related health, behaviour and learning problems.

In 2003, when an entire class of six-year-olds in the UK avoided 39 additives at home and at school for two weeks, nearly 60 per cent of their parents reported improvement in behaviour, cooperation and sleep patterns. This is many more than the 'small subgroup' we have been told about.

As well as behaviour, the side effects can contribute to a wide range of health conditions, which, although not usually life-threatening, can drastically affect quality of life.

'There's nothing wrong'

One of the many conditions increasingly associated with the Western diet, irritable bowel syndrome is thought to affect up to 20 per cent of people in developed countries yet is rare in traditional cultures. This complaint is characterised by abdominal pain, bloating and changes in bowel habits. There can also be feelings of incomplete evacuation (sticky poos) after passing a bowel motion. Other possible symptoms include reflux and colic in babies or adults, nausea, vomiting, urinary frequency, bedwetting or sneaky poos (soiling). Some doctors now recognise that it is food-related and refer patients to dietitians, but most don't. There is nothing more demoralising than being told that nothing is wrong.

A woman in her early fifties with irritable bowel symptoms that improved on an elimination diet reported: 'They did every imaginable test, including sticking things up my bum. The doctor was beaming when she gave me the results. "You'll be glad to know there's absolutely nothing wrong with you." Glad? I was furious. She hadn't listened to me. I knew I wasn't dying of bowel cancer, but something was affecting the quality of my life every single day.'

Why doctors don't recognise the side effects of foods

I have a certain amount of sympathy for doctors. There are thousands of diets around and most of them are unproven. Some people realise they are affected by foods but because reactions are delayed it is easy to make mistakes about identifying the real problem. When patients say 'I've tried diet', they might mean any of the following strategies:

* *Avoiding foods that seem to cause a reaction.* This is not very effective. Some people may have an obvious reaction to some foods. But they may be reacting to other foods in a less obvious way.
* *Avoiding only food additives*. This can help many families but for serious symptoms it's worth considering salicylates, amines, glutamates, dairy and gluten as well. In one particularly successful ADHD study, researchers found that so many children were highly food-sensitive that 'an additive-free diet by itself would be of little benefit.'
* *Diets recommended by naturopaths* often start by excluding wheat, gluten, dairy, yeast and/or sugar. These diets can be unnecessarily difficult and much less effective than they should be for people who are sensitive to salicylates, amines or glutamates.
* *The Few Foods diet* from Britain typically starts with rice, turkey, pears and lettuce. It gets good results but is unnecessarily difficult (see Notes).
* *Diets based on 'allergy' testing.* There are no scientifically proven laboratory tests for food intolerance. The best way

to find out which food chemicals are affecting you is to do an elimination diet followed by careful challenges. Potentially life-threatening allergies to foods such as peanuts are different. Skin tests that measure IgE antibodies to allergens are available from medical allergists.

At last, a scientific approach

It is easy to see why doctors could feel overwhelmed by contradictory information and lack of scientific evidence about diets. In the USA, a prison probation officer named Barbara Reed found that modifying the diets of her probationers produced amazing rates of improvements and decreases in re-offending rates. Her diet was low in refined flour and sugar, food additives, caffeine, soft drinks, grapes, prunes, dates, raisins, figs and alcoholic beverages. One researcher commented, 'The diet is such a hodgepodge of changes that it is hard to know what was important.'

However, from a food chemical viewpoint, Barbara Reed's diet is not a hodgepodge. It is remarkably consistent. The foods that have been removed are very high in additives, salicylates and amines. Once you understand that Barbara Reed's 'grapes, prunes, dates, raisins, figs' and most alcoholic beverages are high in both salicylates and amines, the diet stops looking like a hodgepodge and becomes easy to understand. Reactions to foods also become predictable, instead of being random events that must be tested individually.

The best diet

I like food chemical elimination diets because they are logical. The diet that I recommend as the most scientific and effective in the world is the low-salicylate elimination diet introduced in the United States by Dr Ben Feingold in 1974 and refined over many years by Australian researchers (see Notes).

Sadly, Dr Feingold was in his seventies when he introduced his diet and he died less than ten years later. He was way ahead of his time and had his heroic ideas been widely accepted, millions of people would be better off today.

Feingold proposed that a wide variety of behavioural and medical conditions could be related to artificial additives and natural salicylates in food. Among these conditions were respiratory, skin, gastro-intestinal, skeletal and neurological symptoms including epilepsy, eye muscle problems, the behavioural component of Down Syndrome. He also included symptoms of what would now be called attention deficit disorders, autistic spectrum disorders, Asperger's, tic disorders including Tourette's, developmental disorders and intellectual impairment.

Overall, the Feingold diet achieved mixed results because it used an outdated food list that was not really low in salicylates. In the mid-eighties Australian researchers published a new analysis of salicylate contents in foods showing that there were salicylates in many more foods than previously thought (see Notes). For people who had already been following low-salicylate diets, the new salicylate information was a revelation. 'When I found the Australian salicylate lists I was so excited,' wrote a salicylate-sensitive asthmatic from New Mexico. 'I could finally understand what was happening – I had inadvertently been eating salicylates every day.' (See 'Story 228' on www.fedup.com.au.)

Unfortunately there are numerous salicylate lists of varying quality available on the internet and from health practitioners. A woman whose son was worsening on a so-called 'low to medium salicylate' elimination diet from her doctor was feeding her son lots of broccoli, cauliflower and pumpkin. These are all vegetables we avoid or eat in limited quantities. A low salicylate diet is only as good as the salicylate list you are working from – see the Shopping List in this book (p. 167) or the entire updated food charts in RPAH's *Friendly Food*.

The problems with early research

Diet studies in the 1970s have been criticised on many counts. Elimination diets didn't avoid enough foods, rating scales focused too much on severe symptoms of ADHD, challenges used unrealistically small doses of food colouring and many placebos contained foods now known to cause problems. Researchers at that time concluded that less than five per cent of hyperactive children were affected by foods, but later studies showed that the majority of ADHD children improved on restricted diets and that children without ADHD could also be affected.

When Howard and I organised a series of two-week school trials, parents and teachers found that the majority of children improved on an additive-free diet. In my bread preservative study, *all* of the children who finished two to three weeks of the RPAH elimination diet improved significantly. When children don't improve on the elimination diet it is usually due to reasons such as a high level of stress within the family, lack of support, lack of compliance and mistakes, particularly eating foods not on the Shopping List. Many of these families subsequently try again and achieve success.

How it was

'In my general paediatric practice in Jackson, Tennessee (population 50,000) in the 1950s, my partners and I were "the only game in town". No other full-time paediatricians and only a rare family practitioner. Yet we only saw an occasional hyperactive kid.

'In the 1970s, I saw so many hyperactive children that I kept records of every new youngster with this problem during a period of five years. In 1980, I reported my observations in the *Journal of Learning Disabilities*. The parents of 136 of the 182 children found that their child's hyperactive behaviour was diet-related.' *Informal notes from a presentation by William G. Crook, MD, to the American Academy of Otolaryngic Allergy, Kansas City, 27 September 1991.*

ADHD

The drug Ritalin was first used as medication for children's behaviour problems in the 1960s and its use has increased dramatically since then. By 2000, Australia and New Zealand ranked third in the world for such medication use, after the USA and Canada, and well ahead of European countries headed by the UK.

Unsurprisingly, the amount of ADHD medication used corresponds with the rate of additive use I observed in each country during our travels in 2001. Over many visits to Nepal and the Indian Himalayas I have noticed that the introduction of artificially coloured and preserved products into subsistence villages is accompanied by the appearance of loud, restless behaviours and temper outbursts normally associated with Westernised countries (see http://www.fedupwithfood additives.info/information/world.htm).

Twenty-five years on

By the end of the twentieth century, independent scientists from the Washington-based Center for Science in the Public Interest (CSPI) reviewed 25 years' worth of research in a study called 'Diet, ADHD and behaviour' (http://www.cspinet.org/diet.html) and recommended that parents should try diet before medication for children's behaviour problems.

Families are more likely to succeed with diet if they try it first than if they start diet while the child is on medication. Even if they choose to use medication after an initial trial of diet, I have noticed that families will often return to diet – either alone or alongside medication – after a year or two when they find that medication is not as magical as they have been led to expect. In 2007, NSW judge Paul Conlon told the media, 'I am starting to lose count of [the number of] offenders coming before the courts who were diagnosed at a very young age with ADHD for which they were medicated.'

The official recommendation from the Australian National Health and Medical Research Council is that 'if a special diet is to be instituted, it should be under the careful supervision of a qualified dietitian, preferably with experience in this area.' Some dietitians are more supportive than others. You can write for our list to confoodnet@ozemail.com.au.

Paediatricians who refer families to a dietitian and say directly to the child, 'I'd like you to stick to this for three weeks, then come and see me again' are more likely to see improvements than paediatricians who say, 'You can try diet if you want, but don't do it strictly.'

Diet alone is not necessarily the whole answer. Failsafe parents generally pursue a range of options such as behaviour management, exercise programs, educational strategies, speech therapy and possibly medication, but will often say, 'We had to get diet in place first for the rest of it to work.' Children and adults with ADHD tend to be creative, good at thinking outside the box and do not fit easily into the school system. They will often do better in home schooling or in a smaller more flexible environment where they are encouraged to pursue their strengths rather than their weaknesses.

Autistic spectrum disorders

Children with autism are the most sensitive of all. They can display any of the symptoms of food intolerance, including tantrums, toileting issues and speech delay, but they also have autistic symptoms, such as lack of eye contact, inflexibility, handflapping, rocking and face blindness, all of which can improve on diet.

In a USA study, 49 autistic children followed an extremely restricted diet while staying in a special 'clean room' free of VOCs (volatile organic compounds) such as perfumes, cleaning products, solvents and pesticides. The researcher reported that a 'broad spectrum of severe and chronic autistic symptoms' appeared to be 'fully reversible' since it was observed that 'the children in the program . . . returned to normal'.

This is an extraordinary claim but we do see huge improvements in failsafe autistic children who generally do the strictest form of the diet – including dairy-free, gluten-free and perfume-free as well as additive-free and low in salicylates and amines.

As mothers point out, it is not possible to lock children up in a clean room forever. However, it is possible to reduce exposure to VOCs at home and at school. (See the 'Autism and Asperger' factsheet on www.fedup.com.au.)

Oppositional defiance

Diet works best with the symptoms of oppositional defiance – children who are grouchy, easily annoyed, argumentative, angry, resentful, deliberately annoy others and say 'no' all the time. The core feature of oppositional defiant disorder is irritability. These are the people who have a low frustration tolerance; they are fine when everything is going well, but will overreact to the many small stresses of life. Children – and adults – like this can be hard to live with and hard to teach, yet changing what they eat can have remarkable effects. One grandmother on our DVD described the effect of diet on her three-year-old granddaughter: 'within 7 days it was like God took away *this* child and gave us *this* child.'

Other diagnoses

It doesn't matter whether the diagnosis is ADHD with or without hyperactivity, oppositional defiance, autistic spectrum disorders, developmental disorders, cerebral palsy, intellectual impairment, metabolic disorders such as porphyria, speech delay, semantic-pragmatic disorder, a 'busy brain' (as described by one paediatric neurologist), bad behaviour, or if there is no diagnosis. It is worth finding out if symptoms are the result of food intolerance.

Anyone who works with failsafe families pretty soon realises that it isn't only ADHD children who improve, and this has been confirmed by researchers who suggested that by focusing on children with hyperactivity, early studies may have excluded many other children who are affected by foods. Irritability and mood swings seem to be the most important behavioural effect of foods, along with inattention, restlessness and sleep disturbance – not hyperactivity as previously thought.

Failsafe consumers are in the same position as Captain Cook when he sailed on his voyages of discovery. He knew sauerkraut helped to prevent scurvy, but at that time doctors were still recommending oil of vitriol, which was useless. It took the medical profession 300 years to accept the diet–scurvy connection. We consumers find that failsafe eating works. You have the choice of experiencing the benefits now, or waiting for years while the professionals slog it out.

What the mothers say

People at the coal-face, that is, the ones who spend the most time with children – usually mothers, carers or teachers – are the most likely to notice the side effects of food. In the past, researchers generally have distrusted ratings by parents, but researchers who tested the validity of parents' ratings have commented, 'contrary to the prevailing wisdom, parents were found to be reliable observers and raters of their children's behaviour.' Mothers often report that their failsafe children have gone from one of the worst- to best-behaved in their class, and can see when other children are affected. This mother was surprised by other parents' reactions to her daughter's birthday party:

> We had a good party, lots to eat and drink and games to play. The children all enjoyed themselves and behaved well, no five-year-old fights or tantrums that we have observed at other parties with much the same group of five-year-olds. The allotted three hours passed quickly.
>
> Over the next couple of days, I had mothers coming up to me and asking what I had done to their children, to which I asked, why? Basically they said that their child came home calm and very happy, not noisy and obnoxious. I told them my daughter's party food was all in accordance with her diet. They were stuck for words. I must admit that I was a little stuck for words too as I didn't expect such a result.

What the carers say

Where a working mother spends most of the time away from her child, it is more likely to be the family day-carer or child-care worker who sees the changes. Family day-carers and foster parents attend training and are usually experts in behaviour management. Once they understand failsafe, they are enthusiastic. Describing a nearly-two-year-old, a family daycarer lamented, 'Both his parents work. They give him anything he wants then dump him at my place for me to deal with. I can't cope with him when there are other children here. He's aggressive and he bites the others. I've told them he reacts to certain foods but they won't do anything about it.'

An agency babysitter observed, 'Parents often give their children takeaways before they go out. It makes my job harder. Of the ones who have takeaways, about half are restless and hard to settle, disobedient, won't go to bed, won't listen to me. The parents think it's a treat, but really, the children don't feel good.'

From a worker at a childcare center, dealing mostly with three- to six-year-olds: 'We're not happy about food colouring. Most parents bring in brightly coloured birthday cakes, so we have a policy now. The cakes go straight in the fridge and get served just before home time. This means that the parents get the bad effects. Otherwise we have a whole lot of out-of-control children running around the room, and we can't cope.'

Seeing is believing

An unforgettable demonstration of the effects of foods on behaviour appears in a video of the Shipley Project, in which families of a group of juvenile offenders agree to a trial of an elimination diet. Eight children between the ages of eight and twelve are shown at the initial briefing in a large hall. Their behaviour is no different from that seen in most classrooms. The children are loud, restless, rowdy and uncooperative. They throw things, swing punches at each other and yell. After three weeks on the diet, these children assemble again. In a dramatic turnaround, the children all sit still, and are quiet and attentive. When they play they are cooperative and creative.

Parents and police alike are astonished at the dramatic improvements. As one mother says: 'I really didn't expect it to work. Nothing else we tried had. If I hadn't seen it with my own eyes, I'd never have believed it was possible to change her behaviour just by changing the foods that she ate.' At follow-up the five who remained on the diet had also stayed out of trouble with the law. The three who broke their diet had re-offended. You can see the transformation of these children on our DVD.

I have seen for myself the dramatic improvements in children when they change what they eat. But changes in our Westernised diet have happened so gradually that most people have forgotten how agreeable children can be.

What the grandparents say

Increasing mobility and small families have led to the mystery of parenthood. Parents don't know what to expect and obnoxious children are becoming the norm. But grandparents can remember how children used to be: 'Every time I go out, I look at the children, in the bus, in the streets, in the shops, and I think, "There's something wrong, children haven't always been like that." They're so aggressive and demanding. I used to think they needed firmer discipline, but now you've talked about the food, I can see, that's it.'

At school: eat junk and flunk

The current school generation is underperforming. This can be seen in their grades in school as well as in the significant discrepancies between measured scholastic aptitude and results on standardised achievement scores. According to a professor of education: 'My own research indicates upwards of 40 per cent of children enrolled in a variety of schools . . . at all grade levels are "getting by" in school but according to their natural ability could be doing much better in their schoolwork.'

One high-school student remarked: 'The girl next to me drinks a bottle of cola when she first gets to school. Then she has a packet of yellow-coloured snack food for recess, and starts eating a big packet of lollies. She eats those all day. Her mother packs a sandwich and fruit but she gives them away. She's gone down a grade. She's slow, and she doesn't really try. She gives up easily.'

Teachers are helpless because students cannot concentrate. Parents blame teachers for failing to help their children. Students have low self-esteem and find school boring. The only winners are the food manufacturers.

It is much more difficult to 'see' the effects of foods on learning than on behaviour. One day of difficulty concentrating may not seem so important, but 200 inattentive schooldays makes a year's learning delay. When schools introduce low-additive programs it takes time to see improved concentration translate into measurable end-of-year academic achievement.

During four years of phasing out additives in 800 New York schools in the 1980s, the number of children classified as learning disabled more than halved and there was a 15 per cent increase in academic ranking on national tests. Two years after the introduction of an additive-free tuckshop at Wolney Junior school in the UK, the success rate of 11-year-olds in external exams tripled and the school won praise as one of the most improved in Greater London.

What the teachers say

Classroom behaviour has changed. In Cambridgeshire, England, a school asked parents to stop children's 'tuck' money because, according to the deputy head, 'immediately after morning break and lunch, children are "hyper". They are noisy, rowdy and can't sit still or concentrate. It is not just the exuberance of break-time being carried over, it is much worse. They fill up on ... additives and misbehave immediately afterwards.' Her observation was confirmed by the regional spokesman for the National Union of Teachers: 'There is a problem nationally with this and it is causing a lot of concern. Children are being affected by what they consume at break-times and their behaviour is suffering as well as their health.'

An early-primary-school teacher in Australia describes her week:

> I teach ages five and six. I see these children come to school, all hyped up after the weekend. On Mondays I can't do much with them except try to wear off the energy. We do lots of outdoor activities. Each day they get a bit better, and by Friday I've got them to the point where they'll sit down and listen. I can teach them something. Then it's the weekend and they're just as bad again. I don't know what they do. They must spend the weekend eating junk food.

Older teachers can still remember a time when classrooms were different. A teacher with 30 years' experience had this to say: 'When you've lived as long as I have, you've seen the changes. The foods children eat now are very different from what we had as children. Of course it affects them.'

In a USA teacher survey of behaviour problems in schools, teachers in 1940 identified the top problems in USA schools as talking out of turn, chewing gum, making noise, running in the hall, cutting in line, dress-code infractions and littering. When asked the same questions in 1990, teachers identified drug use, alcohol abuse, pregnancy, suicide, rape, robbery and assault.

Independent scientists have recommended that schools should minimise the use of additives that may contribute to behaviour problems. Schools that follow this advice see a difference.

When I taught in a developing country I could set my class a 20-minute task, and they would all do it. You could have heard a pin drop. Here, I can't turn my back. I have to keep saying, 'sit down', 'be quiet', 'stop talking', 'get on with your work'. I have 12 out of 20 in one class that simply don't want to work at all – I can't get them to do anything. Sometimes I wonder if it's me, if the lessons aren't interesting enough. But I've been a teacher for 20 years and I've never had this kind of problem before. I put a lot of work into preparation and I did one particular session on a subject I thought was fascinating, but these kids don't seem to be interested in anything. 'Everything's boring,' they say.

They seem to lack self-discipline. They can't finish a task without a break, they can't settle down, they can't concentrate for more than five or ten minutes without talking. These kids are the worst I've ever seen. There's something about them, I don't know what it is. I have one particular class straight after recess, and I can't get them to settle. Perhaps it's what they eat. I see them arriving at school and they have a bottle of cola and a packet of chips for breakfast. Or a lollipop, that's the latest craze. No wonder they can't concentrate. Four of them are worse than the rest. I can't get them to do anything. They all work part-time at a fast food outlet. I wonder if that has something to do with it? I just can't get them motivated. *From an experienced teacher who spent three years in a remote high school in the South Pacific.*

At Appleton Central School in Wisconsin, student behaviour was so out of control that the school required its own policeman. However, when vending machines and junk food were replaced by fresh natural foods and water bottles, the number of school dropouts, expulsions, drug use, suicides and weapons violations dropped to zero.

Similarly, when TV chef Jamie Oliver introduced fresh, natural, additive-free school meals for 16,000 schoolchildren in the UK, after four weeks teachers at Wingfield Primary School in London reported improvements in behaviour, reading, writing and concentration. They also noticed that children were calmer and that asthmatics had improved.

In 2005, I took part in the simple two-week trial at Palmers Island Primary School in NSW in which 120 students were taught how to read labels, asked to avoid 50 additives and provided with additive-free breakfasts, as shown on our DVD. Staff, parents and students all saw changes – students were quieter, calmer, 'stopped yelling out in class', had more self-control, concentrated better and classes were more harmonious. When the children again ate artificially coloured treats at the end of the study, they exhibited noisy, argumentative, 'in your face' behaviour. See the 'Eating for Success' factsheet at www.fedup.com.au.

The coca-colonisation factor

'The coca-colonisation factor' is the name given to the rapid socio-economic development over the past 30 years that has resulted in big changes in our lifestyles. Food regulators know that a certain number of additives can cause problems, but food additives are permitted on the understanding that affected people can choose to avoid them. This leaves parents to counteract lunch-swapping, school canteens, peer pressure, billions of dollars' worth of advertising and a lack of alternatives.

Everyone is affected by the side effects of foods, whether directly or indirectly. In the well-known Twinkie Defence case, the mayor of San Francisco was shot dead by a young man who attributed his violent behaviour to coloured snacks called Twinkies. If you are disturbed by murderers, vandals, criminals who steal your property, disruptive children in your child's class, drivers with road rage or paying other people's medical bills through your taxes, then consider yourself affected. Government agencies cannot protect us against multinational food corporations. This is an issue between consumers and food manufacturers. Every time you buy processed food containing additives, you send a message to manufacturers that additives are acceptable. Is that what you want?

As experts identify dramatic increases in literacy problems, irritability, rages, depression, and decreases in attention span and intelligence, they blame television, family breakdown, poor teaching skills, working mothers, pollution, lack of sleep and lack of attention from parents – anything but diet. I suggest that while all of these items are important, food chemicals are a vital factor.

We are slowly creating a new breed of less interesting, less intelligent, less healthy, hard-to-like, hard-to-teach, easily bored, disagreeable, discontented, defiant or aggressive children and adults.

6

Are you affected by foods?

YOU MEAN, FEELING TIRED, IRRITABLE, WHEEZY, HEADACHY, DEPRESSED, ANXIOUS, UNMOTIVATED AND GENERALLY VERY ORDINARY, ISN'T NORMAL?

Why the side effects of foods are so hard to recognise

Everyone knows that medications can have undesirable side effects – for example, a stomach upset by aspirin. Few people realise that chemicals in foods can do the same. Some of the chemicals in foods are the same chemicals we take in medication. Salicylates in foods are the same as salicylates in aspirin and can cause the same side effects. The effects of chemicals, whether taken as drugs or eaten in foods, are related to the size of the dose. Some drugs are addictive and people can suffer distressing withdrawal symptoms when they stop taking them. This can also happen with food chemicals, including additives. When people react to food chemicals in this way, it is called *food intolerance*, not to be confused with *food allergy*.

A true allergic reaction is usually quick, occurring within minutes to a few hours. It involves a measurable development of antibodies by the immune system, called an IgE (Immunoglobulin E) response. In Western countries, food allergies affect about five per cent of children under three and about one per cent of adults. Reactions can be triggered by even a tiny amount of food. The foods most likely to trigger allergic responses in Australia are peanuts (and other nuts), milk, eggs, sesame, seafood, wheat and soy. Symptoms of allergy include itching, rash, swelling, breathing difficulties or diarrhoea that may be confused with other conditions:

> Our three-year-old always had puffy eyes but we didn't realise it was related to allergy. We normally don't eat eggs except for cooking such as in a cake because I used to throw up after eating them as a child. When she ate mayonnaise with raw egg it caused a more pronounced response. Within minutes I saw hives coming up around her mouth and took her straight to hospital. Over three hours the hives went down and then the eyes started puffing up and she developed a runny nose (allergic rhinitis). The Paediatric Registrar told us 'these things sometimes happen when they have a virus – take her home and give her antihistamine' but the next day I insisted on an allergy test referral and my suspicion was confirmed. My daughter was very allergic to both egg white and egg yolk. Not anaphylactic (a major allergic reaction), but one step away.

Food intolerance reactions are much more common, but more difficult to recognise than food allergy. The side effects of drugs often remain unrecognised by doctors and are frequently treated as a separate condition with yet more drugs prescribed. It is with the side effects of foods. A very wide range of foods may be involved and the reaction may happen hours or days later. Because the reaction is related to how much you have eaten, anyone can be affected if they eat enough.

Most people, including doctors, are still unaware of the distinction between these two types of reaction. There are laboratory tests (skin prick or SPT) for true allergy. Unfortunately – despite what many alternative practitioners claim – the only scientifically proven way to test for food intolerance is by using an elimination diet. During this diet potential problem-causing foods are avoided then carefully re-introduced one group at a time, while watching for reactions.

It is possible to have true allergies or food intolerances or both. Mothers of children with both say it is more difficult to live with the threat of a fatal allergy in very young children, but as children grow bigger, food intolerance is more difficult to live with, as this mother explains:

> If he does have any accidental contact with dairy, antihistamines can fix the problem very quickly, whereas with intolerance his reactions would take four weeks to get over, particularly for amines. Intolerance . . . impacts every aspect of his life, his behaviour, his learning, his relationships, his relationships with us, his relationships with his peers.

A family history of allergy

If you have a family history of hayfever, asthma and eczema, and particularly if anyone in your extended family has a known food allergy, your children are at a greater risk of developing allergies. The official advice from the Australasian Society of Clinical Immunology and Allergy (ASCIA) to pregnant women who want to prevent allergies in their babies is to avoid cigarette smoke during pregnancy and breast-feeding, to delay introduction of solids until six months and to fully breastfeed for four to six months or use special formulas (see p. 193 and http://www.allergy.org.au/aer/info bulletins/allergy_prevention.htm).

Food allergies, especially peanut allergies, have increased in the last ten years and experts do not know why. One study found that babies whose mothers had used a UK nappy rash cream containing peanut oil were more likely to develop peanut allergy. Another suggestion is that exposure to per-fluorooctanoic acid, one of the 'Teflon chemicals' found especially in stain resistant fabrics and carpets, may prime the immune system to overreact to allergens.

The official advice (as above) is that breastfeeding mothers shouldn't avoid allergens in their diet as a method of allergy prevention; however, mothers from allergic families need to be aware of allergy symptoms. A breastfeeding mother in our network reported that when she ate peanut butter sandwiches 'to build up her strength', as recommended by a child health nurse, she eventually discovered that her baby's severe and worsening eczema was due to undiagnosed peanut allergy.

There have been a number of reports in our network of young children developing allergies after a reaction to ribonucleotide flavour enhancers (635 and others, see p. 113) that were introduced ten years ago – at about the time peanut allergy started increasing – and one mother whose rash during pregnancy and breastfeeding turned out to be related to additive 635 found her new baby had multiple allergies, unlike her previous children. This is not scientific evidence, but since ribonucleotides are known immune boosters, and allergies are the result of an overactive immune system, it makes sense for at-risk pregnant mothers, babies and young children to avoid exposure to large amounts of these flavour enhancers.

Coeliac disease

Coeliac disease is a permanent autoimmune sensitivity to gluten – the protein found in wheat, rye, barley and some other grains that can damage the lining of the small intestine. This can result in irritable bowel symptoms or various symptoms due to malabsorption and resulting nutrient deficiencies. It was first identified by a Dutch researcher when failure-to-thrive children improved on low wheat rations during World War II. Coeliac disease was originally regarded as rare and obvious but is now thought to occur in one per cent of the population, frequently undiagnosed. When coeliacs eat gluten, it damages the gut and can increase the risk of cancer.

Does your family history include some of the following?

• a relative with coeliac disease • unexplained anaemia (due to malabsorption of iron) • a long history of diarrhoea, constipation and other mild abdominal complaints • longstanding low-key chronic ill-health • unexplained osteoporosis (due to malabsorption of calcium) • poor weight gain in children • an adult who is extra thin and/or short • a rare itchy blistery rash called dermatitis herpetiformis due to gluten intolerance • Down syndrome • schizophrenia • impaired male or female fertility, recurrent miscarriages • insulin dependent diabetes • patchy baldness called alopecia areata • Irish or Scottish heritage.

If so, it is worth considering coeliac disease as a possibility (see www.coeliac.org.au). A number of *Fed Up* readers have reported that they were alerted to coeliac disease by the list above, including one previously infertile woman who brought her new baby along to say thank you.

Blood tests from your doctor for coeliac disease are effective only while you are regularly consuming gluten. If you think you might have coeliac disease, it is best to be tested before starting a gluten-free elimination diet. Gluten can be associated with a range of problems including learning difficulties and children's behaviour. It is possible to have gluten intolerance without having coeliac disease, as I have often observed in relatives of coeliacs whose gluten sensitivity is not picked up by tests.

Gluten-free diets are less nutritious than wheat-based diets, so if going gluten-free in the long term, especially with children, consult a dietitian. Assuming gluten has been completely removed, there should be dramatic improvements within two weeks (see Checklist of Common Mistakes on www.fedup.com.au). Some people are sensitive only to gluten, others to a range of food chemicals (see www.coeliac.org.au and weaning recommendations for babies with a family history of coeliac disease on p. 193).

A family history of food intolerance

The side effects of foods can apply to any age and to a range of problems. People generally have to be desperate before they will give up their favourite foods and often the most desperate are the mothers of difficult children. To know if you have any of the problems often associated with foods, first look at the checklist on p. 83.

IT WAS EITHER GIVE UP THE FOOD, OR GIVE UP THE KIDS!

- Does anyone in your extended family have migraines, irritable bowel symptoms or behaviour problems such as oppositional defiance, difficulty falling asleep or ADHD?
- Have you ever noticed any reaction, ever, to any food?

You may have food intolerance if you answered yes to either question. A 'yes – but' is a 'yes'. For example: 'My daughter used to get hives but she's grown out of it'; 'My sister gets migraines but they're premenstrual'; 'My son gets asthma, but it's not related to what he eats'; 'My husband gets headaches but they're due to tension'; 'I get migraines, but only after I drink red wine'; 'He says he gets stomach aches but he's probably trying to get out of school.'

Regarding noticeable reactions to foods, fathers especially are inclined to say: 'No, he doesn't react to foods. Of course he gets a bit hyped up when he has a can of cola but all kids do that.'

However, there are many families who have never noticed a food reaction and are surprised at how much their children improve on the elimination diet.

A strong family history: Children with a variety of food-related problems such as mouth ulcers, bedwetting, growing pains and others scattered through the family will usually achieve dramatic results on an elimination diet, provided they get it right – hopefully with the help of an experienced dietitian and an email support group.

No family history: Children with little or no apparent family history of food intolerance can still have problems caused by foods. With one such child, his problems turned out to be caused entirely by the preservative in bread. Another did the full elimination diet with challenges because his mother thought she had seen him react to foods. Of the 13 challenges in the elimination diet, this child reacted to only one: monosodium glutamate (MSG), as flavour enhancer (621) and naturally occurring glutamates in foods such as grapes. This family was very glad they did the elimination diet because they now know how to control their child's difficult behaviour. In my experience, people without an obvious family history are likely to react to fewer food chemicals. People with a strong family history can sometimes react to all of the challenges.

The 30-minute rule

People who react to foods have sometimes noticed a connection between certain foods and their symptoms. They usually blame whatever they ate last. But are they right? Reactions can occur within 30 minutes or up to 48 hours after eating a problem food. One study of the effects of aspirin on asthma found people did not connect their attack to the aspirin if it occurred more than 30 minutes later.

Three types of reactions

1. The same-day reaction: Starts quickly, sometimes within minutes or up to a few hours, and lasts for a few hours. Behavioural reactions to food colouring can be like this, easy to see if you're observing carefully during the elimination diet, but frequently overlooked.

I once watched as the entire process from eating to reaction was filmed by a TV crew. Two young boys ate artificially coloured foods then played outside. Within half an hour it was obvious to everyone that they were affected. 'It's as if they were drunk' the presenter whispered as we watched the boys becoming loud, argumentative, uncoordinated and uninhibited, shouting and hitting at each other. What they did was all normal child behaviour and the association between what they ate and how they acted wouldn't be obvious unless you were observing them closely (see Notes). You can see the same kind of reactions at the end of the Palmers Island study on our DVD. As with drunks, it can be funny to watch until you think of parents and teachers trying to control children like that every day.

2. The next-day reaction: This can take up to eight hours to develop and lasts about a day. Reactions to preservatives, annatto colour and salicylates are typically this kind of reaction, although everyone is different. Some children react to food colouring this way, as one mother describes:

> I sometimes think on a good day my ten-year-old son is outgrowing his attention deficit hyperactivity disorder. His behaviour is excellent at school and not too bad at home, but then some uncaring person will buy him a bag of coloured lollies. The next morning I am awoken to a bull in a china shop running at full speed.

It is possible to have one type of reaction to food colours and another type to other food chemicals, as I found with my children. Pre-diet, we used to have pizza once a week. If we had drinks or dessert with food colouring, the children would be climbing the walls by the time we finished dinner, but if we avoided colours they were fine, so we thought, 'Well, that's okay, pizza doesn't affect them.' When we learned about delayed reactions we realised that the morning after eating pizza our daughter especially would be grouchy from the minute she got out of bed. We would have a real walking-on-eggshells morning in an effort to get her off to school without a major blow-up. She would have a bad day at school, adding to her learning delay, and that night she would have difficulty falling asleep. So the next day she would be tired, which wouldn't help at school, and the day after that she would be all right again – if she hadn't eaten another problem food in the meantime. We decided that wasting two whole days for each pizza wasn't worth it. Now we make our own failsafe pizzas.

I see this pattern frequently when a mother phones me early in the morning, in tears, and says: 'My son has always been difficult, but today he wouldn't get out of bed, we had a fight during breakfast, he didn't want to go to school, he was so awful I never want to see him again.' When I ask what they ate for dinner the previous night, the answer is nearly always either some kind of Italian meal, like spaghetti, or takeaway. Italian food, the way we eat it in Australia, is very high in salicylates and amines.

3. The slow build-up: Symptoms can build up slowly over several days, reach their worst on the third day and slowly improve – with occasional flare-ups – over a week or more. I know a child who has no reaction to tartrazine orange colouring on the day he drinks it, a tiny reaction the next day and goes berserk the day after that, recovering slowly over a week. Children who have this kind of reaction and are eating an average Australian diet could be on their way to a detention center. Amines are typically a slow build-up but everyone is different and some people have slow reactions to everything. When migraines or irritable bowel symptoms from salicylates or amines follow this kind of pattern, people are highly motivated to avoid them. You can only detect this kind of reaction with an elimination diet and careful challenges.

One young boy was suspended from school for aggression, at the early age of five. His doctor recommended they try the elimination diet and his parents agreed:

We decided to do a challenge over Easter, so he could eat lots of chocolate and not feel out of it. He was really good and we were starting to think it wasn't going to affect him. Then he went ballistic on day three. He was so bad his father wrote 'ABORT!! ABORT!!!' in the food diary. It took him a week to come down again.

Cumulative effects

Another factor which makes reactions hard to observe is that effects can build up slowly if you eat a certain chemical every day. The bread preservative is a good example. Few children will be affected by the amount of bread preservative in one slice of bread, but when you eat bread every day, effects can build up over several days or weeks, depending on the dose. Synthetic antioxidants in oils and margarines are another example.

CUMULATIVE EFFECTS...

Then there are the natural food chemicals that can occur in more than one food and build up over time. Mothers are confused when their child fails to react to a certain food: 'I can't understand it. I've seen him go off his face after eating chocolate, but he ate a whole bar on Friday and there was no reaction.'

Whether the individual reacts to chocolate on Friday may depend on what he ate on Thursday, Wednesday, or even last week. Spaghetti sauce, cheese, oranges, sultanas, broccoli and some other foods all contain the same problem chemical which is likely to build up and finally cause a noticeable reaction. If eaten frequently, this chemical will cause fluctuating symptoms rather than one dramatic blow-up.

The rules of food intolerance

- food intolerance runs in families
- food intolerance can be triggered by illness, exposure to environmental chemicals or medications
- people who notice the effect of one additive are likely to be affected by other food chemicals
- any symptom may be provoked by any food chemical
- everyone is different
- reactions are related to the size of the dose
- effects can build up slowly over days or weeks
- some people are more sensitive than others
- there are no scientifically proven laboratory tests for food intolerance
- an elimination diet with challenges can show which food chemicals affect you.

If your doctor dismisses the effects of diet and your friends tell you about their wonderful improvements, how are you supposed to know whether it works? The only way is to try it for yourself, preferably with a dietitian helping you.

Keep a record of your score before beginning your elimination diet, and at intervals, for instance, after one week, four weeks and three months. This way you can monitor your progress, instead of having to rely on your memory.

What's your score?

Symptom	Rating

Rate how much each symptom bothers you:
0 is not at all and 3 is very much

Skin

Symptom				
Eczema, hives (urticaria), other rashes	0	1	2	3
Cradle cap	0	1	2	3
Swelling (angioedema), e.g. lips, eyelids	0	1	2	3
Itching with or without rash	0	1	2	3
Flushing	0	1	2	3
Sore vagina, thrush	0	1	2	3
Excessive sweating, body odour	0	1	2	3
Allergic shiners (dark circles under eyes)	0	1	2	3
Pallor (pale skin)	0	1	2	3

Airways

Symptom				
Asthma	0	1	2	3
Asthma cough	0	1	2	3
Hayfever (rhinitis), blocked or runny nose	0	1	2	3
Snoring	0	1	2	3
Nasal polyps	0	1	2	3
Frequent nose bleeds	0	1	2	3
Catarrh or chronic throat-clearing	0	1	2	3
Sinusitis	0	1	2	3
Frequent tonsillitis, colds, flu	0	1	2	3
Frequent ear infections, glue ear	0	1	2	3

Digestive system

Symptom				
Recurrent mouth ulcers	0	1	2	3
Indigestion	0	1	2	3
Nausea/vomiting	0	1	2	3
Bad breath (halitosis)	0	1	2	3
Diarrhoea and/or constipation	0	1	2	3
Stomach ache	0	1	2	3
Bloating	0	1	2	3

Symptom	Rating			
Flatulence	0	1	2	3
Reflux, colic in babies/adults	0	1	2	3
Sneaky poos (soiling)	0	1	2	3
Sticky poos (Incomplete evacuation)	0	1	2	3

Bladder

Bedwetting	0	1	2	3
Daytime incontinence	0	1	2	3
Urinary urgency	0	1	2	3
Cystitis (inflammation of bladder)	0	1	2	3

Skeletal

'Growing pains'	0	1	2	3
Joint pain, inflammation, swelling (arthritis)	0	1	2	3
Muscle weakness	0	1	2	3
Gout	0	1	2	3

Eyes

Nystagmus (involuntary movement)	0	1	2	3
Strabismus (squint)	0	1	2	3
Visual acuity	0	1	2	3

Muscles

Low muscle tone	0	1	2	3
Myalgia (muscle pain)	0	1	2	3
Tremors, tics (involuntary movement)	0	1	2	3

Heart

Rapid heart beat (tachycardia)	0	1	2	3
Heart palpitations	0	1	2	3
Arrhythmias	0	1	2	3
Pseudo heart attack (see factsheet)	0	1	2	3

Nervous system

Headaches or migraines	0	1	2	3
Tinnitus (ringing, noises in ear)	0	1	2	3
Dizziness or vertigo (sense of spinning)	0	1	2	3
Temporary deafness, Ménière's	0	1	2	3

Symptom	Rating			
Unexplained tiredness	0	1	2	3
Feeling hungover	0	1	2	3
Confusion	0	1	2	3
Agitation	0	1	2	3
Hyperacusis (sound sensitivity)	0	1	2	3
Paraesthesia (pins and needles)	0	1	2	3
Dysaesthesia (numbness)	0	1	2	3
Sensory symptoms of MS	0	1	2	3
Salicylate-induced hypoglycemia	0	1	2	3
Epileptic seizures	0	1	2	3

Anxiety & depression

Anxiety	0	1	2	3
Panic attacks	0	1	2	3
Depression	0	1	2	3
Self harm	0	1	2	3
Suicidal thoughts, actions	0	1	2	3

Impaired memory/concentration

Vague or forgetful	0	1	2	3
Unable to concentrate	0	1	2	3
Won't persevere	0	1	2	3
Unmotivated	0	1	2	3
Disorganised	0	1	2	3
Easily distracted	0	1	2	3
Difficulty reading or writing	0	1	2	3
Poor school marks	0	1	2	3

Speech

Loud voice (no volume control)	0	1	2	3
Speech hard to understand	0	1	2	3
Speech delay	0	1	2	3
Selective mutism	0	1	2	3
Stuttering	0	1	2	3
Repetitive noises (vocal tics)	0	1	2	3
Talks too much (empty chatter)	0	1	2	3
Makes silly noises	0	1	2	3
Hums constantly	0	1	2	3

Symptom	Rating

Coordination

Poor handwriting	0 1 2 3
Poor fine or gross motor coordination	0 1 2 3
Frequent accidents	0 1 2 3

Sleep

Insomnia	0 1 2 3
Difficulty falling asleep	0 1 2 3
Frequent night waking	0 1 2 3
Restless legs (RLS)	0 1 2 3
Nightmares/night terrors/sleep walking	0 1 2 3

Mood

Mood swings	0 1 2 3
Premenstrual symptoms	0 1 2 3
Grizzly or unhappy	0 1 2 3
Cries a lot	0 1 2 3
Irritable	0 1 2 3

Oppositional defiance

Uncooperative, argumentative	0 1 2 3
Grouchy, easily annoyed	0 1 2 3
Overreacts to small incidents	0 1 2 3
Temper tantrums or outbursts	0 1 2 3
Constantly says 'no'	0 1 2 3
Breaks rules	0 1 2 3
Blames others ('it's your fault')	0 1 2 3
Deliberately annoys others	0 1 2 3
Angry, resentful, defiant	0 1 2 3
Spiteful	0 1 2 3

Other behaviour

Difficulty in making friends	0 1 2 3
Easily bored	0 1 2 3
Fights with siblings	0 1 2 3
Destructive, aggressive	0 1 2 3
Unreasonable	0 1 2 3
Demanding, never satisfied	0 1 2 3
Disruptive	0 1 2 3

Symptom	Rating			
Discipline doesn't work	0	1	2	3
Overactive, restless or fidgety	0	1	2	3
Head-banging	0	1	2	3
Handflapping	0	1	2	3
Rocking	0	1	2	3
Faceblindness (in autistics)	0	1	2	3

Total

For more information about these symptoms, see the foot of the front page of www.fedup.com.au.

7

And the asthma
went away

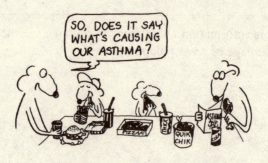

When families go failsafe to support a difficult child, parents generally report that asthma goes away too. This mother wrote:

> We haven't gone the whole hog with the elimination diet yet but for the last four weeks we've avoided additives and have enjoyed a peaceful school holidays with our sons. And their asthma seems to have disappeared. We've only had one asthma 'attack' (if you could even call it that) – which required only one dose of Ventolin.

The same thing happened with well-known TV chef, Jamie Oliver. A month after the introduction of Jamie's additive-free school dinners at Wingfield Primary School in London, staff reported that asthmatic children hadn't needed their asthma medication any more.

Although any of the nasty additives can contribute to asthma, one group of additives is more likely to affect asthmatics than all others: sulphur dioxide and the sulphite preservatives (220–228). Unfortunately, sulphites are probably the most commonly used preservatives in the Western diet, compared to traditional villages where they aren't used at all. While researching the introduction of food additives in the Himalayas, I found that traditional villagers didn't have asthma and they'd never met anyone with asthma.

The sulphite connection

I would have liked to have known about the sulphite connection when my daughter started preschool at the age of four. In a bid to encourage healthy eating, her preschool promoted dried fruit instead of sweets. Unbeknown to me at that time, dried tree fruit such as apricots can contain by far the highest level of sulphites that children will ever be exposed to, particularly in Australia where the maximum permitted level is higher than that in the UK and Europe.

Since Rebecca loved the dried apricots offered at breaktime, I started buying at least a packet a week for her – and the rest of us – to eat as snacks. Over a period of months she developed a night cough, breathlessness during exercise and was eventually diagnosed with asthma. Our doctor handed me a prescription for asthma medication along with a leaflet published by the food industry stating that there was no connection between asthma and diet.

Over the next year, the rest of us developed asthma too. We assumed that our asthma was related to known local triggers such as rye grass allergy until our search for answers to Rebecca's behaviour problems led us to avoid additives – and our asthma disappeared.

The 30-minute rule applies

Asthmatics do not make the connection between their asthma and what they've eaten unless asthma occurs within 30 minutes. I had been vaguely aware that sulphur dioxide was associated with asthma and had noticed it listed on the side of the dried apricot packet as 'preservative 220'. I had watched

Rebecca while she ate dried apricots and she didn't seem to be affected. Like most asthmatics, I had fallen into the trap of thinking that if sulphites or other food additives affected us, we would know because we would see a reaction soon after eating. It is true that some asthmatics are affected that way. But for the majority of sulphite-sensitive asthmatics, regular doses of sulphites seem to cause irritated airways with no obvious symptoms. It is not until you are exposed to an asthma trigger such as cold air, a virus or exercise that you will get asthma. That's how it was for us, and this mother describes a similar experience:

> We haven't done the full elimination diet but with the knowledge I gained from your books I was able to retrace which foods did what. The cause of my three-year-old's asthma became obvious. It was sulphites. He would eat something out of the ordinary, such as two apricot fruit bars, come home, run around outside and have an asthma attack, which he had not had for ages.

If you remove the sulphites or other irritating food chemicals from your diet, you are more likely to manage exposure to asthma triggers without getting asthma.

For our family, sulphites are the only food chemicals that trigger asthma, but we didn't realise that until years later when a supposedly 'pure' fruit ice-cream left us all coughing and struggling for breath within minutes. Afterwards, we realised that we had just experienced our first classic sulphite reaction due to exceptionally high levels of sulphites permitted in processed fruit pulp.

We now avoid all sources of sulphites and no longer consider ourselves to be asthmatics. However, we keep an asthma puffer in our first-aid kit just in case.

Sulphites are so widely used throughout our food supply that they are difficult to avoid unless you are motivated and careful. They are consumed in particularly high doses by young children, especially in dried fruit, fruit-flavoured drinks and meat. Although it is illegal to add sulphites to fresh meat except sausages and rissoles, a NSW food authority survey in 2003 found over 50 per cent of mince samples contained illegal sulphites. For adults, wine and beer are another major source of sulphites.

Possible sulphite intake per serve		legal maximum	
dried fruit	80 mg in 5 dried apricots	3000	mg/kg
sausages	50 mg in 1 sausage	500	mg/kg
hot chips	50 mg in 1 cup of hot chips	200	mg/kg
drinks	30 mg in 1 glass of juice	115	mg/litre

The actual amounts will usually be less, but may sometimes exceed these figures. The Acceptable Daily Intake (ADI) for sulphites is 0.7 mg per kilogram of bodyweight, which means 12 mg per day for a four-year-old. However, *any* sulphites can be too much for some asthmatics.

The rise and fall of sulphites and asthma

Childhood asthma rates in Australia rose from about 10 per cent in the 1970s to nearly 30 per cent at the end of the 1990s. The countries with the highest rates of asthma (see box) are English- and Spanish-speaking cultures where sulphites have been eaten in foods, especially meat, for more than 100 years. Sulphites were banned in meats 50 years ago in the USA, but are still used extensively in other products including French fries.

Asthma's top ten

1. UK	6. Peru
2. New Zealand	7. Costa Rica
3. Australia	8. Brazil
4. Irish Republic	9. USA
5. Canada	10. Paraguay

Lancet (1998) 351(9111), pp.1225–32.

After a number of asthma deaths in the USA due to sulphites in restaurant salads, the World Health Organization recommended that the use of sulphites should be reduced. Since then, food regulators in developed countries have been working to reduce maximum permitted levels and to enforce compliance. The resulting decline in sulphite levels has been accompanied by a reduction of childhood asthma rates in developed countries in the early 2000s, although sulphite intakes and asthma levels are still high.

Bizarrely, most asthmatics are unaware of the effects of sulphites because food regulators don't consider it their job to tell the public. Unless you stumble across information, such as the article 'Sulfites – safe for many, dangerous for some' on the US Food and Drug Administration website (see Notes), you are unlikely to hear about them. As one father wrote:

> . . . from the age of 10, I have suffered terribly from asthma; and yet, over the next 23 years, not a single doctor ever once asked if my condition might be caused by the food that I eat . . . It's been around 6 months now since we actively started amending our diet, and overall, my asthma is now highly manageable . . .

Benzoates

Sulphites are not the only food chemicals that can affect asthmatics. In France, doctors reported the case of a child who was diagnosed with asthma around the time of her first birthday then medicated continuously for the next five or six years. Despite medication, the child was rushed to hospital with severe asthma approximately once a month. Eventually she was checked for additive sensitivity and found to be sensitive to benzoate preservatives, which she was consuming regularly in her asthma medication as well as some drinks and one food. When she avoided benzoates, her asthma stopped.

Benzoates are commonly consumed by young children in drinks, medications, ice-cream toppings and even in flavoured water, so much so that a survey by food regulators found that after sulphites, benzoates are the next most over-consumed preservative by preschoolers.

Adults are at risk too. You can see the story of the cola drinker who developed asthma when she switched to diet cola preserved with sodium benzoate (211) on p. 116.

Colours

Childhood asthma related to artificial colours in foods was first reported in 1958 and followed by reports of asthmatic reactions to colours in medications and vitamins. It is easiest to observe reactions when food additives are eaten infrequently, rather than daily. This explains why there are more reports of additive-related asthma in medical journals in the 1960s and 1970s when the use of food additives was just starting to become widespread in the USA.

Even breastfed babies can be affected because artificial colours and other food chemicals can pass through breastmilk. Although the usual reactions are restlessness, reflux or hives, asthma is possible. Baby Joe's asthmatic cough started on day three, when his mother's milk came in. He also screamed constantly. His family now realises that food chemicals were the problem:

> A GP put him on antibiotics at four months, thinking his screaming might be an infection of some sort. That's when the breathing problems and wheezing started. He was on the nebuliser at least twice a day with corticosteroids, salbutamol and oral steroids thrown in here and there when he got really bad. He had all the tests for causes – dust mites, etc. – which proved negative. Then he started solids at five months and only got worse. When he was two and a half we started him on the elimination diet. His asthma disappeared in the second week.

Challenges showed that Joe reacted to sulphites, benzoates, nitrates and colours. One musk stick (red colours azorubine 122 and erythrosine 127) started him coughing and wheezing within minutes. Annatto (natural yellow colour 160b) took a little longer and tartrazine (artificial yellow 102) turned out to be the worst of all. Additives can also be absorbed through the skin. By experience, Joe's family learned that his asthma could be triggered by coloured antibiotics, toothpaste, shampoo and playdough made with artificial colours.

In 1999, the Center for Science in the Public Interest recommended that the US Food and Drug Administration should 'consider banning the use of synthetic dyes in food widely consumed by children *because dyes adversely affect some children and do not offer any essential benefits*'. In Britain, artificial colours are banned in foods – but not medications – for children under three, and most supermarkets and many large food manufacturers have phased out their use. In the USA and Australia, however, there are still many violently coloured products.

MSG

Some asthmatics know that MSG (flavour enhancer 621) causes asthma, whatever the food industry might say. During one of my school presentations, a young student volunteered: 'My sister and my dad get asthma when we eat Chinese food.' This effect was first reported in 1987 in a study in which twelve patients reacted to MSG with asthma, with half of the reactions occurring unexpectedly many hours later. MSG is widely used in savoury foods, snacks, sauces and restaurant meals and rarely appears as MSG on labels. Instead it will be listed as flavour enhancer 621 or added in natural ways such as yeast extract, hydrolysed plant or vegetable protein. As with any food additive, reactions depend on the size of the dose, but studies also suggest that MSG eaten in a hot soup on an empty stomach will have the greatest effect.

How do you know what's in your food when you eat out? You can ask, but there are no guarantees. In 1993, MSG-sensitive Los Angeles resident David Livingston ate a bowl of vegetable soup for lunch after being assured by the waitress that it was 'made from the freshest ingredients, from scratch . . . every day'. On the way back to the office, Livingston experienced asthma unrelieved by his inhaler and drove five minutes to his doctor's surgery. After suffering an anaphylactic reaction including respiratory arrest he was rushed to hospital where he went into full cardiac arrest without pulse for seven minutes, remaining unconscious on a respirator for three days. Livingston later discovered that the soup had contained a 'beef base' with MSG clearly listed on the label.

Salicylates in natural foods

Asthma induced by salicylates in aspirin has been well-documented for many years, but it is less well-known that salicylates in foods can cause the same problems.

Salicylates are thought to affect about 20 per cent of asthmatics. As with other food chemicals, most people assume they will know if they are sensitive to salicylates including aspirin, but that isn't true. The few people who react within 30 minutes will realise there is a connection, but for most people reactions are delayed for hours or even days, or build up slowly.

A failsafe mother whose fully breastfed three-month-old baby developed an asthma cough 24 hours after she started using teething gel reported: 'I used the teething gel for three days, not putting the connection together, then rang the pharmacist to find out what was in it. When he said salicylate-based and preservatives, I stopped immediately and the cough was gone within two days.'

The mother of a failsafe eight-year-old with formerly

severe asthma described the difference between the effects of salicylates and artificial colours on her son's asthma: 'Salicylates, for example in apples, tend to creep up on him, taking a few days, and the reaction seems milder than with artificial colours.' Since going failsafe nearly a year before, her son has not needed to go to hospital at all – 'and for a child who has been hospitalised multiple times every year since he was six months old this is quite an achievement!' You can see the full story and many others at http://www.fedupwithfood additives.info/stories/storyasthma1.htm.

This kind of dramatic improvement was also observed in a hospital-run trial of an additive-free low-salicylate diet. A salicylate-sensitive asthmatic child who stuck to his diet improved so much in three months with regard to both chronic asthma and lung function that he was able to be weaned off oral steroids.

Added flavours

Parents are most likely to see the effects of salicylates on their babies and children through concentrated flavours such as mint, cherry and other fruit flavours used in children's syrup medications. At the very beginning of the introduction of processed foods forty years ago, Californian paediatric allergist Dr Ben Feingold was way ahead of his time when he blamed salicylates for the effects of added artificial and natural flavours on asthma and other symptoms.

A Sydney Children's Hospital study found that almost one-third of children who attended the emergency department for asthma had experienced 'mirth-triggered' asthma. Asthma diaries showed that laughter while watching a movie caused the biggest increase in asthma symptoms measured by a reduction in peak flow readings. What do kids do while watching movies? Although the researchers didn't consider this, the answer is that they consume additive-laden food.

Microwave popcorn currently contains an artificial butter flavour called diacetyl. When heated, diacteyl gives off toxic vapours that have been linked to an incurable and sometimes fatal respiratory condition known as popcorn workers' lung. Some manufacturers are beginning to remove artificial butter flavour from popcorn following a report that consumers can be affected by popcorn workers' lung too.

Q. Is popcorn failsafe?
A. As well as natural salicylates, commercial popcorn is likely to contain additives linked to asthma. At one cinema, an attendant explained how they add a premix powder. 'I wouldn't eat it,' she said. 'There's a lot of powder, I don't know what's in it.' From reading supermarket labels, I guess it could contain yellow colours – either artificial or annatto – and possible synthetic antioxidants in the vegetable oil, as well as diacetyl butter flavour.

Other additives

Other preservatives and synthetic antioxidants are less commonly associated with asthma. A girl in New Zealand whose asthma cleared up on a wheat-free trial at the age of four then avoided wheat for years. It was only when she did her elimination diet at the age of 12 that she discovered her asthma had not been due to wheat but to antioxidant 320 (BHA) often unlisted in the vegetable oil in bread and also added to most margarines. In New Zealand and the UK most cooking oils contain synthetic antioxidants, compared to Australia where most large containers of oil for commercial use contain synthetic antioxidants, but smaller bottles of oil for home use are usually additive-free.

Asthma and allergy

True IgE-mediated allergies to foods such as milk and environmental allergens such as dust mites, animals or pollen can contribute to asthma, although they are not the major cause of asthma. It is possible to have asthma related to food intolerance alone, allergy alone, or both. Asthmatics are at risk for true allergies if they come from a family with a history of eczema and hay fever.

Milk

Cows' milk allergy is thought to affect about two per cent of asthmatics, so it is not a common cause of asthma, but it is important for those who have it, as Richard's story shows. With a family history of allergies and asthma, Richard's mother followed the recommendation to breastfeed for 12 months and delayed introduction of known allergens such as milk and eggs. At the age of two and a half, Richard was hospitalised for a week with his first asthma attack. Skin prick tests showed he was allergic to 'nearly everything' and he rapidly became a chronic severe asthmatic needing daily preventers and relievers. Avoiding cows' milk didn't help. Much later, when Richard's mother cut out ice-cream, cream, butter, skim milk and whey powder in biscuits, she was able to notice that his asthma attacks came half an hour after ingesting any form of dairy foods. Richard remained additive and dairy-free and suffered asthma only on the rare occasions he ate dairy foods, until university, where he abandoned his diet and resumed his daily medication.

Adults with asthma

About ten per cent of Australian adults are estimated to have asthma, and it is possible to have adult-onset asthma. Any food chemical can be implicated. One woman wrote:

> I was diagnosed with asthma several years ago as an older adult and now finally I think I have solved the problem! For the last 3 to 4 months I have been on low salicylate foods; no asthma, no medication. My bronchial passages just feel calm – under no inflammatory threat. Occasionally I get a slight wheeze and can adjust the food intake accordingly. I think particularly the fruits were a problem, not that I ate huge amounts.

Up to 30 per cent of asthmatic adults may suffer from occupational asthma caused by sensitivity to workplace chemicals such as latex for medical workers, flour dust for bakers, pesticides for farmers, isocyanates for spray painters, and many others. With most occupational asthmas, symptoms start slowly as coughing or chest tightness, shortness of breath or wheezing, particularly at night or in the early morning. Symptoms usually improve during weekends and holidays and the most effective treatment is to avoid exposure by changing jobs.

What you can do

Diet for asthma is only useful if you are prepared to stick to it. If you are going to break your diet you may get asthma, so you should keep on taking your medication (see box p. 100). As with any other food intolerance symptom, people vary in their sensitivity. Some asthmatics are affected by only one group of additives – most likely sulphites, but it can be others – and some are sensitive to everything.

The majority of families I hear from notice that asthma disappears when they do the elimination diet for a difficult child. But there are some asthmatics who need to fine-tune their diet. It can be as difficult to avoid sulphites as doing the full elimination diet, because sulphites are in so many foods.

- If only avoiding additives, see 'How to Avoid Sulphites' on the 'Sulphite Preservatives' factsheet on www.fedup. com.au.
- If doing the full diet or challenges, it is essential for asthmatics to be supervised by a dietitian or doctor. You can write for our list of supportive dietitians to confoodnet@ ozemail.com.au.
- Our email support group for asthmatics can assist with fine-tuning and many other questions, and has helped many asthmatics to achieve success. Email 'subscribe' to failsafeasthma-subscribe@yahoogroups.com.
- See asthma stories on our website at http://www.fedup withfoodadditives.info/stories/storyasthma1.htm

- Always consult your doctor before reducing medication.
- Keep an asthma puffer with you at all times, because every time you eat food you haven't prepared yourself, you could unknowingly be exposed to a sudden high dose of sulphites.

Do you use your Ventolin-type puffer more than twice a week? Do you wake up wheezing or short of breath at least once a week?

Most asthmatics underestimate the severity of their asthma and nearly three-quarters of asthmatics rely only on reliever or Ventolin-type puffers. If you answered yes to either of the questions above, you may need preventer medication as well as reliever medication. Due to better use of medication, asthma deaths have fallen from nearly 1000 per year about 20 years ago to 300 Australians currently. Every asthmatic should have an asthma plan developed with your doctor so you know what to do when symptoms worsen.

8

How to eat fast food

The mother of a fidgety, asthmatic seven-year-old with reading problems said: 'My child doesn't have food additives. We eat healthy food.'

I often hear this. When I explain to the mothers what to look for, they realise just how many additives their children eat every day. The first few daily items this mother mentioned included the bread preservative (282) and diet cordial – 'That's healthy, isn't it?' I asked the mother to read me the label on the diet cordial. It contained preservatives (211 and 223) and colours (102 and 110). Every day this child consumed at least three preservatives – calcium propionate, sodium benzoate and sodium metabisulphite – and two artificial colours – tartrazine and sunset yellow. All five of these additives have been found to cause problems including restlessness, irritability and asthma. When I explained this, the mother complained, 'How are you supposed to know what they put in our food?'

How do you know?

There are approximately 400 food additives currently approved for use in Australia – not counting several thousand flavours – and most of them, such as vegetable gums, emulsifiers, vitamins and citric acid, are no problem. There are only about 60 additives likely to cause adverse effects. Unfortunately, some of these are now used so frequently it is almost impossible to avoid them.

When people think of food additives they think of food colouring, and when they think of food colouring they think of lollies and coloured cordials. People assume sugar is bad. A coach at a training session for elite athletes advised: 'Go and buy yourselves some lunch but don't eat anything sweet.' However, savoury snack foods, pies and hot dogs can contain as many food colourings as lollies, with MSG, preservatives and other problem food chemicals as well.

A packet of chips

When I was a child, you could buy a packet of chips and it would contain potatoes, oil and salt. By the time I wrote the first edition of *Fed Up*, a typical packet of chicken-flavoured chips contained: potatoes, vegetable oil, salt, rice flour, flavour enhancers (621, 627, 631), wheat starch, sugar, hydrolysed vegetable protein, chicken fat, flavours, chicken meat, colour (160b), and antioxidant (319). So in one little packet of chips you had seven additives that could cause problems – counting added flavours and hydrolysed vegetable protein, which is a way of adding MSG without saying so. Ten years later, flavoured chips and crackers are less likely to contain nasty colours and antioxidants and more likely to say 'no artificial colours, flavours, preservatives'. However, they are more likely to contain a range of flavour enhancers, including those that sound harmless, such as hydrolysed vegetable protein, vegetable extract and yeast extract.

A packet of biscuits

You might think you have found a food without additives when you see the following ingredients listed on a packet of biscuits: flour, vegetable oil, sugar, malt extract, salt, full-cream milk powder, baking powder and yeast. However, vegetable oil often contains synthetic antioxidants (in the range 310–312, 319–321) that do not have to be declared on the label (see box). I have seen many people affected by this and the only way to be sure is to phone the manufacturer or check our list of Product Updates on www.fedup.com.au.

The five per cent labelling loophole

If the amount of an ingredient in a product is less than five per cent, any additives in that ingredient don't have to be listed. So you have to phone or email the manufacturer to find out. This loophole affects us most with vegetable oil in a product such as bread, biscuits, frozen potato chips or soymilk. Be pushy. A failsafe mother who suspected her six-year-old's aggression was due to unlisted antioxidants in a gluten-free bread mix was told the manufacturer was 'pretty sure' there were no anti-oxidants. When she insisted, this man was shocked to discover antioxidant 319 in their supposedly 'pure' canola oil (see 'Story 566' on www.fedup.com.au).

How long does a burger last?

If you talk to teenagers, they will insist that there are no addi-tives in burgers and that the food is all natural. This assump-tion is presumably based on advertising about 100 per cent pure beef patties combined with advertising about fresh food. It is true that the meat patty is additive-free, but there can be additives in the other ingredients.

A customer who purchased a burger at the end of winter and left it in his overcoat pocket by mistake was surprised at the beginning of the next winter to discover it still in his pocket, mould-free and in excellent condition. You can try this for yourself. A burger I purchased as a demonstration for a talk in Christchurch, New Zealand appeared on the New Zealand news in good condition nine years later. This is a convincing display of preservatives doing their intended job very well indeed. The trouble is that preservatives 282, 202, 320, 211, 200 and annatto colour 160(b) in my burger have been associated with health, learning or behaviour problems in some people.

As well as problem additives in the burger, a serving of French fries or chips will probably add antioxidant 320, a milkshake another dose of 211 and an ice-cream another serve of annatto 160(b). But unless your children are preschoolers and you buy a soft drink with colour or a birthday cake with colours (102, 110, 123, 124, 133), you are unlikely to see a quick, over-the-top reaction. Most reactions to these kinds of additives and natural chemicals are delayed. So you may have to wait for up to 48 hours to see irritability, forgetfulness, headaches, bedwetting, sleep disturbance or asthma, which can all result from such a meal.

A young woman confided: 'My fiancé started a new job two weeks ago. He's really changed, like Jekyll and Hyde. He's been so grouchy, I thought he must have met someone else and he didn't love me any more. But then I realised it's because he's been eating lunch at a fast-food restaurant every day.'

In a child with behaviour problems you are likely to have a grumpy child the next day who has a fight before breakfast and spends the day standing outside the classroom, adding yet another wasted day to his learning delay. The mother of a four-year-old phoned me one Saturday afternoon: 'He can't sit still to watch television. He's trashed his room. His eyes are glazed. I can't get through to him. Could it be because we ate fast food last night?'

How to eat fast food

Nearly all fast foods, especially from the big chains, contain additives and natural problem-causing chemicals. From the food chemical viewpoint, baked potatoes with sour cream, Chinese fried rice with egg and shallots (no MSG, no sauce), or grilled fish and limited chips are some of the safest take-aways, although the oil will contain synthetic antioxidants. BBQ or rotisseried chickens used to be additive free but are now usually covered in flavour-enhanced seasoning. Pizzas are very high in the natural chemicals that often cause problems.

Nutritionally and chemically, you are better off eating at home. Fast foods are generally high in kilojoules, fat and salt, and low in fibre and complex carbohydrates. If eaten frequently these may contribute to a poor diet, which increases the risk of diet-related health problems including coronary heart disease, high blood pressure, obesity, diabetes and possibly even some types of cancer.

If you still want to eat fast foods, ask about the ingredients. This is not always easy. When I phoned Pizza Hut head office to ask if their pizza toppings contained MSG, a product development officer declined to comment. When *Choice* magazine looked at fast foods in 1990, all the meat toppings on Pizza Hut pizzas contained MSG, as did KFC chicken batter mix. The Australian Consumer Association suggests that ingredient information should be available at point-of-sale. McDonald's provide a useful product ingredient list (see Notes). At the time of writing, their meat patty and lettuce are additive-free, and you can take your own bun; chicken nuggets are free of nasty additives although not failsafe due to spices; and the French fries would be failsafe if not for antioxidant 320. The vanilla soft-serve mix is failsafe although the chocolate contains artificial colours. Bottled water is available to drink.

Salads usually contain additives in dressings and any ingredients that aren't fresh vegetables. One woman was shocked to find two artificial colours (102, 110) and two preservatives (202, 211) in coleslaw from her local supermarket. At McDonald's, although there are two additives to avoid in a Crispy Cut chicken salad, the Garden Mixed Salad is additive-free.

Colours

Discovered in the late 1800s, 80 different coal tar dyes were available for food colouring in the USA at the turn of the century. By 1980, only eight certified colours remained. Some of these colours were banned because animal studies demonstrated potential health hazards, others were abandoned because industry had no further use for them. Expressing the attitude of the time to these newly introduced food colourings, the heroine in a novel first published in 1912 wrote: 'We had delicious pink ice-cream for dessert last night. Only vegetable dyes are used in colouring the food. The college is very much opposed, both from aesthetic and hygienic motives, to the use of aniline dyes.'

Colours can cause almost instant restlessness, as the mother of this five-year-old boy in Connecticut, USA, reports:

> When we did the food colour challenge his day-care teacher and I both noticed that he was extremely fidgety and I noticed that he started to do his 'chanting' again. By this I mean that he likes to make repetitive noises. A wide variety of them, but he latches onto one and repeats it over and over. He doesn't do this when he sticks to the diet. This is an example of his 'tic' behaviours, according to the occupational therapist and doctors.

I always ask if parents have ever noticed their child react to food colouring, even once in their lives. One surprised mother replied, 'Yes, my son reacts to food colouring. They all do, don't they?' In my experience, the families who miss this connection are the ones who never had food colouring when their children were under five, or the ones who give their children coloured food or drinks every day.

Other people who don't know that food additives affect children are the ones who don't spend a lot of time observing children or who can't read. This includes most doctors, scientists and people who make the regulations about food, some teachers, especially the younger ones, working mothers who spend little time with their children, disadvantaged mothers with dyslexia or poor reading skills, mothers from a non-English-speaking background, and, in general, men. Literate, observant women who spend time with children are the ones most likely to see the effects of food additives.

Why didn't someone tell me?

The father of a three-year-old expelled from a childcare center for uncontrollable behaviour exclaimed: 'You mean it's not an old wives' tale? Food colouring really does affect kids?' Like this boy, most very young children who are expelled or suspended from day-care centers and schools turn out to be sensitive to a range of artificial and natural food chemicals, sometimes with a very delayed response. Before he changed his food intake, this boy had been having large quantities of food colouring in a soft drink for breakfast every day, as well as frequent lollies and processed snack food.

A mother who had never heard of food additives affecting children had given her son coloured icypoles or cordial every day of his life since he was a baby. She described how she had taken her son, always a poor sleeper, to a doctor when he was seven for suspected hyperactivity: 'The doctor weighed and measured him, took his blood pressure, and told me he was a normal, healthy boy. I tried being firmer with him and tried to convince the school there was something wrong . . . Now he's doing badly in high school and his behaviour is getting worse. I've tried everything. Sometimes I think the only thing left to do is to kill him!'

Colours in drugs

We have often seen the ridiculous situation where hyperactive or asthmatic children – those who are most likely to react to food colours – are given food colouring every day in their medication. There are still ignorant doctors and pharmacists who protest when I request plain white tablets: 'Food colours have been shown not to affect children.' I hate to think how many artificial colours elderly patients take in their medications.

Vitamin supplements are another trap for consumers. You would think vitamins with the label 'free from salt, yeast, starches, gluten, wheat, corn, dairy products, egg' would avoid food colours. It took three phone calls to a vitamin manufacturer to find that the coating was coloured with artificial colour sunset yellow (110), definitely a problem for many sensitive people. Pharmaceutical products don't have to list all ingredients on the label (see p. 182).

Natural colour annatto

One natural colour can cause the same problems as artificial colours. It is listed as annatto, annatto extracts or colour 160b on labels. A study of people with urticaria (hives) found annatto affected more people than artificial colours. Failsafe families have reported a wide range of symptoms from irritability, oppositional behaviour, head-banging in toddlers and headaches, to irritable bowel symptoms, rashes, asthma and severe allergic reactions.

Annatto is widespread in seemingly healthy 'all natural' products – yoghurt, breakfast cereals, vanilla ice-cream and crumbed products such as fish fingers – as well as in biscuits and sweets. In our family, annatto causes a grouchy-all-the-next-day reaction. Some parents say it has the worst effects of any additive. One mother described a typical reaction in her 15-year-old daughter after eating 'the slightest amounts' of annatto in foods such as ice-cream, sliced cheese or sweets:

The scenario sounds like a typical teenager but don't be fooled, it is unprovoked and quite out of character for her. It starts with 'You don't understand me', and escalates through to 'You're mean, you hate me, I hate you, everyone hates me, I won't be here tomorrow, nobody will miss me'. She has threatened to kill herself and once tried to jump out of a moving car.

Preservatives can be worse than colours

What most mothers mean when they say 'my child doesn't have food additives' is that they avoid obviously coloured drinks or sweets. Some will give their children a can of cola or lemonade because there is no artificial colour. Most have no idea about preservatives, especially in bread. The fact is that although most mothers perceive artificial colours as the main problem, studies have shown that preservatives can be at least as important as colours. The reaction to colours is the easiest to see because it can be quick and dramatic. Reactions to preservatives are often delayed.

Preservatives found to cause problems include:

- Sorbates (200–203) in fruit products like drinks, fruit yoghurt, processed cheese, dips, soft drinks, flour products other than bread (for example, cakes).
- Benzoates (210–213) in fruit drinks, cordials, sports drinks, flavoured water, many soft drinks, some jams, fruit topping and imitation fruit.
- Nitrates and nitrites (249–252) in processed meats such as salami, pressed meats like devon and other luncheon meat, corned meats and ham and bacon.
- Sulphites (220–228) in processed fruits and vegetables, salad bars and prepared fruit salad, cordials, juice drinks, dehydrated vegetables, and in fresh meat like sausages and manufactured meat. All sulphites may be dangerous to asthmatics.
- Propionates (280–283) in bread, also in dairy products such as cheese in north America.

Most preservatives are colourless, odourless, tasteless powders. The consumer can't tell whether they are there or not. They are often added by the handful, not measured out. I asked a seafood shop whether they used preservatives in their fish. 'Yes, we just sprinkle it over, when the fish is packed in ice. It's just a white powder, in a big sack. We call it "metta". Hang on, I'll check with the boss . . . No, we only use it on the prawns, not the fish.'

This woman was undoubtedly referring to sodium metabisulphite, which is strongly implicated in asthma and other adverse reactions. 'Metta' is the same preservative often used in mince by unscrupulous butchers. 'Does this mince contain any preservative?' I asked a butcher, who answered 'No'. 'You mean it's just meat, nothing else?' I persisted. Looking uncomfortable, he replied, 'Well, just a little bit.' 'Of what?' I asked. 'Preservative,' he replied. He didn't know the name of it. 'It's a white powder.' (See Notes.)

People obviously feel more comfortable about using a white powder than a colour. So how do we know whether there is preservative in our foods? We have to rely on the honesty of the supplier.

A glance at the applications from manufacturers to the Australia and New Zealand Food Authority suggests that the use of additives is on the increase. For example, one company applied 'to increase the level of benzoic acid or its salts permitted to be added to icings from 0.1 g/kg to 1 g/kg.' This is an increase of ten times the amount of preservative used in icings. Another manufacturer applied for approval to use 'sulphur dioxide as a processing aid in pastry products. Furthermore, because of the negligible amounts of sulphur in the final products, the applicant also requests the deletion of "preservative added" from the labelling requirements.'

I was lucky to find a butcher who felt the same way about additives as I do. He made preservative-free sausages for our support group and suggested these sausages to all his customers. He said: 'You've been good for business. People are sick of preservatives.' Of course, with preservative-free sausages, you have to eat them the same day or freeze them. They will not keep forever.

As a food scientist, Howard questions whether preservatives are good for the human gut: 'We rely on bacteria to help us digest our food. These preservatives are designed to kill bacteria. I wouldn't want to eat a food which was preserved so it kept for weeks without refrigeration. I think preservatives must interfere with beneficial gut bacteria.'

Antioxidants

Synthetic antioxidants were some of the first additives found to cause problems by Dr Feingold in the 1960s. They are widely eaten yet often overlooked, because few children will react to one dose. It is more likely that effects will build up from small doses eaten nearly every day.

Antioxidants (gallates 310–312, TBHQ 319, BHA 320 and BHT 321) are found in vegetable oils and products that contain oils including margarines, bread, biscuits, takeaways, fried foods such as hot chips and chewing gum. Natural antioxidants such as Vitamin C (300–304) and Vitamin E tocopherols (306–309) are harmless. Synthetic antioxidants can be present in foods labelled 'no preservatives'. This range of additives can cause all the usual symptoms of food intolerance, including depression (see the 'Antioxidant' fact-sheet at www.fedup.com.au). They can even cause problems when unlisted, see the five per cent labelling loophole on p. 103.

MSG (monosodium glutamate)

MSG was introduced into American food in 1948 and so-called Chinese Restaurant Syndrome was recognised soon afterwards. Symptoms may include sensations of warmth on the face, a burning sensation on the skin, sweating, heart palpitations, cardiac arrhythmia, anxiety, light-headedness, headaches, dizziness, muscle tightening, heartburn, stomach ache, nausea and vomiting, weakness in the upper arms, pains in the neck, migraine, flashing lights, hallucinations, respiratory distress and asthma. Symptoms can develop soon after eating or many hours later.

Flavour enhancers are used in sauces, soups, stock cubes, gravy mixes, tinned food containing meat and vegetables such as casseroles, stews, pasta, curries and Chinese foods, frozen diet foods; and especially in savoury snack foods including biscuits and chips, seasonings sprinkled on BBQ chicken, in stuffing in fresh chicken, seasoned salt sprinkled on hot chips, sausages, manufactured meats and sea foods, marinated meats and many others.

Food manufacturers are wary of listing MSG in the ingredients label because of the bad publicity. So they list it as 'flavour enhancer (621)', or add it in another form as hydrolysed vegetable or plant protein (HVP/HPP), beef or chicken broth, vegetable or yeast extract.

Most consumers are outraged when they learn that the banner 'no artificial colours or flavours' on two-minute noddles can include MSG (flavour enhancer 621) in the ingredients (see Notes). Yet this claim is legal because technically MSG is 'natural'. That's if you consider it natural to add extracts from high-protein yeasts grown on molasses in factories that produce 1.5 million tonnes of MSG each year.

The new flavour enhancers from hell
In the 1990s new flavour enhancers (ribonucleotides 635, sodium inosinate 627 and sodium guanylate 631) were introduced to intensify the effects of MSG by up to 15 times. The trouble is, for some people the nucleotide group intensifies bad effects as well. Foods that say 'NO MSG' in big letters will often contain hydrolysed vegetable protein or similar as well as nucleotide flavour enhancers (see the 'Ribo Rash' factsheet at www.fedup.com.au).

Symptoms can include children's behaviour, anxiety and pseudo heart attack, but one effect in particular that we have noticed is long-lasting itchy rashes appearing up to 30 hours after eating. The following report is typical:

I have never suffered food allergy in my life (43 years) until ten weeks ago when I developed an extremely intense and constant itch of my hands and arms. After two days I came out in hives, starting on my upper chest, abdomen and back. It then spread to my arms and my legs and from then on each day in different locations, worse at night, causing intense itch and lack of sleep. I can't begin to tell you how unbearable the itch was and how it affected my everyday living and ability to work. On several occasions my lips have been swollen and once my eyelids puffed up too. Through studying the foods that I had eaten I became almost

100 per cent certain that it was 635 causing my problem.

For almost two weeks I avoided all foods containing this additive and was finally able to come off the antihistamines I had been forced to live on. Then I ate a seasoned lamb steak from my local butcher and the next night the hives were back. Guess what? The butcher told me that the seasoning used on those steaks contained 635. I wish this additive had never been put on the market. I'm sure it is what has caused me absolute hell almost continuously for over two months.

Chemicals in drinks

Water is the best drink. But no matter how healthy your eating habits at home, once your children are at school peer pressure sets in and you will probably find your children drinking soft drinks sooner or later. I hear from mothers who choose cola or lemonade because they are free of artificial colour, or who choose diet drinks because they are healthier. Unpreserved lemonade is the lowest in problem chemicals, but Magic cordial (see p. 227) is better still.

Soft drinks usually contain preservative sodium benzoate (211), which has been found to affect more children than any food colour. But don't expect instant hyperactivity. This additive is more likely to produce a delayed reaction, and a daily intake of preserved soft drinks is more likely to cause constant low-level problems than a big blow-up.

Caffeine can have adverse effects on anyone in large enough doses. It is present in drip coffee (115–175 mg per cup), brewed or iced coffee (80–135 mg), instant coffee (65–100 mg), tea (30–70 mg), cola drinks (30–100 mg per can) and in chocolate (5 mg). The recommended maximum is 250 mg per day for the average adult. In large doses caffeine stimulates the central nervous system and may increase the heart rate. A counsellor once told me, 'I was seeing a patient for anxiety. After a while, he asked, "Can too much coffee make you anxious?" He admitted he was drinking about 40 cups a day. I encouraged him to cut down gradually and his symptoms improved.'

A survey of the effects of caffeinated drinks on behaviour found that teachers rated the high caffeine consumers nearly three times higher than the low caffeine consumers on a behaviour rating scale which measures hyperactive behaviours. A teacher from an inner-city primary school remembered, 'I had one boy in my class who was completely uncontrollable – we couldn't do anything with him. He was eating a lot of junk. We also found out he was drinking eight litres of cola a day.'

Caffeinated drinks often contain other food chemicals. For instance, the formula for Coca-Cola is believed to include essential oils of lemon, orange, nutmeg and cinnamon, which are all high in salicylates, so caffeine is not necessarily the only cause of the reaction.

A teenager with ADHD dropped out of school after several years of behaviour problems and truanting. He started an apprenticeship at the age of 15, which suited him far better than school. He became settled and happy and the family enjoyed previously unknown harmony. But his mother commented: 'We had to increase his Ritalin dose from six tablets to eight per day. It might be because now he's working, he's drinking a lot more cola.'

Caffeine is the most widely used drug in the world. Toxicology Professor Bernard Weiss suggests its effects on the developing brain, which is always the most vulnerable to toxic insult, need to be considered in the light of increasingly high consumption by young children. An exceptionally difficult and food-sensitive little boy, suspended from a day-care center at age three, responded well to diet but needed medication as well. His mother remembered: 'He used to love iced coffee. He lived on it. He was weaned onto it.'

Forty years ago it would have been unthinkable to offer a strong cup of coffee with five teaspoons of sugar to a baby or toddler. Because a high level of sugar disguises the bitterness of caffeine in packaged food, this is exactly what young children now drink in iced coffee and cola drinks.

Diet drinks

If you choose diet drinks because they are 'healthy', think again. Diet colas are more likely to contain preservative sodium benzoate (211) than regular colas. When a woman in her thirties who wanted to lose weight switched from regular cola to diet cola, over a period of four months she developed a night cough then chronic asthma. Realising that nothing else had changed in her life, she switched back to regular cola and her asthma disappeared.

Then there is aspartame (artificial sweetener 951) in diet drinks. Aspartame has not been shown to cause children's behaviour problems but there are safety concerns and some people have reported aspartame addiction. One mother confessed: 'I need to lose weight. I drink seven litres of diet cola a day. I know I should cut down.' Another drank 16 cans of diet cola per day – one can an hour during the day and one during the night – including throughout her pregnancy.

Aspartame was approved for use with humans based on studies allowing for two cans of diet soft drink a day, and there have been no studies on the long-term effects of continuous consumption of this additive on humans. In 2007, an independently funded Italian study of more than 4000 rats allowed to live until they died naturally showed that a lifetime of consuming high doses of aspartame raised the likelihood of leukemias, lymphomas and breast cancer. In previous studies that had shown aspartame was safe – virtually all industry funded – the rats had been killed at the age of two. As a result of the Italian study, independent scientists at the Center for Science in the Public Interest advised that people should stop buying products with aspartame and acesulfame potassium (950).

Aspartame can be found in about 6000 products worldwide, including soft drinks and diet or low-sugar products such as chewing gum, sweets, desserts, yoghurts, tabletop sweeteners, medications, sugar-free cough drops and vitamin supplements.

How aspartame was approved

For over 20 years, scientists debated the safety of aspartame. Although an independent panel of reviewers recommended that the US Food and Drug Administration withhold approval, the manufacturers, Searle Laboratory, kept pushing. The day after the new Republican administration took office on 21 January 1981, they petitioned for approval from the newly appointed FDA commissioner, Arthur Hull Hayes. Aspartame was approved for use in dry cereals in July 1981 and in drinks in 1983. (see Notes).

Don't blame sugar!

Sugar is often blamed for causing hyperactivity in children but that is wrong. I have described our ineffective sugar-free diet in the first chapter. However, a diet which gets a lot of its kilojoules from sugar is not healthy, because the kilojoules it provides are 'empty', contributing no nutrients to the diet. Sugar is also associated with tooth decay.

White sugar is so refined it contains no food chemicals other than sucrose, so should not be a problem for food-sensitive people. Mothers who have undertaken a properly supervised elimination diet, complete with careful challenges, nearly always find their children react to other food chemicals such as additives or salicylates, rather than sugar.

I don't recommend any artificial sweeteners and I recommend caution with sugar-free sweeteners including sorbitol that have been found to cause irritable bowel symptoms such as bloating, diarrhoea or stomach cramps in some people (see the 'Sugar-free Sweeteners' factsheet on www.fedup.com.au).

Life without additives: is it impossible?

Americans are leading the way in the obnoxious children stakes (see Notes) and Australians are hard on their heels. A failsafe family reported:

> We have just been lucky enough to go to Vanuatu for a week, self-catering, where we bought fresh food at the market every day and guess what? We all felt *so* good. What are we doing to ourselves in the so-called developed world?

Similarly, the Australian parents of a difficult child described their son as the 'most settled he's ever been' during a visit to relatives in Sri Lanka, eating simple additive-free food such as eggs and homemade bread. Others were surprised at how much easier it is to buy fresh, additive-free foods in Europe and Asia – although getting harder every year – and reported their children were 'much better there than at home'. All agreed their children were the 'worst ever' during holidays in the USA.

In the late 1990s, I belonged to a USA-based ADHD email support group with about 500 posts a week. There were numerous stories of small children doing the rounds of psychologists, paediatricians, psychiatrists and neurologists. As well as attention deficit hyperactivity disorder, they often had multiple health problems such as asthma and sleeping difficulties. Some as young as five had tried up to six different types of medication and one teenager was so disabled by his inability to sleep that he was hospitalised. Problems like this may well respond to diet, if families are prepared to give it a go.

The mothers often swapped hints for fussy eaters. A common suggestion was, 'If your child is happiest eating takeaways, do it.' Some of those children ate fast food every day and virtually all of the children were on medication. Yet many were still experiencing enormous problems and in some cases the problems were caused by the drugs. A mother who found diet worked commented: 'I am glad to have your support for this. Aside from my husband, everyone here is sceptical. Everyone here seems so eager to try medication; I think Americans have this "quick fix" mentality.'

A mother from Scotland reported: 'The Scottish diet is now reputed to be one of the worst – so much processed food . . . many children now drink litres of soft drinks – highly coloured, flavoured, preserved and artificially sweetened . . . meanwhile, we have more and more disruptive pupils in schools and parents at their wits' end.'

In the original *Fed Up*, I concluded that 'the overwhelming picture of the late twentieth century is of societies where it is now so difficult to avoid food additives that it isn't worth trying.' Ten years on there have been big changes. The bad news is that it is becoming more difficult to find additive-free foods in developing countries such as Nepal, due to increasing introduction of Westernised foods. The good news is that the UK is leading the charge to protect our children and rid our food supply of harmful additives.

UK to the rescue

Around the beginning of the new millennium, some UK supermarket chains and food companies started to phase out the use of additives due to consumer concerns. This trend accelerated in 2002 after results from research from the University of Southampton psychology department reported a link between certain additives and hyperactivity, restlessness and tantrums in preschoolers.

In 2003, new EU guidelines required medications containing certain additives – artificial colours, preservatives and synthetic antioxidants – to carry warnings of possible 'allergic reactions', 'mild irritation to the skin, eyes and mucous membranes', 'severe hypersensitivity reactions' or 'bronchospasm (difficulty in breathing)'.

In 2006, artificial colours were replaced by natural colours in the British version of the iconic candy-coated chocolates called Smarties.

In 2007, when a second University of Southampton study confirmed the link between additives and hyperactivity, the tipping point was reached. As lawyers warned that manufacturers may be sued for long-term harm resulting from the use of harmful food additives, food regulators hastened to assure manufacturers there was no safety risk. However, lead author Professor Jim Stevenson pointed out that there is a risk to children's psychological health, through difficulty learning to read and later behavioural difficulties at school.

As I write, all of the major British supermarket chains and many of the large food companies in Britain are in the process of removing various additives, especially artificial colours, from their own-brand products.

It is too early to know whether these changes will extend to Australian foods. It is likely that consumers will have many more fights ahead. You can help by emailing company websites or phoning consumer hotlines to request the removal of nasty additives in products you would like to eat.

9

What's wrong with fruit and other healthy foods?

Since the 1930s, fruit consumption per person per year in Australia has nearly doubled. While nutritionists tell us that 'fruit is the healthiest food', a growing number of mothers have discovered that orange juice and sultanas are just as bad for their children as coloured drinks and sweets. One mother commented: 'I have a friend who thinks that fruit is the healthiest food there is. Her attitude is, you can't have too much of it. Her children just about live on fruit and fruit juice. That's all you ever see them eat. What are they like? Well, when I think about it, they're uncontrollable. Real little terrors.'

Nearly two thousand years ago the co-founder of modern medicine wrote that his father had lived to be a hundred by avoiding fruit. Unlike Dr Galen, I am not suggesting that *all* fruits are bad for *all* people. However, in the last 30 years, people in developed countries have consumed increasing amounts of fruits, often through processed foods.

> My little boy is nearly three. He's getting to be a real problem when we go out, like shopping. I can't control him, and at home I don't know what to do with him. He's into everything. Right now he's climbing the furniture. He hates going to bed and always ends up with us. I've been talking to Nanna about what she fed to my mother, and she says everything was different then. Much plainer foods, like meat and barley. A lot less fruit, and it was home-grown. And no juice. My little boy drinks juice all the time and loves fruit.

The trouble with fruit

Fruit and other natural foods were not designed to be perfect foods for humans. It is easy to forget that fruits are primarily the sexual organs of plants. Plants are made up of thousands of natural chemicals, some of which can cause unfortunate reactions. Rhubarb leaves and green potatoes are examples of natural foods that can kill. Salicylates are one group of natural chemicals that occur frequently in fruits and have been identified as causing problems. Reactions are dose related and some people are more sensitive than others. Since we are eating increasingly higher amounts, in more concentrated forms, more people are likely to be affected.

Do you know about salicylates?

Hard to pronounce and in nearly every mouthful we eat, salicylates (*sal-i-sill-ates*) protect plants from pests and diseases. The best known form of salicylate is aspirin, originally from willow bark. At first, aspirin was regarded as perfectly safe, but in the last 50 years there have been reports of side effects such as heartburn, nausea, tinnitus, headaches, gastric bleeding, stomach ulcers, asthma, rashes, mental confusion, irritability and behavioural disturbance in children. Any of the known effects of aspirin can also be caused by salicylates in foods, but are rarely recognised as side effects of either medication or foods because the effects usually build up slowly over days.

Some people are more sensitive than others. In rare cases, people have died from a single 300 mg dose of aspirin, so it is easy to see that some consumers could be affected by much smaller amounts in foods.

Concentrated plant products such as tomato sauce, spices and most fruit contain a high level of salicylates, so Italian, spicy and vegetarian diets are higher in salicylates than, for example, the traditional Australian 'meat and three veg'. As families change their eating styles to eat larger doses of salicylates, more people are more likely to react. People who are sensitive to salicylates usually react to similar chemicals such as food colouring and preservatives.

Salicylates in added flavours

Salicylates give food a sharp, acidic, tart, tangy, zesty flavour – think citrus, kiwifruit, berries, Granny Smith apples, tomatoes and olives. On the other hand, fruits that are low in salicylates such as pears and bananas tend to be bland, sweet and mild.

Most people think that artificial flavours are bad and natural flavours are good, but they are all made in giant chemical factories and, chemically speaking, there is little difference between them. For example, a strawberry flavour, whether artificial or natural, may contain a hundred chemicals including methyl salicylate.

The problem with flavour additives is the size of the dose. Since laboratory-made chemicals are much cheaper than real fruit, the doses used are likely to be much higher than can be found in nature, and therefore more likely to affect sensitive consumers. As early as 1968, Dr Feingold wrote about the effects of salicylates in added flavours. Some parents see their child affected by flavours for the first time in strongly fruit-flavoured medication. Fruit, flower and eucalyptus fragrances made in the same chemical factories as flavours also contain salicylates that can be inhaled and affect some people.

If you think your family isn't affected by salicylates

Consider this: research shows that *the majority* (nearly 75 per cent) of children with behavioural symptoms will react to salicylates, followed by preservatives (60–70 per cent), artificial colour (about 50 per cent), synthetic antioxidants, amines and MSG (about 40 per cent). The figures are similar for other food intolerance symptoms. Salicylates generally affect the majority of those with irritable bowel symptoms, headaches and rashes, although only about 20 per cent of asthmatics.

'We're lucky, we're not affected by salicylates,' mothers often say. How do they know? Since these chemicals are eaten many times each day, reactions are not obvious. Salicylate-sensitive children and adults are likely to have a chronic health or behaviour problem that is not regarded as food-related. You won't know how good you or your child can be until you remove all salicylates from your diet for a few weeks. People are amazingly resistant to doing this, as I know, because I was one of them. However, as our dietitian Marion Leggo commented, 'It's only three weeks of your life.'

Salicylates in foods

Analysing food for salicylates is difficult and expensive, so it is rarely done. In the most comprehensive survey of over 300 food items, researchers found a wide range of salicylates in fruits and vegetables (see box). Very few consumers are affected by one dose of salicylates in foods. More often, as people are exposed to salicylates many times every day, effects build up slowly causing occasional outbreaks of symptoms and no one realises what is happening. For someone who is very sensitive, even an apple a day will be too much. There is only one way to see if a person is affected by salicylates and that is to do the elimination diet with a careful challenge.

Food	Salicylates in mg per 100 mg of food
Pears, Packham, ripe, peeled	0.00
Potatoes, white, peeled	0.00
Cabbage, green	0.00
Apples, Golden Delicious, peeled	0.08
Mangoes	0.11
Carrots	0.23
Strawberries	1.36
Oranges	2.39
Tomato sauce (up to)	2.48
Mint-flavoured sweets (up to)	7.58
Sultanas	7.80
Worcestershire sauce (e.g. in barbecue-flavoured crackers)	64.30

From: Swain, A., and others, 'Salicylates in Foods', *J Am Diet Assoc* (1985) 85 (8), pp. 950–960, see Notes.

The mother of a 15-year-old in a village in northern Italy, when hearing about salicylates, commented, 'I don't think we could give up olive oil and tomatoes.' At that time, fast-food restaurants and processed food were unknown in their village, but their all-natural diet was very high in salicylates. This mother eventually decided to try an elimination diet because her son was underachieving at school. My guess is that he would have suffered major learning and behaviour problems and been diagnosed with attention deficit hyperactivity disorder if he had been eating an Australian diet.

After several weeks of elimination, they tried a salicylate challenge:

On Friday we started the salicylate challenge. In less than a day there was forgetfulness, a critical attitude and a silly mistake, due to distraction. On day three he said he had trouble following what the Economics and Maths teachers were saying, 'like old times'.

On day four he left his art case on the steps near the bus stop. We got it back the next day but all the professional pens and pencils had been stolen. We were very upset about this and he said he felt depressed and no good at anything. On day five he said salicylates made him depressed and he had it in for everyone instead of everything being wonderful. 'Isn't it terrible to be sensitive to salicylates?' He has been dull-looking and his posture and movement are disharmonic, he drags himself around. He made the connection before I did that salicylates were affecting him.

Two years later this mother reported the family was still 'fairly strictly on the low-salicylate diet and my son is doing quite well at school despite minimum effort put in.' In the meantime, a cousin had been found to react to salicylates and colours. He 'has become docile and amenable and no more accidents (he was previously off to the hospital nearly every two weeks).'

Life without fruit

Most parents are reluctant to consider a low-salicylate diet. 'How can children live without fruit?' they ask. However, I have spent months in remote subsistence villages in the Himalayas where children eat very little fruit. These children are happy, healthy, well-spoken and eager to learn, sometimes walking up to two hours each way to school. They are mostly vegetarians living on home-grown rice, potatoes, lentils and a range of other vegetables, with a few fruit trees around the house resulting in less than one piece of fruit per week in season. As well there might be fresh milk and yoghurt in season from their own yak-buffalo cross and eggs from their own chickens. Their intake of additives is zero, and is much lower than ours of high salicylate-containing foods. My daughter, who follows a low-salicylate diet in Australia, does well on the Himalayan subsistence diet.

No free lunch

Nutritionists promote the Mediterranean diet as the healthiest in the world. There are suggestions that some ingredients may contain factors that are particularly protective of health, but the main reason this diet is recommended is for the proportion of foods eaten. Foods that are emphasised are the plant foods like grains, vegetables, dried beans, fruit and nuts. Foods that are eaten less frequently are the animal products like dairy foods and meat.

However, despite being low in additives, the Mediterranean diet contains foods very high in salicylates and amines such as tomatoes, olives, eggplants, mushrooms, broccoli and grapes. Like so many Australian children with behavioural or learning problems, the Italian boy above was affected by these.

Melbourne scientists conducting a long-term study of children's temperaments have found that children of Mediterranean families are five times more likely than others to be born with a 'difficult temperament', including withdrawal from new situations, a low ability to adapt, moodiness, a high activity level and difficulty settling into a routine. Half of the difficult children also suffered from colic, and 37 per cent from sleeping problems. Sounds like the effects of foods to me. One teacher observed: 'When I was teaching in Melbourne, the most difficult children in my class by far were the ones from Greek and Italian families. Some of them were extremely bright, but they had trouble concentrating. One boy in particular just couldn't sit still for a minute.'

These problems may not be due to 'inborn temperament' but the high level of salicylates, amines and glutamates in the Mediterranean diet. There is no free lunch. Mediterranean food may decrease your chance of a heart attack, while increasing your chances of being irritable and hot-tempered.

Amines

Salicylates are the most common but not the only natural food chemical to cause bad reactions. Amines are another group of problem chemicals that also occur in many fruit and vegetables, including grapes, oranges, bananas, broccoli and tomatoes. They are caused by protein breakdown, or fermentation, and so are high in, for example, cheese, chocolate, processed or less-than-fresh meat and fish and many alcoholic drinks. In 2003, amine responders noticed problems when Australian supermarkets started using vacuum-packed meat that can be up to three months or more old when it is repacked and sold as 'fresh'.

Effects of salicylates and amines can be different. This mother describes her nine-year-old son's reactions to the elimination and challenge diet: 'When we challenged with salicylates he became hyped-up and couldn't sit still. Even his writing was affected. The next morning he had that old familiar spaced-out look, and it was the first morning he wasn't ready for school on time. The challenge with amines resulted in my son at his worst. He became extremely argumentative and defiant.'

Amine-rich foods such as chocolate, cheese and red wine are traditionally associated with migraine, but amines are also linked to the full range of food side effects. People with migraines who avoid a few amine-rich foods often say 'I tried avoiding foods and it didn't work.' This is because migraines can still be provoked by eating other amine-containing foods or other food chemicals such as additives or salicylates. The mother of a 14-year-old tells a common story with regard to the differences in reactions to various foods:

> He goes off his face with food colouring but it only lasts a couple of hours so we can put up with that. Salicylates aren't too bad either at home, although it must be terrible at school. He gets bouncy and silly. In class he wouldn't be able to sit still or listen to the teacher. He would be too busy poking and prodding the kid next to him.

Amines are the really big problem though. When he eats amines it's World War III at our place. We need an air-raid siren. He'll get up in a foul mood, kick the wall, swear, throw things, yell. Absolutely revolting. After we started the elimination diet we had five months of a perfect child, but when we started our challenges that was the end of our wonderful existence. With his amine challenge he took nearly four weeks to calm down again.

Natural glutamates and MSG

Glutamates occur naturally in many of the best-tasting foods, including grapes and tomatoes. The only difference between MSG (monosodium glutamate) as a food additive and natural glutamates in foods such as tomatoes is the size of the dose (see box).

For two families who attended one of my workshops, understanding the effects of glutamates has turned out to be extraordinarily important. I doubt that any health professional would ever have suggested dietary management for these children's behaviour problems. What makes the story of these families so interesting is that there was no family history of

Glutamate contents of foods		
Food	portion size	mg glutamate per serve
Chinese soup with MSG	1 bowl	5000.00 (approx)
Marmite/Vegemite	2 grams	850.00
Parmesan cheese	25 grams	48.00
Peas	½ cup	2.00
Tomato juice	1 cup	1.73
Mushrooms	50 grams	0.90
Tomato	3 slices	0.70
Cow's milk	1 cup	0.02

(See the 'MSG and other flavour enhancers' factsheet on www.fedup.com.au.)

food intolerance. They did not have 'allergic' symptoms. They had never been seen to react to food colouring, and challenges confirmed this. They had not been diagnosed with attention deficit hyperactivity disorder.

One of the families completed their elimination and challenge diet within two months because the answer was extremely easy. Glutamates were the only food chemicals that affected their child. The other family took a little longer because the child reacted to four challenges: two classes of preservatives, one natural colour and MSG. 'MSG was the worst. I realise he used to eat a lot of natural glutamates every day. He's been on his diet for over a year. His new teacher has had him for four months. She doesn't even know what I'm talking about when I ask if his behaviour is okay. He used to argue and talk back. There's none of that now.'

This family found the high level of glutamates in their son's diet came mostly from natural sources such as tomato paste, Vegemite, broccoli, sultanas and grape juice. Common foods like stock cubes, gravy powder and soy sauce are also high in natural glutamates, even without added MSG.

Failsafe for health

Most people are understandably reluctant to try failsafe eating if it means giving up most fruit and some vegetables. It's difficult to accept that for some people – including my family – these so-called 'healthy' foods can actually contribute to chronic ill-health and family disharmony.

The nutritional benefits of failsafe eating are two-fold. First, you are avoiding the anti-nutritional effects of some chemicals. For example, soft drinks high in phosphorus can deplete calcium reserves in the body, contributing to osteoporosis. Similarly, high levels of sulphite preservatives in foods such as meat and dried fruit can prevent your body from being able to use thiamine (Vitamin B1), even in vitamin supplements that are taken at the same time. In Australia, cats and dogs have died from thiamine deficiency due to highly sulphited pet meat. Early signs of thiamine deficiency can include irritability, inability to concentrate, forgetfulness, insomnia, depression, agitation, sensitivity to noise, appetite loss, constipation, fatigue, nystagmus (eye movements) and a decreased sense of touch.

Second, there are nutritional benefits in what we can eat. For example, Brussels sprouts and cabbages are among the most nutritious of all leafy vegetables. They also contain compounds that seem to protect against a wide range of cancers, including breast, lung and colon cancer. Brussels sprouts in particular are a good source of minerals, fibre, protein, carotene, Vitamin C and folic acid, as well as a chemical called sinigrin that has been shown to suppress the development of precancerous cells.

Failsafe eating covers the full range of foods that are considered essential for good health (see p. 189). I've seen for myself that villagers on a restricted traditional diet can be much healthier than most Westerners. It's like returning to the simple foods our grandparents ate. The restrictions of failsafe eating have to be balanced against the happier and more fulfilled lives that people find they can lead when they avoid the foods that cause them problems.

10

How do you get difficult children to eat failsafe?

Find your own way

Motivated adults have little trouble with failsafe eating. They generally stick strictly to permitted foods at home and choose the foods that cause the least problems when out. Families have to find their own way. For children used to takeaways, home-cooked chicken and chips are likely to be the most popular option, at least at first. My-husband's-a-meat-and-potatoes-man-type families probably only have to make a few changes. Vegetarians need to adapt to different vegetables and less fruit. This is a lifestyle change, a long-term investment for better health. 'I believe that people need time to think and commit themselves to do the diet. It certainly took us a long time,' admits a mother of an eight-year-old boy. Some need to try it twice. A mother of a preschooler found: 'I tried the diet last year, but to be honest, I didn't do it properly. The Ritalin isn't enough so I'm doing the diet right this time. His temper's toned right down, and he's easier to manage.'

Helping children to cooperate

Children cannot be forced to do this diet through threats and punishment. One father of a four-year-old said, 'I'm not going to give up my colas and iced coffee. We'll just have to put a padlock on the fridge.' Another family told how they all ate home-delivered pizza while telling the five-year-old son, 'You can't eat this.'

Children in situations like this will break their diets at the first opportunity, through lunch swapping at school or stealing money to buy food at the shops, and who can blame them? It is best for children to feel they are supported by the whole family doing their diet, at least at home.

If you can't say 'no'

Some parents are unable to say 'no' to their children. Mothers often refuse to try the diet, even with young children, because 'My son loves peanut butter/tomato sauce/fruit. I couldn't ask him to give that up.' In that case, I suggest you start by watching *1-2-3 Magic*, which is the most entertaining and useful introduction to behaviour management that I have come across. This program should be shown continuously in all maternity hospitals. It would save everyone a lot of effort (see p. 329).

School problems

Children who are unhappy at school sometimes have good reasons, such as a personality conflict with a particular teacher, lack of friends, or bullying. Those who have difficulty learning to read and poor coordination will need help to feel good about themselves in the classroom and schoolyard. What are these children good at? For some children, diet alone can turn these problems around. Others have difficulties that are not food-related. One boy who improved dramatically on the diet became irritable during a week in which he was bullied so badly after school that the principal suggested calling the police. Dr John Irvine's comprehensive parenting manual *Who'd Be a Parent?* provides ideas on how to deal with such issues (see Notes).

Keep in touch with teachers and school counsellors, let them know you are working with your child, and ask for their help. A boy whose teacher gave him merit points when he stuck to his diet and a girl whose school provided suitable foods at social occasions succeeded, whereas a boy who was punished during withdrawal symptoms started breaking his diet. A change of school is sometimes effective. For children who are really miserable, home schooling for the rest of the year or longer can be a relief for everyone. (See the 'Home Schooling' factsheet on www.fedup.com.au.)

Praise and bribery

Gain children's cooperation through praise, positivity, bribery and making sure you have a 'safe house' – that is, all the food in the house is okay for them to eat and they are not constantly confronted by temptations. You can offer frequent rewards or even a large reward, such as a bike, and give them a number of points every day they stick to the diet towards their goal. Perhaps there could be a bonus for finishing all the challenges. If they break their diet, for instance, because there was food offered at school, don't scold them or punish them for telling you. It is counterproductive to remove points. Instead, you can

say, 'Thank you for telling me . . . now, what can we do to stop that happening again?'

It is good if they can suggest alternatives themselves, like having special food available at school. Or they might like to miss out on the treat at school if they know you will definitely buy them a toy or a special treat to make up. Quality time with parents is one of your most valuable bargaining tools. Doctors sometimes complain that it is not the food but the fact that parents spend more time with their children that makes them improve on the diet. What is wrong with that?

With older children there are more options. If they realise they are not doing well, and would like to do better, you can often talk them into agreeing to a three-week trial, 'Just so we can see how good you can be . . . I know it will be hard but I think it might be worth it, don't you?'

Involve your children

Try to involve your children in all the decisions. If a recipe fails, admit it. Encourage them to recommend alternatives, do taste testing and have a go at cooking. I earned the admiration of my children one night while we were eating on the verandah by admitting the soup was completely inedible and pouring my bowl over the railing onto the garden. The meal ended in giggles as they followed my example but, more importantly, they knew I was on their side.

Dietitian Joan Breakey suggests that children become 'diet detectives' by keeping their own food diaries and trying to discover what affects them. This is a wonderful way of getting them involved and taking responsibility for their own actions.

Junk food addicts

For teenagers, the decision to eat failsafe must be their own. Some will benefit from cutting down at home, even if they break out when with friends. A 15-year-old who refuses to change his lifestyle may become a 19-year-old who is disappointed with his life and would like to improve himself.

Inspiration

We have been surprised by the number of mothers who say their children or partners have been inspired by the examples on our DVD (see Notes). One mother wrote, 'After watching your DVD, my husband is now a firm believer and is ready to go the whole way, not just in front of the kids', and another reported:

> It came as a very pleasant surprise that my six-year-old failsafer devoured the DVD with the same passion as I have every single *Fed Up* book. She watched the entire DVD, mesmerised, pausing and rewinding, nodding and calling out to me that this was just like her.

Jaded palate syndrome

The more frequently you have a treat, the less of a treat it becomes. As food manufacturers continue to make food ever more delicious, the amount of flavour necessary to make people feel they are indulging themselves has reached ridiculous levels. It is possible to change your tastes. If you go without food for a few days even a humble food like a carrot will taste strong and sweet to you. People who change their lifestyles usually find they can adapt to a whole new range of foods – for example, a low-salt diet – in about three months or less. Your taste buds actually get used to the new flavours. The best way to enjoy food is to be hungry before you start eating. The same routine-regularity-repetition which works well for managing children's behaviour also works well with their mealtimes.

Fussy eaters

Children and adults with food intolerance are often fussy eaters. They may have cravings for the food chemicals that give them a high, like the amines in chocolate and cheese or the salicylates in strawberries and cherries. Just as these people often have developmental delays in ball-handling or reading skills, they may also have a developmental delay in learning to like vegetables. Yet vegetables are important nutritionally. Don't give up. The way to accustom children to eating vegetables is to offer a tiny taste of a new food, perhaps 20 times or more before you can expect them to like it. I did this successfully with my children by offering small rewards (a small toy or sticker) every day for two weeks for eating small but increasing amounts of blended vegetable soup. I started with a few acceptable vegetables, mostly potato, pureed with a wand blender. On the first day, they didn't have to eat any, just put a loaded teaspoon in their mouths and take it out again, then collect the reward. The next day they had to take a small lick, then a spoonful, and so on. After two weeks the rewards stopped and they had to eat a cup of soup before dinner would be served. After a while the soup included more vegetables such as highly nutritious Brussels sprouts.

Our grandmother's trick of withholding a delicious dessert until vegetables have been eaten may work, but don't expect difficult children to eat large quantities. Be reasonable. Try offering very small quantities, often, with as much trickery, bribery and praise as you can manage, like these mothers: 'My kids love mung bean sprouts because we call them fishing rods and I encourage them to play with them while they're eating'; 'We take the outer leaves off then cut a lettuce into cheeks. We eat lettuce cheeks like other people eat apples'; 'My son has a thing about textures. The only vegetable he likes is mashed potato. Now I put other vegetables in with the potatoes'; 'I've found my boys will eat Brussels sprouts if I call them baby cabbages'; 'We eat lots of your vegetable soup, my teenager calls it Sue's Poo Soup, but he eats it', and 'The only way I can get vegies into my kids is to serve stir-fries all the time.'

Introduce your child to gardening

Studies show that children who are involved in growing vegetables will eat more vegetables of any kind and in particular more of those they grow themselves. It doesn't mean you have to produce all your own food, even a few pot plants will help.

(See our 'Failsafe Gardening' factsheet on www.fedup. com.au.)

Teach your child to cook

You can't do better for food-sensitive children than to teach them to enjoy cooking. Start with party treats. Rebecca's gingerless pigs (p. 290) are fun to roll out and cut. Psychologist Steve Biddulph recommends that a boy of 10, having been taught care with sharp knives and hot stoves, should be able to prepare a meal for the family, and that boys need to see their dad working in the kitchen. Teenagers can put on a roast with potatoes, so that working parents come home to a delicious smell of a nearly cooked meal.

Kitchen gadgets can help

With a home donut-maker, failsafe children can have a treat like everyone else – fresh donuts to share when their friends come to visit. The basic donut mix is failsafe, and fresh, hot donuts can be dusted with caster sugar instead of cinnamon. Others recommendations from failsafe families include ice-cream makers, home Fairy Floss (cotton candy) makers, automatic egg cookers and breadmakers that can be easily used by children. (See Product Updates on www.fedup.com.au.)

Try new recipes

One mother whose child had been breaking his diet by sharing lunches at school wrote, 'I bought your cookbook. Now he is getting enough interesting things and variety so he feels that he is not missing out!'

Avoid advertising

Advertising works, otherwise nobody would do it. Nutritionist Rosemary Stanton comments that increasingly we purchase 'what food manufacturers want us to buy and forget the body's basic needs'. One of the world's most successful advertisers, McDonald's, considers television to be the most powerful advertising medium. In the so-called McLibel trial,

McDonald's spent nearly $20 million on a libel case that became the longest trial in British history. Two unemployed activists from a small environmental group in London were sued for libel for distributing leaflets called 'What's Wrong with McDonald's?', one of many protests and campaigns against McDonald's in over 24 countries. The court transcripts make fascinating reading, on every topic from nutrition (when asked if Coca-Cola was nutritious, McDonald's Senior Vice President of Marketing said that it was 'providing water, and I think that is part of a balanced diet'), to McDonald's employment of spies who infiltrated the environmental group, to the aggressive nature of their advertising. It was revealed in court that a former Ronald McDonald actor, Geoffrey Guiliano, had quit and publicly apologised, stating: 'I brainwashed youngsters into doing wrong. I want to say sorry to children everywhere . . .'

Although judgement was eventually handed down in McDonald's favour, a number of aspects went against McDonald's. The judge ruled that the leaflet's claims about advertising were true: that McDonald's is 'exploiting children' through its advertising, deceptively promoting company food as 'nutritious' and putting the health of their most regular, long-term customers at risk (see Notes).

Australian television has the world's highest level of food advertising aimed at children, and most of it is highly flavoured snack, fast and breakfast food. A good way to help your children avoid this influence is to stick to the ABC and advertisement-free cable channels, or limit television and hire DVDs instead. Some movies are better than others for avoiding fast-food brainwashing. Try anything set in the past or the future. No fast food there, sometimes not even any identifiable food. You can forget about pizzas while watching *Star Wars* without advertisements.

A social disaster?

Any dietary restrictions are difficult socially. In the 1980s when my family started on the Pritikin diet for healthy heart reasons, our dietitian commented, 'Nutritionally it's excellent but socially it's a disaster.' I suppose most people would regard failsafe eating like that. One mother explained, 'My sister and her family came to stay with us for a week. I think they were expecting terribly boring food and were surprised to find we ate normal, delicious meals. But when we went out they saw the problems.'

You find out who your friends are. Rebecca was occasionally told, 'I'd like to have you round for a sleepover but Mum says she couldn't cope with your diet.' I would have preferred that these people discussed the problems with me so I could send something suitable, but they were in the minority. Most were supportive and helpful. It is handy to make friends with families who are eating the same foods. Some people do this through the failsafe local or email groups (p. 328).

When my children went to someone else's place I would usually provide food for them, from preservative-free sausages and bread for a barbecue, to permitted lemonade, dip and crackers or chips and lollies at parties, to homemade pizza to share, or noodles with a chicken dish to be reheated in the microwave, or a cake or a tub of permitted ice-cream. And I was always prepared to deliver a 'Dengate takeaway' of ready-to-eat lamb stew on rice or similar, packed in a takeaway container, as described on page 19.

Sometimes we managed by having other children over to our place instead, although I was pleased by the supportive attitude of many of my children's friends. At one party, instead of the usual fast-food restaurant and a movie, there was a home-cooked meal followed by trail riding on horseback, which was a big success.

For difficult children, social isolation is often their lot anyway. Children with food-induced behaviour problems are often left off the invitation list to parties because of their behaviour. So they may as well avoid certain foods and enjoy their friends. There is nothing wrong with failsafe eating at parties. You can have a great feast with good company if suitable alternatives are provided. One mother reported that the failsafe dishes she contributed to a street party were the first to disappear – and she had thought only her own family would eat them. Another sent her daughter to friends' places with a stylish cane basket filled with failsafe treats. She reported that her daughter would arrive full of confidence and find herself being asked for some of her food.

Support from food suppliers

I hear many, many complaints that suitable foods are not available. One middle-aged woman complained: 'I've been on this diet for five years. The health benefits are worth it, but every year it is more difficult to buy additive-free foods and I've often attended social occasions where there wasn't a single thing I could eat or drink.' The mother of two young children complained that her boys were being 'starved out of the food chain'.

Many smaller manufacturers, such as Brumby's and Bakers Delight bread shops, are exceptionally helpful, and there are signs that the giant food manufacturers are starting to move away from artificial additives.

Support from the medical community

There are some dietitians and general practitioners in our network and many more doctors are referring children for a trial of the elimination diet now than ten years ago. Bernard Weiss, Professor of Toxicology at Rochester University in New York, was one of the original sceptical researchers who conducted trials of the Feingold diet. What he saw changed his mind. He now recommends that doctors and nutritionists should take a stand on cosmetic as opposed to functional additives. He says, 'food colours are cosmetic ingredients and are not added to promote nutritional value or safety. The same is true for most synthetic flavours and for flavour enhancers such as MSG. Few additives are devoid of risk. If the benefit is zero, the risk:benefit ratio becomes infinity.' In other words, the risks are too high.

What great-grandma ate

The typical Australian diet of 50 years ago was lower in problem-causing chemicals than today's diet. Roast chicken, grilled meat and three veg without spicy sauces; old-fashioned vegetables like potatoes and cabbage; plain home-baked cakes and biscuits and homemade ice-creams are low in problem chemicals. These days, mothers are more likely to work outside the home. A working mother who is tired at the end of the day would rather grab a takeaway on the way home than have to cook. It is difficult to buy convenience food without additives. You have a choice. You can either get organised, prepare meals on the weekend and eat simply during the week, or you can ask the food suppliers for plainer food.

In the long term

Families who see results with diet will stick to it, as in this study of 62 overactive children with physical problems: 'Being on an acceptable diet did seem to make a remarkable difference to the lives of many of these families ... 92 per cent were continuing the diet when last seen.'

In a two-year follow-up of families using diet, another group of researchers found: 'Thirteen out of 14 mothers described their children's behaviour as having improved since the end of the study. Typically they reported a steady, gradual increase in self-control and a marked improvement in school-work.'

This is what I hear. Mothers report that children using diet as well as, or instead of, medication develop greater self-control and self-discipline. Remember the 'marshmallow test' (p. 8) where researchers found that self-control was an indication of future success?

Families report that the diet is hard, but it is worth the effort. This family is using a combination of medication and diet. They have found the health of all members of the family is affected by what they eat:

> We were reluctant to try the diet. It sounded hard, and we felt we had enough on our plate . . . Well, the results were astounding. My son's behaviour changed dramatically and after only three days the teachers were all commenting about the positive changes . . . negative, oppositional attitude gone, pleasant manner, trying harder, concentrating better, relating to teacher better, completing more work. At home we noticed that the temper tantrums disappeared, he was more organised, got ready for school, did his homework and was generally happier. He even looked better. Diet was obviously an answer for us.

The biggest vote of confidence comes from the children. When I see teenagers who choose to eat failsafe, I know it is important to continue supporting these families. One asthmatic and difficult 15-year-old boy, two years after starting his elimination diet, said: 'I want to tell the doctors that diet works. I think they ought to know.'

The message is that we are what we eat. If food chemicals affect you, avoid them. As tastes change, in the long term work towards eating foods low in fats and sugars and high in fibre, including vegetables and fruit that are safe for you.

11

Non-food factors

For readers who feel that diet is helping but there is further to go, this chapter looks at some factors that can make your symptoms better or worse. If you don't feel ready for the information below, sort your diet out first.

Medications

Medications are supposed to make us better but all drugs have side effects, some of them serious. At the extreme end of the range, in the USA, over a quarter of a million people per year die from the adverse effects of healthcare, mostly the unintended side effects of prescribed medication, and many more are disabled. Most patients and doctors do not recognise symptoms as drug side effects because they can occur days or much longer after starting the drugs. It is the same with the effects of food chemicals.

A drug called thalidomide was marketed in the late 1950s

as a safe sedative and anti-nausea drug for morning sickness, but by 1961 it was identified as the cause of severe birth defects in more than 10,000 children around the world. More than 30 years later, in 1994, researchers realised thalidomide had caused some cases of autism when taken by pregnant women between days 20–24 after conception. Another drug implicated with autism, sodium valproate, is used for epilepsy. Minimise the use of medications that aren't essential (see p. 180).

Antibiotics are designed to kill nasty bugs, but unfortunately they kill beneficial bugs in the gut at the same time. This unwanted side effect can lead to irritable bowel symptoms that are usually temporary but sometimes permanent depending on dose and individual sensitivity. It is not unusual for mothers starting failsafe to report that their child has had five or more courses of antibiotics in the past year. One woman was very clear. 'I know when my food intolerance developed. I was in hospital for surgery and was given a course of strong antibiotics to prevent infection. I've had problems ever since.'

Probiotics are living bacteria that can improve health by altering the balance of good and bad bacteria in the body. It is thought that in the gut alone there is a mixture of more than ten billion bacteria from more than five hundred species. Probiotics occur naturally in traditional fermented foods such as yoghurt and are sold as supplements in their dried form. Scientists have only recently started to study the beneficial effects of probiotics for a variety of disorders from irritable bowel symptoms to prevention of allergy.

There are over a thousand strains and sub-strains of beneficial lactic acid bacteria that occur naturally in traditional fermented milk products. A single batch of traditional Indian dahi (yoghurt) or kefir from Eastern Europe may contain many more strains than found in Australian yoghurts. Consumption of such fermented milk products during a meal can prevent the flatulence normally associated with bean dishes, which may explain why yoghurt is traditionally served as a side dish or drink with meals in India.

It seems that some strains of probiotics may be more useful than others and that combinations of probiotics as found in traditional products may be more effective than a single strain. Of the few probiotics studied so far, *Lactobacillus GG* taken in late pregnancy by the mother and given to the baby in the first six months of life was found to protect against the development of eczema, but *Lactobacillus acidophilus* did not. Another study showed that kefir, traditionally used as a weaning food, reduced specific IgE antibodies (involved in allergy) in mice, leading researchers to hope that it may help to reduce food allergies in babies. See the 'Probiotic' factsheet at www.fedup.com.au.

Vaccinations: Some parents report that their children became more food intolerant after vaccinations. Nearly 5000 families in the USA and over 2000 in the UK claim that their child's regressive autism was associated with MMR (measles–mumps–rubella) vaccinations, although doctors say there is no evidence for this. At first parents blamed mercury-based preservatives in the vaccines and this preservative has been withdrawn. One mother wrote about her son's experience with a mercury-free vaccination:

We went through the supervised elimination diet for my son's hyperactivity, humming, flapping, being loud and defiant, days of little language and lack of toilet training. He was intolerant of salicylates (hyperactivity), amines (language and toileting), antioxidants (defiance), colours, preservatives and all other additives (loudness and hyperactivity). Afterwards we had a different child.

Two years on he is still very sensitive. Since he had his five-year-old immunisations a month ago, he has become a lot louder, more defiant and most alarmingly the humming and flapping and hyperactivity has returned. This has been commented on by his teacher at school so we know it is not just our observation. His diet has not changed. [This mother wrote later to report that the symptoms started improving again after two months.]

Should you have your child vaccinated? Parents need to understand that a decision not to vaccinate exposes their child and society to significant risks. My children are vaccinated because I know of a GP who chose not to vaccinate his children and one of them died of whooping cough. The bottom line is that vaccinations save lives.

Sunlight

We are warned to avoid the sun because of skin cancer, but our main source of vitamin D is from exposure to sunlight on the skin. Vitamin D is essential for normal bone and muscle growth and helps with immune function. Some researchers think it could prevent auto-immune diseases such as multiple sclerosis, rheumatoid arthritis and type-one diabetes. 'You don't need very much sunlight to produce adequate amounts of Vitamin D,' says Associate Professor Graeme Jones from the Menzies Research Institute. 'This might be as little as five to 15 minutes, four to six times a week.' While most people get that in daily life, it can be more difficult for people with debilitating conditions such as chronic fatigue syndrome and fibromyalgia.

Age and stages of life

Food intolerance symptoms can change throughout life. Babies may appear to grow out of 'allergies' such as hives or reflux. However, they may grow into different problems such as learning difficulties or depression later on.

- Babies and young children are most vulnerable to the effects of chemicals because of the so-called Bambi factor: they breathe, drink and eat more than adults, so have a higher intake of potentially toxic substances. As they get bigger the dose per kilogram decreases and they should develop better tolerance, especially boys. Girls have the additional problem of female hormones.
- Breastfed babies can be affected by chemicals in the mother's diet that pass through her breast milk. Since

breastfeeding contributes to development of the immune system, it is important to breastfeed if you can by avoiding problematic food chemicals in your own diet. When babies are so sensitive that your diet would be too restricted, your dietitian can advise about special formulas such as Neocate (see p. 328).

- Women are likely to be more sensitive premenstrually and during their childbearing years, due to hormonal influences. They may improve after menopause.

- Men in the prime of their lives are least likely to be affected by food intolerance, although individual sensitivity varies.

- The elderly become more vulnerable, due to a reduced capacity to eliminate toxic chemicals.

- People of any age can develop food intolerance or experience worsening symptoms as the result of an illness, particularly giardia or travellers' diarrhoea, or chemical exposure including medications.

Stress management

Stress can make symptoms of food intolerance worse. Reduce the stress and your food intolerance symptoms are likely to improve.

Laughter therapy: Laughter really is the best therapy. Watching a comedy movie has been show to stabilise blood sugar, reduce stress hormones, blood pressure, pain, anxiety and depression, and improve mood, immunity or eczema in diabetics, children, heart patients, schizophrenics and more. Hormones associated with relaxation were found in breastmilk and researchers found breastfed babies slept better and their eczema improved if their mothers watched a comedy hours before feeding. Belly laughs – laughing out loud – are more effective than silent laughter or snorting. A family struggling in their second week of diet with a difficult child noticed a big improvement in attitude after a 'home holiday' – homemade chicken and chips, a favourite dessert and a comedy DVD for the whole family.

Exercise: Exercise stimulates the brain's natural 'feel good' chemicals. These can have a calming effect and counteract the effects of food chemicals. Choosing an exercise can be difficult for children with poor coordination. It is best to find an activity that really suits your child, probably non-competitive – such as bike riding, swimming, jogging, walking, using a climbing wall or going to the gym – but all regular exercise is good.

The relaxation response: Other stress management techniques include relaxation, meditation or yoga. Watching a waterfall, an open fire, or waves crashing on rocks will produce a state of relaxation, but these tranquil scenes are not always available. You can achieve the same effect by meditating for 20 minutes. The health benefits of meditation have been investigated over the last 30 years by cardiologist Dr Herbert Benson from Harvard University. Dr Benson became interested when he saw that heart patients using what he calls the relaxation response were able to lower their blood pressure without drugs. From this beginning he went on to establish the Benson-Henry Institute for Mind Body Medicine at Massachusetts General Hospital. He says, 'to the extent that any disease is caused or made worse by stress, the relaxation response can help'. Children can use their age as the time – e.g. 10-year-olds meditate for 10 minutes – and choose their own focus word, something that is important to them, such as 'racing car' (see http://www.mbmi.org/basics/whatis_rresponse_elicitation.asp).

Take a holiday: Research shows that blood pressure, static muscle tension, perceived strain, adrenaline levels and 'psychosomatic' symptoms, or what we would see as food intolerance symptoms, decrease during holidays compared to working days.

Behaviour management programs can promote family harmony by reducing negativity. There is an important difference between management and punishment. Children who feel their whole lives consist of criticism and punishment are unlikely to improve with diet alone. They need to feel valued through recognition, positive feedback and encouragement, yet when parents were asked whether their management style was more like the best or worst boss they ever had, most confessed they were more like the bad boss. If this sounds like you, consider using the *1-2-3 Magic* program (see Notes) that can help you avoid criticism by providing 'discipline without too much talk or too much emotion'. The same principle applies to the classroom. Not surprisingly, studies show that children behave better for teachers they believe like and care about them.

The gift of time: Experts now recommend that spending time with your children is the most important gift you can give them. 'Spend as much of the early years with them as possible,' says Judy Radich of Early Childhood Australia. 'If you don't need to work or study, stay home and join other parents like yourselves.' According to Melbourne psychotherapist Ruth Schmidt Neven, 'the most important resource parents can give their kids is their own relationship with them, it is these relationships that really matter, not whether they make the team or top the class. Parents' presence is vital.' Former USA first lady Jacqueline Kennedy once commented, 'if you bungle raising your children, I don't think whatever else you do well matters very much'.

After starting diet, we used a behaviour management

system that required parents to rebuild a positive relationship by spending 15 minutes three times a week in one-on-one play sessions, doing something the child enjoyed while making positive comments. The psychologist who developed the program observed that parents who are too busy to do this have not attached enough importance to childrearing. The best thing we ever did for family bonding – other than switch to failsafe eating – was an extended backpacking/campervan style holiday while our children were teenagers. In countries like Nepal and Egypt where traditional food was still available, food was not an issue; in developed countries we cooked for ourselves. Other failsafe families have reported similar experiences travelling within Australia (see p. 308).

Home schooling: Schools are not always the best places for food intolerant children due to peer pressure and chemical exposure. Home schooling can be the quickest and most effective way to reduce stress in a family. One mother wrote about her nine-year-old daughter:

> Not only is she behaving better because she eats only failsafe but her concentration has improved, she enjoys learning and is learning more and is a far happier child as a result. Before we started home schooling, my daughter exhibited strongly oppositional defiance behaviour patterns and was becoming a very unhappy and unsettled little girl. It's so good to see her playing happily with the others and being able to hold a conversation instead of fighting and tormenting her siblings – not to mention us, her parents.

A good way to try home schooling can be until the end of the term or the end of the year. Children who have been home schooled for even a short time have a chance to discover how to enjoy learning. Two of the failsafe families whose stories appear in this book home schooled their children for years while travelling around Australia in a caravan. Research has shown that home schoolers as a group score better on achievement tests, do well at universities and have significantly higher self-concept than that of their publicly schooled peers. The internet has revolutionised home schooling by providing well-organised supports and resources including socialisation (see the 'Home Schooling' factsheet on www.fedup.com.au).

Academic support: After diet, a child with a learning delay due to years of food effects may require help to overcome the gaps. For example, most poor readers cannot 'sound out' the five vowels, yet this is a very basic skill. One girl needed only a few sessions with a private tutor to learn this and was then able to catch up. Others have recommended basic hearing or vision tests for problems previously hidden by bad behaviour.

Man-made chemicals

Avoiding perfumed products: People doing the elimination diet are asked to avoid perfumes, perfumed products and aerosols because fragrances can contain synthetic salicylates and other chemicals. Fragrances are made in the same giant chemical factories as flavours and, as with flavours, it's the size of the dose that matters. Salicylates, benzoates and others can be absorbed into the bloodstream by inhalation or contact with the skin through lotions and cosmetics, as well as by mouth. Synthetic salicylates in air-fresheners are likely to be higher doses than would ever be found in fresh air – although some people will be affected by strong-smelling flowers and trees too.

A businesswoman who enjoyed perfumed products, essential oils and air-fresheners decided to take a 'smell free' holiday when failsafe eating didn't produce the change she wanted in her son. She wrote:

> After two days, our son's behaviour was above reproach. For the first time we have a 'normal boy' who we are enjoying spending time with. We are now without perfume at home and using vinegar and bi-carb for cleaning. After a lifetime of lovely smells, I have traded vanity for an angel.

Sensitivity to perfumes is common. A national survey in the USA found 30 per cent reported adverse reactions to fragranced products, nearly 20 per cent experienced breathing difficulties and other health problems when exposed to air-fresheners, 11 per cent reported unusual hypersensitivity to chemical products such as perfume, fresh paint, pesticides and other petrochemical-based substances, and 2.5 per cent had been diagnosed with multiple chemical sensitivity.

Don't clean: In the UK, studies of new mothers and cleaning chemicals found more headaches and depression in mothers and more asthma, diarrhoea, vomiting and ear infections in babies with increasing use of air-fresheners and/or aerosols.

People sometimes ask 'Why are our children so sensitive?' Some scientists think that certain manmade industrial chemicals act as 'sensitisers' – meaning that exposure to these can make people more sensitive to other common chemicals. I've noticed that the most intolerant children in our network – kids who have been on special infant formulas, can only tolerate a few foods, and are sensitive to environmental chemicals – often have a parent or grandparent in a high-risk occupation for chemical exposure, such as a pest controller, farmer, nurse, hairdresser, panel beater or chemical factory employee. I suspect the effects of thousands of manmade chemicals introduced in the 1960s are just beginning to be apparent through a two-part process: first we expose our children to chemicals that make them more sensitive and then we increase the chemicals in their food and environment that are most likely to affect them.

VOCs (volatile organic compounds): A Sydney resident who is considered to be one of the most sensitive people in the world, Jonathan Wilson Fuller was shown in the TV movie *The Boy in the Bubble* as a seventeen-year-old breathing purified air and unable to leave his own home since the age of ten. After 35 years of working as an industrial chemist with chemicals such as formaldehyde, Jonathan's father retrained as a maths teacher when it became obvious that Jonathan's health improved while his father was on holidays and worsened when his father came home from his job with toxic fumes on his breath and skin.

Jonathan is sensitive to both food chemicals and VOCs, which Jonathan describes as 'anything that smells', including perfumes, pesticides and industrial chemicals. These are the chemicals that caused a wide range of autistic symptoms in Dr Slimak's study (see Notes).

There are thousands of volatile organic compounds that give off gases at normal temperatures. While in the form of a gas they can drift around and be inhaled. This is the characteristic smell of new buildings, furniture, fabrics and cars. As the temperature cools, they settle out on furniture or food where they can be ingested or absorbed through the skin. VOCs are associated with sick building syndrome, a range of symptoms that include eye, skin and throat irritation, headaches, lethargy, dizziness, nausea, memory disturbance and depression.

In Australia there has been little monitoring of VOCs. In 2007, overseas alerts led to the discovery of imported blankets from China with levels of formaldehyde – one of the most common VOCs and a known carcinogen – at almost ten times the international upper safety limit. An earlier study by Australia's Commonwealth Scientific and Industrial Research Organisation (CSIRO) found that homes less than one year old in Melbourne contained up to twenty times the limit of VOCs recommended by health authorities. New cars were even worse: another CSIRO study found that levels of VOCs in three new cars were up to 128 times as high as the recommended Australian exposure limit.

The standard recommendation for dealing with toxic emissions is to allow new cars, buildings and furniture to 'gas off' with good ventilation for about six months. However, certain flame retardants are not so easily dealt with. A Swedish study of triphenyl phosphate (TPP) used in the plastic casings of computer monitors found that the monitors emit the compound when their temperature rises during normal operations, causing health problems in computer workers. The emission levels declined with use, but remained ten times higher than background level after two years of working use.

Although TPP has not been safety tested on humans, numerous rat studies have showed it causes depression. This is how it affects me, although it is the only chemical that does, as depression is not one of my usual food intolerance symptoms. I am convinced my VOC sensitivity originated with TPP overexposure in a computer monitor and have subsequently experienced problems with a new mattress and lounge suite. These days I avoid items with flame retardants, buy them second-hand, or allow them to gas off for months in the garage before bringing them into the house.

Since VOCs are not listed on labels, consumers cannot find out whether these chemicals are used in products, or in what quantities. In a 2002 NSW health survey, a quarter of more than 12,000 adults answered yes when asked 'Do certain chemical odours or smells regularly make you unwell?' Despite the large numbers of people affected, there are no regular monitoring programs, no avenue for consumer complaints, and no sanctions for exceeding recommended guidelines.

Chemical sensitivity: Anyone with food intolerance should consider keeping their exposure to manmade chemicals to a minimum. A dietitian from a banana-growing area noticed that the families who lived among the farms were much more sensitive to food and chemicals than those on the coast. She reported: 'One family's diet was so restricted they could hardly eat anything. When they moved to the coast, they improved, and could eat a much wider range of foods.'

'But we don't use chemicals!' one mother exclaimed. If you breathe, drink water, drive in a car, live in a city, live in the country, travel on roads, buy anything plastic, use household cleaners, insect repellents, live or work in a house or building containing synthetic building materials or furniture, watch television, use a computer, eat food you haven't grown yourself, wear clothes made of synthetic fibres or treated fabrics, smoke, take medication or swim in a chlorinated pool, you are exposed to artificial chemicals.

Chemical sensitivity can result when a person is exposed to an accidentally large dose or from small exposures over a long period of time. Frequent exposure to heavy metals such as lead, mercury or cadmium, solvents such as paint thinners or nail-polish remover, metal degreasers and industrial fuels have been shown to cause brain damage, memory and attention deficits, personality changes and depression (see Notes).

In the USA alone, 250 billion kilos of chemicals are manufactured each year. You cannot avoid them all, but it is worth trying to minimise exposure.

In the short term:
- Buy fragrance-free soaps, shampoo, conditioner, deodorants, cosmetics and other personal care products (see Product Updates on www.fedup.com.au for brand suggestions and alternatives to perfumed hairsprays, shaving foams, gels and body lotions).
- Buy fragrance-free washing powders – see Shopping List for alternatives. Soakers and aerosols such as fabric conditioners and ironing sprays are not okay.
- Most household cleaners are harmful and unnecessary – you can clean a house with sodium bicarbonate, vinegar, dishwashing liquid and powder, microfibre cloths and a vacuum cleaner.
- Avoid air-fresheners, essential oils, pot pourri, incense, cut flowers and other smells.
- Avoid products that claim to be fragrance-free but contain strong-smelling ingredients, such as lime or mandarin essential oils.
- Avoid scented children's products such as pens and even dolls.
- Minimise time spent in indoor shopping malls.
- Do not renovate your house, have your carpet cleaned, buy a new car, television, computer, mattress, drapes, carpets,

lounge suite or other furniture while doing the elimination diet.

- Drink filtered or spring water if tap water has an unpleasant odour.
- Minimise use of heavily chlorinated swimming pools during the elimination diet, or wear goggles and rinse off quickly afterward.
- Avoid contact with nitrogen-based lawn fertiliser (e.g. playing barefoot on a recently fertilised lawn).
- Minimise your intake of medications (see p. 180).

In the longer term (especially for children, for women intending to become pregnant, or if chemically sensitive):
- Avoid or minimise your use of garden pesticides and weed-killers and keep them stored outside your house.
- Minimise pest-control treatments for house, avoid chlor-pyrifos – which has been banned in the USA – and use cockroach traps instead of sprays, or use small local treatments while you're out of the house for a few days.
- Avoid flea collars and diazinon – banned in the USA – in hydrobaths for dogs, and minimise the use of pesticides on your animals.
- For headlice in children's hair, comb in a failsafe oil each night, sleep on a towel-covered pillow and wash out the next morning.
- If your garage connects to your house, always keep the

door closed and well sealed because engines continue to give off toxic gases for several hours after being turned off.

- Keep your house well aired and ventilated.
- Avoid dry-cleaning.
- If you need a new car, consider buying a second-hand car and ask your children to comment on the smell during a test drive.
- Minimise your use of plastic; store food in glass or hard rather than soft plastics which release toxic gases or gas off for longer; avoid plastic cling film.
- Minimise your use of perfluorinated chemicals (the 'Teflon chemical') in cookware, stain-resistant carpets, furnishings and clothes, grease-resistant fast-food wrappings and some cosmetics.
- Until industry changes the lacquer lining in metal cans – as is happening in Japan – minimise your use of canned drinks and foods (a source of bisphenol-A).
- Avoid reusable plastic water and baby bottles (a source of bisphenol-A).
- If building or renovating a house, it is possible to find low-emitting furnishings and non-toxic building materials with low levels of VOCs and formaldehyde (see the 'Environmental chemicals' factsheet on www.fedup.com.au).

Some good news

Exposure to harmful substances can be reduced. A failsafe lifestyle can be protective because:

- By avoiding nitrate preservatives in processed meats such as bacon and ham, you reduce your risk of colorectal cancer.
- By avoiding salicylates in the skin zone of fruit and vegetables – discarding the peel and outer leaves – you reduce your intake of pesticides.
- By avoiding takeaway food you reduce your intake of Teflon chemicals in grease-resistant takeaway packaging.
- By avoiding cans of soft drink, you reduce your intake of bisphenol-A, suspected of causing birth defects, prostate and breast cancer.

- By avoiding amines in salmon you reduce your risk from the extra high levels of polychlorinated biphenyls (PCBs) found in farmed salmon – this salmon now accounts for about 50 per cent of all supermarket salmon.
- By avoiding perfumed beauty products you reduce your exposure to phthalates, chemicals that have been linked to health concerns including reduced fertility, reduced sperm counts, premature breast development in young girls, liver and kidney damage and asthma.

Research shows that when toxic substances are banned, children's health improves. For example, lead can cause developmental delays, reduced IQ, learning disabilities, attention deficits, hyperactivity and health problems, especially in babies and young children. Blood lead levels in children have dropped dramatically in developed countries since leaded petrol was phased out in the last two decades of the twentieth century. Similarly, the effects of PCBs were first noticed in the children of pregnant women who ate fish from the polluted Great Lakes in the USA. However, since PCBs were banned in the USA in 1976, blood PCB levels have been dropping steadily. Also in the USA – although not yet in Australia – when common household pesticides chlorpyrifos and diazinon were banned in 2000, researchers saw an immediate improvement in newborn birth weights.

Although animal studies show that the effects of chemicals on behaviour and learning can be passed down to the next generation, scientists think this is due to a temporary 'hijacking' of the genes by environmental chemicals, not a genetic mutation. So the bottom line is, if women can avoid exposure to these chemicals before and during pregnancy, they can avoid these effects on their children.

For more information and detailed references about topics in this chapter, see the 'Fumes and Perfumes' factsheet on www.fedup.com.au.

12

Failsafe eating

Before you can consider doing an elimination diet, you have to have a problem. Second, you have to be prepared to change what you eat. Some people, when they hear about this diet, say, 'Fantastic, this answers my questions. I'm going to do it,' and start right away. Some families binge on their favourite foods before starting. That's what we did and it probably makes withdrawal symptoms worse. Others cut out a few additives, maybe artificial colours and the bread preservative, and wait until they are more desperate, sometimes years later.

A disadvantage of the last approach is that I have seen so many mothers with nine-year-olds and under, which is a reasonable age group to do the diet, wait until they have unmanageable teenagers and a real crisis on their hands. When they find the diet actually works, there is no way their rebellious adolescent is going to stick to it. It's too late.

160

We didn't hear about the diet until he was nearly fourteen. It really worked. Nothing else we'd tried had, including medication. For three months he was really good, and we had peace at home for the first time ever. Then he started going out with his mates and breaking the diet. He wouldn't stick to it. We've lost him. He's dropped out of school, and he's running wild.

Your chance of success

You will do better if your partner is supportive and the whole family does the diet together. It is very tempting to think, 'I know about food, I can do this by myself', but for families who are very sensitive, one daily mistake can ruin your chance of success. It's good to have as much help as you can.

In this chapter, I go step by step through the elimination diet, additives to avoid and where to find them, the Shopping List that will become your lifeline, and pitfalls of medications with some failsafe alternatives.

How we did our elimination diet

1. The diet that was a magic answer for us is called **the RPAH Elimination Diet** from the Royal Prince Alfred Hospital Allergy Unit in Sydney, Australia (www.cs.nsw.gov.au/rpa/allergy). It is additive free and low in salicylates, amines and glutamates.

2. There are numerous **salicylate lists** on the internet but they can be wrong, usually don't include amines, and if, for example, cauliflower appears on the low end of the scale, then the list is out of date. The best food charts are in the RPAH book *Friendly Food*, available through their website above or in bookstores.

3. It is best to be supervised by an experienced dietitian. **Our list of supportive dietitians is available from confoodnet@ozemail. com.au.** A dietitian can increase your chance of success, write a report for school, check nutrition and help with challenges.

4. We had already consulted doctors but there are stories of people doing diets for **conditions that need medical treatment**, so check with your doctor first. Children on ADHD medication often start the diet during holidays as medication makes it more difficult to succeed.

5. The dietitian weighed our daughter. **If weight loss is a problem**, caloric supplements such as Polycose can enhance appetite, but we only used it a few times years later during an illness.

6. We decided to avoid **dairy foods** but not **gluten** at first, but it depends on the severity of your symptoms. I later needed to go gluten-free when my intolerance worsened due to travellers' diarrhoea.

7. When I first saw the dietitian's booklet, like most mothers I was overwhelmed. The trick is to stop focusing on what you can't eat, and to **focus on the Shopping List** (p. 167). Compared to the Few Foods diet that starts with turkey, rice, pears and lettuce, failsafe eating is easy.

8. Ingredients change frequently. See **Product Updates** on www.fedup.com.au for the latest changes.

9. We established **a failsafe house** by eating or giving away all the unsuitable food in our kitchen. It is best for the whole family to do the diet for support, although fathers often only appear to support the diet while at home. Children who are expected to stick to this diet while others at home eat tempting foods will very reasonably sneak food or money.

10. I negotiated **incentives** with our children – 'What's this worth to you?' Daily credit points and weekly rewards with a bonus after three weeks worked better than one big bribe. In our case our children settled for cash, but I bargained them down. Your chance of success is higher if your partner is supportive so you might need to negotiate for this too.

11. We marked **D-day** – diet day – on our calendar, waiting until special occasions like birthday parties and school camp were out of the way.

12. I wrote down what we normally ate then drew up a **week's menu plan** (p. 210) and personal **shopping list** using the Shopping List on p. 167. Some families have a lot of homemade chicken and chips in the first three weeks, when it's important to get over food cravings.

13. For the first shopping trip I took my prepared **shopping list** (above) and the list of additives to avoid (see card at end of book). It took a long time because I had to read labels but is now very quick because I know exactly what I want.

14. I tested some **recipes** before D-day, cooked and froze some meals and treats, such as failsafe mince, pear muffins and rolled oat bars, and had Magic cordial, pear jam and icypoles ready.

15. I scored my child's behaviour on a **rating scale** like the one on p. 83 so that there was a starting point against which to measure progress.

16. On D-day, **we started the diet**. The first few days were difficult, and sometimes we had a bowl of Rice Bubbles because I couldn't think of anything else, but after that we settled into it.

17. I would have liked to talk to others doing the diet. You can join an **email group** by emailing 'subscribe' in the subject line to failsafebasic@yahoogroups.com. See www.fedup.com.au for local or special groups.

18. Keep up with **new products** by joining the newsletter list. Email 'subscribe' in the subject line to failsafe_newsletter-subscribe@yahoogroups.com.

19. I kept a **diary** of food and symptoms. Include toothpaste, medication, anything that goes on the skin, changes in behaviour, learning and health, and comments such as 'fed dog without being asked' in a special exercise book.

20. Expect **withdrawal symptoms** that can occur within the first two weeks, in our case on days four and five. These can be tearfulness, strong food cravings, irritability, any symptoms that existed before the diet or flu and other illnesses. Having been through it myself, I feel that children shouldn't be punished for outbursts during withdrawals, but should be kept home from school and away from stress if possible.

21. It is easy to make a mistake that stops the diet from working, see the **Checklist of Common Mistakes**, on the website www.fedup.com.au. Some children improve within days, others improve slowly, going through the second week blahs and only coming good in the third week. If there is no improvement after a week or two, ask your dietitian, failsafe contact or email group.

22. **Children cannot be punished into sticking to this diet.** My children said what helped them most was the example I set by sticking to the diet too. I gave them extra love and hugs, outings and board games, and praised them for sticking to it. We treated it as a family adventure that we were all in together. When we started the diet I had been at the end of my tether so I had to work on rebuilding love, positivity and fun (see p. 148).

23. When diet kicks in, you can introduce a **behaviour management** program to double the effect of the diet (see p. 133 about *1-2-3 Magic* – or go to www.parentmagic.com or www.parentshop.com.au).

24. We found **challenges** tricky. After three weeks you're supposed to reintroduce one group of food chemicals at a time according to your dietitian's booklet. You can challenge anything you want – from additives to salicylates to fish oil supplements – but it has to be according to the rules of challenge. That is, wait until you are symptom free, then take the recommended doses every day for about a week while sticking strictly to your diet and keeping a food and symptom diary, then review your diary. It is never enough to eat one serve and conclude that the item is safe. See the 'challenges' factsheet on www.fedup.com.au. If you are confused about challenges, ask your failsafe group or write to confoodnet@ozemail.com.au.

25. After failing the salicylate challenge, we had to work out our tolerance. We were instructed to introduce half a cup of salicylate foods (such as carrots, sweet potatoes, Chinese greens, snow pea sprouts, mangoes or Golden Delicious apples) every second day for two weeks, then daily for two weeks, then one cup every second day for two weeks, and so on, until we reacted, then go back one step. We all have differing sensitivities, with the most sensitive on half a cup every second day except during holidays.

26. After we had finished challenges, we went back to our dietitian and had our **nutrition** checked, particularly because we had to avoid salicylates and dairy products. We were doing fine except that my dairy-free son who doesn't like soymilk had to work at getting enough calcium.

27. During our elimination diet we changed our washing powder, deodorant and toothpaste, but didn't take **environmental chemicals** seriously until we stayed in a smell-free home and realised how good it felt (see p. 156).

28. Most children like to eat fatty and sugary foods while being weaned off processed food, and mine were no exception. As our tastes settled down, we reduced our intake of fats and sugars, and ate more **permitted vegetables** (see p. 173). I must have succeeded because my children have continued to eat vegetables including Brussels sprouts since leaving home and cooking for themselves.

Food chemicals to avoid

ARTIFICIAL COLOURS
102 tartrazine, 104 quinoline yellow, 107 yellow 2G,
110 sunset yellow, 122 azorubine, 123 amaranth,
129 allura red, 132 indigotine, 133 brilliant blue,
142 green S, 151 brilliant black, 155 chocolate brown

NATURAL COLOUR
160b annatto – in yoghurts, ice-creams, cereals etc.

PRESERVATIVES
200–203	sorbates – in margarines, dips, etc.
210–219	benzoates – in drinks, medications etc.
220–228	sulphites – in dried fruit, sausages, etc.
249–252	nitrates, nitrites – in meats like ham
280–283	propionates – in bread, bakery products

SYNTHETIC ANTIOXIDANTS
310–312	gallates – in oils, margarines, fried foods
319–320	TBHQ, BHA, BHT – as above

FLAVOUR ENHANCERS
620-625	MSG and other glutamates
627, 631	disodium inosinate/guanylate
635	ribonucleotides
HVP, HPP	hydrolysed vegetable protein, yeast extract

ADDED FLAVOURS
There are thousands of flavours that don't have to be identified by name or number because they are considered to be
trade secrets. Vanilla flavoured products are safest.

SALICYLATES, AMINES, GLUTAMATES
See what you can eat in the Shopping List, what you can't eat
in *Friendly Food* (www.cs.nsw.gov.au/rpa/allergy), or more
information in the 'Natural Food Chemicals' factsheet at
www.fedup.com.au.

Shopping List

These are the foods you will need to make the recipes in this book, listed by supermarket categories. There will be more products on your dietitian's list, including vanilla-flavoured custards, biscuits, yoghurts, dairy desserts, cake mixes, creamed rice puddings and sweets that we rarely buy because they can cause problems. Some people may be affected by some items (see Checklist of Common Mistakes on www.fedup.com.au). The brands mentioned in the following paragraphs are what we use. If buying an unlisted product with a vegetable oil content of less than five per cent you will need to check with the manufacturer for possible unlisted antioxidants.

Asian foods
Bean vermicelli noodles (e.g. Lion brand, gluten-free)

Japanese buckwheat soba noodles (Spiral Foods are 100 per cent buckwheat, but most contain wheat)

Rice noodles (e.g. Pandaroo, Fantastic, gluten-free)

Rice paper (e.g. Banh Trang, gluten-free)

Wheat noodles (no antioxidants, colours, flavours, e.g. Changs)

Baby needs
Baby pear puree (e.g. Heinz)

Baked beans and spaghetti
None (make your own, see recipes, or use canned butter beans instead)

Baking aids
Baking powder (gluten-free if necessary, e.g. Wards)

Bicarbonate of soda (sodium bicarbonate, e.g. McKenzies)

Citric acid (e.g. McKenzies)

Colours (natural by Queen, for playdough and special occasions)

Cooking chocolates Nestlé White Melts (*The following are not suitable for your elimination diet: for people who tolerate amines, plain unflavoured chocolate and cocoa, e.g. Nestlé dark choc bits, Nestlé baking cocoa*)

Cream of tartar (e.g. McKenzies)

Gelatine (e.g. Davis)

Glucose syrup (contains
sulphites driven off when
boiled, e.g. Herb Valley)

Hundreds & Thousands
(natural colours, e.g. Nemar)

Pectin (for jam-making, e.g.
FowlersVacola Jamsetta)

Vanilla essence (natural or
artificial, e.g. Queen – we
use rarely, *see Cleaners*)

Yeast (not brewer's yeast)
(e.g. Lowan, Tandaco,
Kitchen Collection dried
yeast, some brands may
contain gluten)

Biscuits, crackers and crispbreads

There are numerous plain and
sweet biscuits seemingly
made from safe ingredients,
but you will need to check
the following • Arnott's
have removed unlisted
antioxidant BHA 320 from
their vegetable oil, for other
brands you will need to ask
manufacturers • we prefer
to avoid any biscuits listing
'flavour' • if dairy-free, avoid
milk powder and preferably
butter in biscuits

Biscuits with dairy: Arnott's
Sao, Wholemeal Sao,
Cruskits, Milk Arrowroots,
Scotch Finger, Milk Coffee,
Glengarry shortbreads or
any other shortbread with
flour, sugar, butter, such as

Walkers shortbread, Unibic
Shortbread Fingers and
Petticoat Tails

Biscuits without dairy: Arnott's
Original water crackers,
Salada, Saltine, Vita-Weat
original, Shredded
Wheatmeal, Kavli and Ryvita
crispbreads

*Biscuits without gluten or
dairy:* SunRice plain Rice
Cakes (not with corn), plain
Rice Crackers (no flavour
enhancers, no synthetic
antioxidants, e.g. Sakata)

Bread

Choose plain white or
wholemeal breads without
• preservatives or mould
inhibitors 280–283 • vinegar
• sulphites or dough
conditioners 220–228
• seeds except poppy
seeds • fruit or flavours,
e.g. Brumby's or Bakers
Delight plain breads,
Country Life Bakery pita
bread, Quality Lebanese
wraps, Brumby's white iced
finger buns. *See more
brands* in Product Updates
on the website. For gluten-
free breads *see Health
Foods*

Breadcrumbs

None (no preservatives or
flavours, *see Crumbs in
Health Food section*)

Bread mix

Numerous brands (without
   nasty additives, especially
   calcium propionate 282,
   e.g. Laucke's)

Breakfast cereals

Rolled oats (no additives or
   flavours, traditional or quick,
   e.g. Uncle Toby's, Home
   Brand) • Kellogg's Rice
   Bubbles, Rice Bran • All
   Bran, Special K, Uncle
   Toby's Weeties, Sanitarium
   Weet-Bix and other plain
   additive-free wholewheat-
   based cereals

Cake and pancake mixes

Pastry mix (e.g. White Wings)
Plain pancake premix (many
   brands, e.g. White Wings
   Original Shaker pancakes –
   I prefer to avoid added milk
   and flavours so mostly use
   the buckwheat pancake mix,
   see Health Foods)

Cakes and croissants
(bakery)

Woolworths baked in-store
   croissants
*See also Sara Lee Pound
   Cake and Sara Lee
   Croissants in Frozen Foods*

Canned fish

None suitable for your
   supervised elimination diet
   (For people who tolerate
   amines: tuna, salmon or
   sardines in spring water or
   failsafe oils, no flavours, e.g.
   John West sandwich tuna in
   canola oil)

Canned fruit

Pears in syrup (not natural
   juice, e.g. supermarket own
   brands, eat only the soft
   pieces of pear)
Coles Diced Pears Fruit Cups
   in syrup, *see also pear
   puree under Baby Needs*

Canned meals and meats

None

Canned and dried
vegetables

Canned beans (no spices or
   flavoured sauces as in
   baked beans), e.g. red
   kidney beans, chickpeas,
   butter beans, borlotti beans,
   three (or more) bean mixes,
   green beans, Surprise dried
   green beans, *see also dried
   beans and lentils in Soup
   Mix section*
   (*Not suitable for your
   supervised elimination diet:
   beetroot no spices, asparagus,
   corn kernels, canned green
   peas no mint, Surprise dried
   green peas no mint*)

Chips and snacks

Arnott's 'French Fries' potato
   straws

Colvan plain chips
Kettle Original Salted chips
Pretzels (no flavours, e.g. Parkers)
Red Rock Deli plain chips

Chocolates

Nestlé Milkybar Chocolate (limited)

See also Baking Aids section and carob as a chocolate substitute in Health Foods

(The following are not suitable for your elimination diet: for people who tolerate amines, plain unflavoured chocolate and cocoa, see Baking Aids section. For nut allergies, Kinnerton and Willow nut-free brands)

Cleaners

Dishwashing powder
Microfibre cleaning cloths
Plain low-scented dishwashing liquid (e.g. Earth's Choice)

See also sodium bicarbonate and vinegar as natural cleaners

No aerosols, use vanilla-flavoured water in a spray bottle as an air-freshener

Coffee and tea

Decaffeinated coffee (many brands, we use Vittoria natural decaffeinated espresso coffee and Nescafé Instant decaffeinated coffee)

Tea – none

(Carob powder, see Health Foods)

(The following are not for your elimination diet: for people who tolerate amines, unflavoured cocoa powder, e.g. Home Brand)

Confectionery

No colours, preservatives or flavours except limited vanilla. Commercial fudge may contain unlisted synthetic antioxidants in margarine or vegetable fat. Cornflour will contain gluten unless specified from corn. Glucose syrup may contain sulphite residues. The following are for occasional treats not daily use. See also www.smashi.com and www.hullabaloofood.com

Homemade fudge (may contain unlisted synthetic antioxidants, check with manufacturer)

Pascall vanilla marshmallows (white, limited due to flavours)

Werthers Original Butter Candies and Chewy Toffees (as above)

White Rabbit sweets (Cane Sugar, Liquid Glucose, Butter, Milk) from Chinese supermarkets

Cook-in sauces
None (see recipes for
   alternatives)

Cooking oils
Canola cooking spray (e.g.
   Pro chef)
Canola, sunflower and
   safflower oil (not cold
   pressed, no synthetic
   antioxidants 310–321, e.g.
   Golden Fields Canola,
   Crisco Sunflower), Soy oil
   (no synthetic antioxidants,
   cold pressed okay). Check
   labels as large containers
   usually contain synthetic
   antioxidants.
Rice Bran oil (e.g. Alfa one)

Cordial
None (make your own, see
   Magic cordial recipe).

Crumpets and muffins
None (make your own muffins,
   see recipes)

Cosmetics and deodorants
As unperfumed as possible,
   best minimised (my
   daughter uses Natio lipstick,
   mascara and eyeshadow,
   Revlon eyeliner and
   eyeshadow, Maybelline
   Express 3 in 1 foundation
   and blush, Revlon powder),
   see also Hair Care
Unperfumed deodorant (no
   aerosols, we use Simple
   roll-on)

Desserts
Easiyo yoghurt premixes
   (natural and vanilla flavours)
Sago (e.g. Lion Brand)
Tapioca (e.g. Lion Brand)

Dried fruit and nuts
Cashew nuts (raw, e.g.
   Naytura Natural Cashew
   Kernels)
Dried pears (peeled, no
   sulphite preservatives
   220–228, from health food
   stores e.g. Totally Pure Fruits
   freeze dried pears or home
   dried, see recipe)
(Not suitable for your
   supervised elimination diet:
   for people who can tolerate
   amines, additive-free dried
   bananas, e.g. Lion of
   Sahara Crispy Fruit Banana,
   other brands in health food
   stores)

Drinks
Gin, unflavoured vodka,
   whisky

Eggs
Fresh eggs, preferably free
   range (for egg allergies, see
   egg replacers in Health
   Foods)

Flour
Arrowroot flour (gluten-free,
   e.g. McKenzies)
Cornflour (gluten-free if made
   from corn, e.g. White Wings)
Custard powder (no artificial
   colour, no annatto 160b, e.g.

Orgran gluten-free custard powder)

Plain or self-raising flour (e.g. Defiance)

Fresh fruit and vegetables

Pears (soft, ripe, peeled, pear-shaped varieties such as Bartlett and Packham – not apple-shaped varieties such as Nashi or Ya), potatoes (large, old, white-skinned), green beans, cabbage, celery, iceberg lettuce, leeks, shallots, chives, garlic, Brussels sprouts, swedes, chokos, red cabbage, mung bean sprouts, bamboo shoots, parsley for decoration

(Not suitable for your supervised elimination diet • for people who can tolerate limited amounts of salicylates: Golden or red delicious apples, mangoes, rhubarb, tamarilloes, persimmons, custard apples, carrots, butternut pumpkin, beetroot, sweet potatoes white or orange, asparagus, Chinese greens such as bok choy, snow peas and snow pea sprouts, fancy lettuce such as butter lettuce, fancy potatoes such as red skinned, coloured flesh or small new potatoes, corn, marrow, parsnips, turnips • for people who can tolerate limited amounts of glutamates: green peas • for people who can tolerate amines: pawpaws, bananas except the ladyfinger or sugar banana variety)

Frozen foods

Pastry (no preservatives or synthetic antioxidants, e.g. Pampas Puff Pastry sheets not rolls, Pampas Butter Puff Pastry sheets not rolls, Borg's Puff Pastry and Home Brand Puff pastry but not Pampas shortcrust or filo)

Sara Lee Croissants, All-purpose Pound Cake

Spring Roll Pastry (e.g. Trangs)

Ice-cream: (no colours, no annatto 160b, e.g. Peter's Original vanilla, Nestlé Milky Bar, Norco Natural, Sara Lee French Vanilla, Sara Lee Honeycomb and Butterscotch, Toppa Hokey Pokey, Pure Chill or Dairy Bell organic vanilla from Coles)

(Not suitable for your supervised elimination diet: for people who tolerate amines: additive-free chocolate desserts)

Dairy-free ice-cream: *see recipes,* or Mototo vanilla (www.mototodairyfree.com) at selected IGA stores, limited to one serve per week due to some salicylates and amines in the vegetable fat

Fruit and vegetables: green beans, Brussels sprouts, frozen chips, fries and hash browns (no annatto 160b), e.g. Woolworths, Logan Farm. Some brands contain unlisted antioxidants, see website

(Not suitable for your supervised elimination diet: green peas not minted, frozen mango pulp, frozen corn cobs)

Gardening

Seeds or Grow Your Own kits (e.g. parsley and chives)

Gravy

None (*see recipes for alternatives such as leek sauce*)

Hair care

No perfumed products or aerosols (one teenager used beaten eggwhite for shaping his Mohawk instead of hair gel or spray), *see also Shampoo section*

Health foods (or health food stores)

(All products in this section are gluten-free)

Agar Agar (gelatine substitute, e.g. Gold Cup powder from health food stores)

Buckwheat gluten-free

pancake mix (Orgran)

Carob buttons (no added flavours, with milk or soy)

Carob coated buckwheat or rice cakes (contain milk, e.g. Naturally Good)

Carob powder for drinking and cooking (e.g. Abundant Earth)

Cashew nuts, raw

Crumbs (e.g. Orgran All Purpose Crumbs, Casalare Rice Crumbs)

Egg replacer (if allergic to eggs, e.g. Orgran No Egg)

GDL glucono-delta-lactone (baked products texturiser)

GF bread (many brands, e.g. R&R Bakery Wholegrain Rice Bread, Dinner Rolls, Pizza Bases, www.rrbakery.com.au)

GF bread mixes, e.g. Laucke's Gluten Free Easy Bakers Instant Oven Bread Mix, Orgran Bread Mix

GF crackers, pretzels and rice cakes (no corn, no rye, e.g. Eskal crackers, Eskal Pretzels, SunRice Original Rice Cakes, Naturally Good Buckwheat Crispbreads)

GF flour mixes (plain or self-raising e.g. Orgran, Freedom Foods, FG Roberts)

GF flours, e.g. rice (McKenzies), buckwheat (Kialla), millet (Lotus), besan (Lotus)

GF pasta, many brands, e.g. Orgran GF spaghetti, San Remo GF lasagna sheets

GF pastry and pizza mixes, e.g. Orgran Pizza and Pastry Multi-mix, FreeFrom Pizza Dough Mix

Lecithin granules (from soy)

Millet (e.g. Lotus French hulled millet, Demeter whole millet for home grinding)

Puffed rice, millet, buckwheat, amaranth (many brands, e.g. Good Morning, Micronized Foods)

Rice flakes (no added fruit or juice, e.g. Rice Flakes Medium from JK International)

Rice malt (e.g. Colonial Farm) and Rice syrup (e.g. Nature First)

Roasted chickpeas (e.g. Chic Nuts garlic flavour)

Rolled oats (e.g. Freedom Foods contamination free quick oats)

Soy flakes

Xanthan gum (e.g. Nu-Vit) and Guar Gum (e.g. Lotus)

Indian foods

Besan (chickpea) flour, also in health food stores

Dried chickpeas, lentils

Pappadums (may contain unlisted BHA 320, e.g. Sharwood's plain Ready to Cook, not Ready to Eat snacks)

Jellies and puddings

None (make your own, *see recipes*)

Juices

None (*see recipe for Magic cordial and other suggestions*)

Laundry needs

No perfumed products, aerosols or enzymes (we use Omo Sensitive, Planet Ark and Lux Flakes)

Longlife milk

See Soymilk, ricemilk and longlife milk

Mayonnaise

None (make your own, *see recipes*, e.g. Mighty mayo)

Meat, poultry and fish (refrigerated section)

Meat: buy fresh meat (preferably not supermarket meat that may have been vacuum packed for three months or more – ask your specialist butcher) and use the day you buy or freeze and eat within one month
• beef or lamb, e.g. preservative-free mince (you can test for preservatives with sulphite test strips from our website), beef roast, T-bone or sirloin steak for pan frying, lamb leg for roast,

diced lamb for stew, lamb steak, lamb loin chops for grilling, chump chops for stewing • rabbit • veal for schnitzel • failsafe sausages (excellent frozen sausages are available on Australia's East Coast by courier from www.honestbeef.com.au or ask your specialist butcher if he will make up the recipe (p. 233) or *see Product Updates* on the website for butchers who will make sausages to order)

Chicken: Whole fresh or frozen chicken (no seasoning, stuffing, self-basting or manufactured meat), chicken breast fillets, thighs, pieces (no marinade or flavour enhancers)

Fish: Very fresh (not frozen or canned) white fish or seafood, e.g. snapper, barramundi, whiting, crab, lobster, oysters, calamari, scallops (but not salmon, tuna or prawns). Best from specialty fish shops, ask for the freshest and eat that day *(Not suitable for your supervised elimination diet: for people who can tolerate amines: pork chops, roast pork, additive-free ham and bacon from organic butchers or health food stores, chicken skin, (e.g. wings), offal (e.g. steak and kidney, lamb's fry and chicken livers), frozen and canned fish. Not prawns which contain sulphite preservatives, not imitation crab sticks, seafood salad mix or seafood extenders which contain flavour enhancers)*

Mexican foods
None (make your own tortillas and burritos, *see* Failsafe Cookbook)

Milk
See Soymilk, ricemilk and longlife milk, and Refrigerated section

Muesli bars
None (make your own, *see recipes and* Failsafe Cookbook)

Noodles
See Asian foods

Nuts and snacks
Cashew nuts (raw, not roasted, not suitable for people with nut allergies)
Pretzels (no flavours, e.g. Parkers Baked Wheat Pretzel Twists)

Pasta
Couscous (e.g. San Remo), *see Health Foods for gluten-free pasta*

Plain pasta in any shape (no colours, flavours, fillings, e.g. spaghetti, twists, alphabet)

Refrigerated section

Cheese: cream cheese (no preservatives 200–203, e.g. Philadelphia Cream Cheese in blocks not tubs, own brands), cottage cheese (no preservatives, e.g. Jalna from health food stores), ricotta cheese (no preservatives, e.g. Pantalica), mascarpone cheese (no preservatives, e.g. Clover Creek) *(The following are not suitable for your elimination diet: for people who tolerate amines: additive-free mild cheddar cheese, mozzarella cheese; for people who tolerate amines and some glutamates, tasty cheese, parmesan cheese, blue cheese, soft ripe cheese such as camembert)*

Cream, sour cream

Margarine (no sorbates 200–203, no antioxidants 310–321, no artificial colours, no annatto 160b, e.g. Meadow Lea Original with dairy, Nuttelex dairy-free margarine)

Milk (unflavoured, we use A2 milk www.A2australia.com.au)

Pure butter (e.g. Mainland Butter Soft, supermarket own brands), butter blends only if additive-free (e.g. Helga's Continental Style Light Butter Blend)

Yoghurt (natural or vanilla, no artificial colours, no annatto 160b, no preservatives, e.g. Vaalia natural, Bulla Lite 'N' Healthy vanilla)

Dairy free: Soy cream cheese (e.g. Kingland), Tofu (plain and silken, e.g. Pureland), Soy yoghurt (natural, e.g. Soygurt)

Rice

Plain rice (e.g. Sunwhite, medium or long grain, Arborio, Doongara, glutinous rice but not flavoured such as basmati, jasmine or wild rice)

Salad dressings

None (make your own from oil and citric acid, *see recipes*)

Salt and pepper

Sea salt or rock salt preferably iodised (no vegetable or flavoured salts except McCormick garlic salt – we use MasterFoods sea salt grinder on the table and Saxa iodised salt for cooking)

No pepper

Sauces

None (make your own, *see recipes, e.g. Leek sauce, Birgit's pear ketchup*)

Shampoo

Preferably no perfume (we use DermaVeen shampoo and conditioner from pharmacies and Melrose Everyday shampoo and conditioner from health food stores)

Skin care and sun care

Moisturisers (fragrance free, e.g. Redwin Sorbolene moisturiser with Vitamin E and Duncan's Ointment which is zinc based and preservative free, or see your dietitian's list)

Sunblock (free of parabens or benzoates and preferably unperfumed, we use Megan Gale Invisible Zinc from health food stores and Cancer Council Everyday sunscreen, or see your dietitian's list)

Soap

Handwashing Liquid (fragrance free, we use Redwin Sorbolene Handwash or EnviroCare body and hair cleanser from health food stores, or see your dietitian's list)

Soap (fragrance free, we use Redwin Sorbolene Moisturising Bar or Simple Soap)

Soft drinks

Lemonade (no preservative 211, e.g. Schweppes bottled, only for occasional parties due to salicylates and amines in natural lemon flavour, or make your own, *see the Magic cordial recipe*)

Soda water (no flavours, no additives)

Sparkling mineral water (no flavours, no additives)

Tonic water (no preservative 211, e.g. Schweppes, as above)

Soup and soup mixes

Dried beans and lentils (e.g. red, brown and green lentils, chickpeas, split peas, red kidney and all other dried beans except broad beans)

Pearl barley (e.g. McKenzies)

Soup mix (e.g. McKenzies)

Soymilk, ricemilk and longlife milk

Longlife milks (e.g. Nestlé sweetened condensed milk, Nestlé canned reduced cream)

Dairy free: soymilk (be careful with flavoured soymilks and unlisted antioxidants in oils. I prefer calcium enriched, these are the brands we drink: Sanitarium So Good, Sanitarium So Good Soyaccino, SoyLife Original, PureHarvest Organic Soymilk gluten-free) • rice-milk (e.g. Vitasoy, gluten-free)

Spices and cooking needs

Garlic powder or granules (e.g. MasterFoods)

Poppy seeds (e.g. MasterFoods)

Saffron threads (powder can be adulterated with artificial colours) e.g. MasterFoods

Spreads, honey, jam, etc.

Golden syrup (CSR)

Malt extract (e.g. Saunders)

No honey, no jam (make your own pear jam), no Vegemite, no peanut butter (make your own cashew butter, p. 272)

Sugar

Caster sugar

Icing sugar (pure icing sugar is gluten-free, icing sugar with cornflour is not)

Light brown sugar (not raw, no molasses for colouring)

White sugar

Tissues and toilet paper

Preferably no perfumes (e.g. Sorbent hypoallergenic)

Toothpaste and dental care

Plain dental floss (not mint flavoured)

Unflavoured toothpaste (e.g. Soul Pattinson's Plain toothpaste from Soul Pattinson pharmacies, Oral Hygiene Solutions Plain toothpaste, www.plaintoothpaste.com, or use a wet toothbrush or battery operated toothbrush)

Toppings and ice-cream cones

Betta natural ice-cream cones

Gluten-free ice-cream cones, see www.hullabaloofood.com

Nestlé Caramel Top 'n' Fill

Pure maple syrup (no added flavour, e.g. Camp, sometimes in the Health Food section)

Vinegar

None (except as a household cleaner)

Vitamins

Multivitamin and mineral supplement (additive free, free of herbal ingredients, bioflavonoids and flavours, we use Amcal One-a-day multivitamin and mineral supplement from pharmacies, see 'Supplements' factsheet on www.fedup.com.au for other supplements)

Vitamin C for cooking (we use Melrose ascorbic acid powder from pharmacies)

Water
Spring water (all brands, e.g.
  Mount Franklin), still mineral
  water, *see also Soft drinks*

Always read labels: ingredients change!
For recent changes and new failsafe products, premixes
and treats check Product Updates on www.fedup.com.au or
subscribe to our free newsletters (email failsafe_newsletter-
subscribe@yahoogroups.com with 'subscribe' in the subject
line). For readers inside and outside Australia: your local
failsafe group may have a shopping list of suitable foods in
your region or country.

Medications and alternatives

While on the elimination diet you need to consider everything that goes in your mouth, nose or on your skin because chemicals can be absorbed very well through skin and inhalation. Obviously you need to avoid medications containing salicylates, amines or nasty additives if possible.

Drugs containing salicylates

If you are sensitive to salicylates, be careful of any drug that lists any kind of salicylate, e.g. in many prescription and over-the-counter medications including aspirin, oil of wintergreen, anything with a warning for asthmatics in the Consumer Medicine Information sheet, arthritis creams, sports creams like Dencorub, Vicks VapoRub, teething gel and oral gels like Bonjela and Ora-Sed, wart removers, acne cleansers and wipes and some insect repellents. Herbal remedies like echinacea and herbal preparations in multivitamin supplements can cause salicylate reactions and our family members have had salicylate reactions to homeopathic remedies. Technically, non-steroidal anti-inflammatory drugs such as ibuprofen (with brand names such as Nurofen), diclofenac (Voltaren and others) and naproxen (Naprosyn and others) do not contain salicylates. However, most people who are sensitive to salicylates are also sensitive to these painkillers. Paracetamol (acetaminophen) is much less likely to cause problems.

Drugs containing amines

Drugs that can contain amines include over-the-counter cold tablets, decongestants, nasal drops or sprays, some pain relievers, general and local anaesthetics and some antidepressants.

Additives in drugs

Syrup, capsule or tablet medications may contain artificial colours, benzoate or sulphite preservatives and concentrated flavours such as cherry or menthol that are extremely high in salicylates. One mother who had to give antibiotic syrup to her active four-year-old complained: 'It is turning him into one very nasty tantrum-throwing s—'. Even plain white paracetamol tablets can contain benzoate preservative (see Product Updates on www.fedup.com.au for alternatives).

Supplements

The active ingredients in vitamins, herbal remedies and fish oils can cause problems, and so can added colours, preservatives and flavours. Colours and flavours do not have to be listed on the label. It's best to avoid all supplements except those recommended (see the 'Supplements' factsheet on www.fedup.com.au) during your supervised elimination diet, then reintroduce supplements one at a time as challenges according to the rules of challenge – that is, wait until you are symptom free, take the recommended dose of the supplement every day for at least a week while sticking strictly to your diet and keeping a food and symptom diary, then review your diary.

What you can do

- Don't take medication unless it is really necessary. Asthma drugs are necessary, never reduce asthma medication without consulting your doctor.
- Always check ingredients in medications and supplements (see box on p. 182).
- Assume that any new symptom you develop after starting a new drug – including worsening asthma – might be caused by the drug.
- Empty contents of coloured capsules (e.g. antibiotics) and mix with golden syrup or a tablespoon of ice-cream that numbs the tastebuds.

What's in your pharmaceuticals?

Pharmaceutical labels don't have to list all ingredients. You can ask your pharmacist, look for the Consumer Medicine Information sheet (CMI) which has an ingredients list at the end using http://www.appgonline.com.au/browse.asp?t=cmi or do a Google search for <name of drug> ingredients.

Example 1: What's the yellow colour in Ritalin 30 mg LA?

Google search: Ritalin 30 mg LA ingredients

At the time of writing, the CMI listed the colour in Ritalin LA as yellow iron oxide. You can then search for <name of additive> on our website's additive list at http://www.fedupwithfoodadditives.info/information/additivesall.htm. Iron oxide is natural colour (172), therefore failsafe.

Example 2: Our paediatrician recommended Fergon elixir iron supplement which contains glucose liquid, ethanol and saccharin sodium. Is it failsafe?

Google search: Fergon elixir ingredients

As well as the glucose liquid, etc., on the label, the CMI listed 'apricot superarome' – in other words, strong apricot flavour. It's not failsafe because all fruit flavours are high in salicylates. See the 'Supplements' factsheet on www.fedup.com.au for alternatives.

If there is no list of inactive ingredients on the CMI, contact the supplier on the toll-free number listed or ask your pharmacist.

- Wash hard coloured coatings off pills by rubbing between thumb and fingers under the tap.
- See Vitamin icypoles recipe (p. 229) for getting unflavoured vitamins into children.
- White tablets (e.g. paracetamol) can be cut into smaller doses for children – the failsafe email groups have a similar useful recipe for children's paracetamol.
- Ask a compounding pharmacist (search for Compounding in the online Yellow Pages), for example:

> Our three-month-old breastfed baby has to take oral antibiotics so I explained to our local pharmacist that I wanted no added colours, preservatives or flavours. He had no idea what was in antibiotics other than the active ingredient, conceded that I knew more about it than he did, and gave me a contact for a compounding pharmacist. They made me up a liquid that is just the antibiotic suspended in water, with nothing else added, and made it concentrated so that I could give her less at one time. It tastes bitter but she takes it squirted into her mouth with a syringe with no problems.

Most people find they are much healthier and experience far fewer colds, flu and infections after they go failsafe. Our bodies have their own defences to fight off sickness with rest and good food (see Notes).

Some natural alternatives (always consult your doctor when necessary)

• **Colds, flu, cough:** drink lots of fluids, breathe hot-water vapours to loosen mucus (head over a basin of very hot water, make a tent with a towel), see hot lemon drink (p. 185). • **Treat sores** by scrubbing with soap and water and use hot soaks for infected wounds. • **For pain**, try ice packs or hot-water bottles. • **Sore throat:** gargle hot salt water. • **To soothe a ticklish throat:** suck slowly on a hard sweet like a Werther's Original butter candy • **Stuffed-up nose:** sniff up warm salt water. • **Fever:** rest, drink plenty of liquids. The latest medical thinking is that fever is the body's way of healing itself. Let the fever run its course. • **High fever:** cool the body with tepid water. Use plain white preservative-free paracetamol tablets when necessary.

• **Sores, pimples:** scrub with soap and water. • **Itching, burning, irritations of the skin:** for relief, cold compresses. See soothing failsafe creams for itchy rashes in the 'Eczema' factsheet on www.fedup.com.au. • **Minor burns:** hold in cold water for ten minutes. • **Cold sores:** hold ice on blister for one hour at first sign. • **Diarrhoea and vomiting:** drink plenty of liquids to avoid dehydration. When the person is vomiting or feels too sick to eat, give 'sips and chips' – sips of commercial rehydration preparations such as unflavoured Gastrolyte, or 1 litre water, 2 tbsp sugar, ¼ tsp salt, ¼ tsp sodium bicarbonate; or water and chips of ice. Progress to clear soups (chicken or vegetable), icypoles, plain boiled rice. Slowly introduce crackers, pears, potato, other low-salicylate vegetables, progress to chicken, lean meat, beans, lentils, eggs, no fatty foods. If wheat/gluten has ever been a problem, avoid it during diarrhoeal illness. A backpacker's trick I learned in India is 24 hours with nothing but boiled water and boiled rice. Consult your doctor, especially with a young baby. • **Constipation** can be due to lack of fluids and fibre or to food sensitivity. It can range from hard, dry stools or 'rabbit pellets' to a feeling of incomplete evacuation (also called 'sticky poos' – faeces are sticky and hard to clean up). If due to food sensitivity, in the long term, aim to get your diet right. Suspect any of the usual culprits, especially dairy foods and salicylates. The mother of a previously often constipated preschooler wrote about the benefits of failsafe: 'her bowel motions are normal now (despite only eating one pear a day . . . who would ever have thought!)'. To manage constipation: drink lots of water and Magic cordial, eat more fibre, for example All Bran if tolerated or psyllium husks if not (see p. 204), pears, celery, cabbage, other vegetables including dried beans, chickpeas, cashews, rhubarb (medium salicylates but the laxative effect of rhubarb is well-known in Chinese medicine), rolled oats, gelatine in jellies (p. 280) and marshmallows (p. 301) and dried pears (see Product Updates on www.fedup.com.au). The antidote below may help for food-intolerance-induced consti-pation. See 'Constipation' factsheet and Product Updates on www.fedup.com.au for suitable laxatives.

Hot 'lemon' drink
A soothing drink for colds and flu.

1 mug boiling water
1 tbsp Magic readymix or more to taste (p. 228)
1 pinch plain white ascorbic acid or calcium ascorbate (Vitamin C) powder

Add Magic readymix and vitamin powder to boiling water and stir well. Adults can add a splash of whisky.

Probiotics
There is increasing evidence that probiotics can help with irritable bowel symptoms and possibly other aspects of food sensitivity (see p. 145).

Antidote for food reactions
People have noticed that certain over-the-counter remedies can ease the symptoms of food intolerance for a short time. Antacids (Eno's: sodium bicarbonate, sodium carbonate, citric acid – regular not lemon flavour) and calcium supplements (plain Caltrate: calcium carbonate not chewable with flavour)

can reduce hyperactivity, reflux, stomach aches, irritability, restless legs and difficulty falling asleep. Calming effects begin almost immediately and last for about an hour. As with any medication, there can be side effects such as diarrhoea so it is essential to stay within recommended doses and best to use only when necessary. We usually have a dose as soon as possible after having to eat at a non-failsafe social occasion, as the antidote hastens the excretion of salicylates. Ask your pharmacist about doses for children.

Weight loss

Failsafe eating is a way to reduce your intake of harmful food chemicals, not a weight-loss diet. However, many overweight people find they lose weight when they go failsafe, particularly if they have previously eaten heaps of processed foods high in hidden fats, sugars and additives designed to make you overeat.

Even natural chemicals can be addictive and contribute to being overweight. A woman who went failsafe for irritable bowel problems found that salicylates and dairy foods were the cause of her symptoms and her obesity. She wrote: 'I'm back to size 12 clothes and have bought lots of new ones. I turn fifty next week and feel like forty. I'm a bit evangelical when I tell people why I've lost so much weight.' There are more details on the 'Weight Loss' factsheet on www.fedup.com.au.

If the weight doesn't fall off when you go failsafe, you might have to work at it. There's a fascinating study in the USA where scientists are observing 5000 super-successful weight losers. To join the National Weight Control Registry, you have to lose at least 13 kilos and keep it off for at least 12 months (http://www.nwcr.ws/Research/default.htm). These super losers originally lost their weight in different ways: on their own, consulting a nutritionist, in organised programs or using liquid formulas, but the question is, how do they keep it off?

It turns out that super losers eat a diet lower in fat than average, so the message is • reduce your intake of fats and oils • choose low-fat dairy and soy products • buy lean meat • trim obvious fat and drain mince while cooking • halve the recommended oil level in recipes if possible or choose cooking methods that require no oil • avoid cream and fatty desserts.

Super losers exercise more than average, the equivalent of walking 4–5 kilometres a day for women and 6–7 kilometres a day for men.

The principles of routine, repetition and regularity work just as well with eating as they do with children's behaviour. Studies with laboratory rats show that the way to create obesity is to provide self-feeders so the rats can eat whenever they like. The super losers regularly eat five meals a day including breakfast and are more likely to watch the size of their portions and weigh themselves frequently.

'A real variety queen'

Interestingly, the super losers eat fewer takeaways and meals out than the rest of the population. They prepare nearly all of their food themselves, so with failsafe you are halfway there. Super losers also eat less variety than average, and again this is a feature of failsafe eating, as a mother describes:

> It's amazing how everything looks (or seems) similar these days. Pre-intolerance I was a real variety queen. Never the same food twice in one week, let alone the same recipe more than once in a month. I would be so sick if I ate those foods now. Anyway, healthy, happy boys are worth it.

They also watch considerably less television than average. Although researchers didn't say, I can't help wondering if this is due to the avoidance of junk-food advertising.

Over 95 per cent of successful dieters claimed the quality of their life had improved as a result of the weight decrease, listing energy levels, self-confidence, mobility and improved mood among the benefits.

Weight gain

Food intolerance can contribute to being underweight through malnutrition due to, for example, coeliac disease (see p. 75) or irritable bowel symptoms, so in some cases welcome weight gain can result from avoiding gluten. For people who need to gain weight, the principles are the opposite of weight loss. Eat frequently, eat more fat – preferably vegetable oil that won't clog your arteries – and provide more variety in meals. For instance, offering three types of pasta, bread rolls or vegetables will make people eat more than one type.

Dietitians can help with weight loss or gain when needed, as well as supervising the elimination diet for food intolerance.

Children and sugar

Children who are used to eating processed foods will prefer to eat high fat and sugar foods during their elimination diet. For the first few weeks, until they lose their food cravings, it is more important to worry about food chemicals than nutrition: for example, it's okay if they want home-cooked chicken and chips most nights. Although sugar doesn't cause behaviour problems, it doesn't provide long-lasting energy either, so it is best to minimise children's intake of sugary foods and save sugary drinks and sweets as occasional treats. Sugar is best served as part of a balanced meal or in a snack that contains other nutrition, e.g. rolled oat bars (p. 289) or lunchbox muffins (p. 216). One mother was pleased to hear that you can feed children dinner recipes such as pasta or quiche for lunches and snacks – 'I never thought of that,' she said.

What about nutrition?

If you are prepared to eat permitted vegetables such as Brussels sprouts and hummus, failsafe eating can be very nutritious. An analysis of three-year-old Ethan's menu (p. 294) found that his daily intake of calcium, iron, A, B and C vitamins and other nutrients were all at the recommended levels and folate was considerably higher than the recommended level. One of his favourite meals – Darani's amazing chicken noodle stew (p. 231) – which he ate nearly every day, was found to be highly nutritious.

Vitamin C and Vitamin A can be low for children who can't eat fruit and won't eat vegetables; calcium can be low for children who are dairy-free; and thiamine and iron can be low for children who are gluten-free, especially for vegetarians. If your children are on a restricted diet, you need to have their nutrition checked by a dietitian.

Nutrition gurus recommend five serves of vegetables and two serves of fruit a day. One serve is half a cup. A failsafe seven-a-day could be a tinned pear with cereal for breakfast, a chunk of lettuce and a stick of celery with lunch, fresh peeled pear for afternoon tea, a mug of vegetable soup (which is two serves), potato and green beans, cabbage or coleslaw with the main meal.

Children's eating habits generally become much healthier after a few weeks and there are hints about how to get vegetables into children throughout this book. Calcium supplements or fortified soy and rice milks are available for those who are dairy-free, and people who are gluten-free are encouraged to eat two serves per day of meat or eggs to keep up iron and thiamine levels.

There are some low-dose multivitamin and mineral supplements that will fit into failsafe eating (see Shopping List). After challenges and establishing a routine, you can encourage more vegetable eating (p. 136) and visit your dietitian for a nutrition check. The recommended daily intake for Vitamin C in Australia for children ranges from 30–50 mg per day. Vitamin C is found in breastmilk, all fresh fruit and vegetables and fortified cereals like Rice Bubbles (10 mg per serve). The amount of Vitamin C in an average failsafe day (potato, green beans, cabbage, lettuce, celery, pears) is more than double the RDI. Two medium potatoes or one serve of Brussels sprouts equals the RDI. Vitamin C is reduced by storage and overcooking. Large doses of Vitamin C supplements may be counterproductive as salicylates and Vitamin C compete for excretion in the kidney. This means that Vitamin C can have the effect of 'damming up' salicylates and causing them to stay in the body much longer, with increased adverse effects.

Food additives can have anti-nutritional effects. For example, sulphite preservatives (220–228) are known to inactivate folate and Vitamin B1 (thiamine) in the body, with results severe enough to cause death from thiamine deficiency in pet cats and dogs. When families go additive-free, the nutrients in their foods will be more available to them.

Calcium

The recommended daily intake for calcium is from 800–1500 mg a day. There is a theory that we need only 200–300 mg daily if we avoid calcium depleters such as • phosphates – in cola drinks and excess animal products • sodium, especially salt hidden in processed foods (for example, a bowl of cornflakes contains more salt than a packet of salty crisps) • caffeine • animal protein, including dairy products • tobacco • a sedentary lifestyle. Some readers have reported constipation or diarrhoea from calcium supplements, so I prefer to buy calcium-fortified soymilk or ricemilk than to take calcium as a supplement, but have used it as an antidote (p. 185). Check with your dietitian or doctor regarding dosages for children.

Low chemical sources of major nutrients

Nutrient	Food sources
Protein	meats, fish, poultry, eggs, dairy foods
Fat	oils, margarine, meat, eggs, dairy foods
Carbohydrates	rice, potato, bread, pasta, cereals, white sugar
Fibre	wholegrain cereals, wholegrain bread, cabbage, Brussels sprouts, lentils, beans, pears
Essential fatty acids (omega-3 fats)	canola, sunflower and safflower oils and margarine, flaxseed oil, egg yolk
Natural antioxidants	foods containing vitamins A and C (below) and Vitamin E (canola, sunflower and safflower oils and margarine)
Vitamin A	dairy foods, eggs, margarine, fish, lettuce, Brussels sprouts, beans, cabbage
Vitamin B1	breads (brown and white), brown rice, wholemeal pasta, fortified breakfast cereals
Vitamin B12	meat, chicken, fish, eggs, milk
Other B vitamins	dairy products, meat, chicken, fish, lentils
Vitamin C	wholegrain cereals, potato, parsley, Brussels sprouts, cabbage, peas, swedes (rutabaga)
Folic acid	Brussels sprouts, lettuce, cabbage, lentils, pulses, wholegrain cereals, fortified breakfast cereals
Iron	meat, chicken, fish, eggs, lentils, wholegrain cereals, calcium dairy foods, calcium-fortified soy products

Reproduced with permission from *Friendly Food* (by Anne Swain, Velencia Soutter and Robert Loblay, Murdoch Books Australia, 2004)

Changing nutrients

Changes in the way our food is produced and stored have led to decreases in essential nutrients. Comparisons of government food nutrition tables show that in the last 50–60 years • the iron content of the average rump steak has fallen by 55 per cent • the iron content of milk has fallen by more than 60 per cent • the calcium content of cheddar cheese has fallen by 9 per cent • calcium, magnesium, sodium and copper levels in fruit have declined significantly • potassium, iron, magnesium and copper levels in vegetables have declined significantly • the vitamins in bagged salad are reduced significantly by storage • farmed fish are likely to have a poorer ratio of omega 3 fatty acids to omega 6 fatty acids compared with wild fish, especially if fish feed is based on soy.

It seems likely that our fruit and vegetables are only as good as the soil they are grown in and our animal foods are only as good as the food fed to the animals. Depletion of soil in farms that rely on synthetic fertilisers, and dilution of milk due to the use of high-yield A1 producing cows – compared to the much lower yield A2-producing cows – could be to blame. The message seems to be to choose more natural, old-fashioned, organic farming methods, and less processed foods wherever possible.

Experts recommend that women who are planning a pregnancy or who may become pregnant accidentally should take 400–500 µg daily folic acid supplements before conception and during the first three months of pregnancy to prevent neural tube defects.

Introducing food to babies

Recommendations about weaning foods are changing as experts grapple with increasing allergies. Everyone agrees that introducing solids before the end of the third month should be avoided.

For a family history of allergy

At the time of writing, for children with a family history of allergies (eczema, asthma, hay fever, known food allergies) the Australasian Society of Clinical Immunology and Allergy (ASCIA) experts recommend delaying introduction of solids until six months and delaying the introduction of the most common food allergens according to the following schedule:

- cows' milk and other dairy foods other than formula (12–24 months)
- egg and egg-containing foods (age 12–24 months)
- fish (age 12–24 months)
- peanuts and tree nuts (age 36 months or up to 5 years if there is a family history of this allergy)
- shellfish (age 36 months or up to 5 years if there is a family history of this allergy).

But this may change. You can check the most up-to-date official recommendations at http://www.allergy.org.au/aer/infobulletins/food_allergy.htm. (See the 'Probiotics' factsheet on www.fedup.com.au as it is likely probiotics will soon be recommended for breastfeeding mothers and possibly babies.)

For non-allergic babies with a family history of coeliac disease

Studies have shown that breastfeeding is the best protection against coeliac disease. At the time of writing, a number of researchers recommend that if you are breastfeeding non-allergic babies at risk of coeliac disease, introduce gluten in small amounts in the diet between four and six months while breastfeeding and continue breastfeeding for at least a further two to three months (see Notes). Consult your doctor.

For a family history of food intolerance

Food-intolerant babies can be sensitive to many of the foods on the ASCIA list. The following suggestions fit within official guidelines and were developed in consultation with mothers from the failsafebaby group.

- Introduce new solid foods one at a time, every one to two weeks, so that reactions can be identified.
- Keep a food and symptom diary in an exercise book. Include symptoms such as rash, diarrhoea, reflux, sleep disturbance, unsettled behaviour, crying.

From six months old

• baby rice cereal – use pure rice cereal (see Shopping List), or cook plain white rice with water, formula or breastmilk and puree it in a blender. For a quick and easy cereal, use rice crumbs (see Shopping List) with water added and heated in the microwave for about one minute. Some mothers recommended contamination-free oat porridge (see Shopping List).

• pureed fruit and vegetables. We suggest this order, see salicylate and amine content in brackets: pear (0.00, Packham, should be ripe, soft and well-peeled), swede (0.00), choko (0.01, you can add a little sugar if needed), celery (0.00), green beans (0.11, but are better tolerated than expected), cabbage (0.00), Brussels sprouts (0.07), potato (0.00, should be large, white-fleshed and brown-skinned, old and well-peeled), Golden Delicious apple (0.08, but are not as well-tolerated as you would expect), butternut pumpkin (0.12), Red Delicious apple (0.19), carrot (0.23), sweet potato (0.48), other pumpkin.

Remember that the effects of salicylates and amines can build up slowly, and if you are breastfeeding, the food chemicals in your diet can add to the effect. If problems occur with these foods, talk to members of the failsafebaby group and a dietitian. (p. 328)

Eight to twelve months old

Introduce other foods one at a time: • Other fruit and vegetables: bananas (0.00 and amines), watermelon (0.48), peaches (0.58), cucumber (0.78), zucchini (1.04), rockmelon (1.50, AKA cantaloupe), cauliflower (0.16 and amines), plums (up to 0.21 and amines), avocado (0.60 and amines), broccoli (0.65 and amines), grapes (up to 1.88 and amines) • Meat – chicken, veal, lamb • Wheat products – such as preservative-free bread, egg-free pasta.

Soymilk, ricemilk, allergies and infant feeding

- If breastfeeding isn't possible, prescription formula is available from your doctor for children with confirmed cows' milk and soy allergies.
- Ricemilk and soymilk enriched with chickpeas are not suitable for children or adults with cross reactivity problems due to nut, legume or soy allergies.
- Ricemilk is not suitable for infant feeding. Any infant not breastfed to 12 months must be given an appropriate infant formula.

13

Failsafe recipes

What can we eat instead of . . .?

Some families are horrified when they read the list of foods they need to avoid. 'What *can* we eat?' they exclaim. You won't have to give up chicken and chips, hamburgers, pizza, roast dinners, fresh fish, stir-fries, spaghetti, noodles, ice-cream, cakes or lollies – you'll just have to cook them yourself. One mother commented, 'My time is distributed differently. I'm spending more time in the kitchen and less time arguing with him. It's more relaxing this way.'

Some people complain, 'but the food is so bland'. The food industry has worked hard to turn you into a flavour junkie. Buy the best-quality fresh ingredients rather than relying on spices and glutamates for flavour. It is cheaper than eating out and your tastes will change. For some people strawberries are a disaster whereas chocolate cake has no effect. For others it is the reverse. You will have to choose the options that suit you.

Throughout the failsafe recipes, fruit and vegetables that contain moderate amounts of salicylates, amines and natural MSG are listed as options. These are not suitable for your supervised elimination diet, they are for people who have completed their elimination and challenges and have worked out their tolerance for salicylates and amines. If you are very sensitive your allowance will be one moderate serving of salicylates every two days, or less. Some people will tolerate one moderate serve every day. You could spend your salicylate allowance on commercial lemonade and lollies but it's healthier to choose Golden Delicious apples, carrots and fresh corn cobs. If you eat too many salicylate- or amine-containing foods, your problems will probably build up slowly until one day you realise 'the diet isn't working as well as it did at first'.

Symptoms of food intolerance can change with age. Most children reach their peak of hyperactivity around the age of four, but while their hyperactivity improves they grow into other problems. I hear frequently from parents who say, 'They've grown out of their food reactions. We don't have to stick to the diet so strictly . . . but they still have problems with inattention (social skills, lack of motivation, learning difficulties, defiance . . .)'. Growing out of one problem generally means growing into another, and will usually improve when families tighten up on their foods again.

Tomato sauce
This is one of the most difficult items for many families. Try Birgit's pear ketchup (p. 270), mayonnaise (p. 268), leek sauce (p. 263), pear puree, or salt, depending on the situation.

Pasta topping
Forget tomato sauces and flavour sachets, instead use failsafe mince (p. 234) or cream cheese sauce (p. 269). Even easier is butter or failsafe margarine with salt and garlic. See the recipes in the pasta section (p. 264).

Baked beans
Not failsafe. Cook your own and serve with pear ketchup.

Soy sauce

Strange as it sounds, golden syrup can give a soy-sauce-type flavour to Asian-style cooking but you have to be careful not to burn it.

Salt

Although health authorities advise against adding salt in home-cooked recipes, it doesn't apply to failsafe eating because we have to avoid so many salty foods, from yellow cheeses to takeaways, packet snacks and most processed cereals. Health authorities now recommend the use of iodised salt.

Vegemite

Vegemite is high in salicylates, glutamates, amines and salt. Instead of Vegemite on toast you can use butter with a good sprinkle of salt. Pioneering Australian families did that and it tastes delicious. For a sandwich spread, see the Vegemite Substitute recipe (p. 272).

Peanut butter

Cashew butter (p. 272) – commercial cashew paste from roasted cashews is not okay; failsafe hummus (p. 253); Freedom Foods Soy Butter if you can find it in your supermarket.

Cheese

Use preservative-free cream cheese.

Nutella

Cashew paste with the carob or carob and maple-syrup variation (p. 272); maple butter (see Shopping List).

Chocolate

Use carob instead, as a powder for cooking and hot drinks or in carob bars (avoid flavours) and carob-coated rice cakes. Try different carob powders until you find one you like. Certain batches from Turkey seem to cause adverse reactions. For people who are dairy-free, some carob products are made with soymilk.

Honey

Maple syrup, rice malt, rice syrup, golden syrup, white sugar, caster sugar, icing sugar, light brown sugar.

Jam

Homemade pear jam (p. 271), maple butter (see Shopping List).

Pizza, burgers, KFC, chicken nuggets, fish fingers

Make your own (see recipes).

Fries (hot chips)

Make your own (p. 226) or look for frozen oven-bake fries without unlisted antioxidants (see Shopping List).

Takeaways

Plain BBQ chicken if available – no stuffing, no seasoning, no seasoned salt; grilled fresh fish; potato cart baked potato with sour cream; steak sandwich, no sauce, no onions, provide your own buttered bread; fresh hot cob of corn is not failsafe but a reasonable compromise; fried rice with egg and shallots only (but the oil will not be safe). Commercial fries or hot chips are rarely failsafe – if you have to eat them, reduce the dose by eating a tiny amount. You can fill up by taking your own buttered bread rolls and salad instead.

Soft drinks

See Magic cordial and Magic readymix (p. 227). You can also drink soda water, spring water and limited preservative-free tonic water or preservative-free lemonade (less than one small glass per week).

Lemon juice

Real lemon juice contains salicylates and amines. Use 4 tbsp warm water, 1 tsp sugar, ¾ tsp citric acid or to taste, pinch ascorbic acid (Vitamin C) (optional) as a substitute.

Snacks in a packet

Plain unflavoured potato chips (see Shopping List), but keep them for treats due to high fat content. Pretzels are OK.

Icypoles

Make your own (p. 228) or see Shopping List (special occasions only).

Ice-cream

There are a few vanilla ice-cream brands without artificial colours or annatto 160b. Read labels or see Shopping List.

Sweets

Toffees, caramels, butterscotch, fudge and white marshmallows could be failsafe but generally contain too much flavour or other additives, see Shopping List.

Food colouring

Avoid artificial colours and annatto natural colouring (160b) (p. 108). Cochineal red (120) made from insects is failsafe but not kosher and a possible allergen. Beta-carotene 160a is failsafe. See p. 289 for other suggestions. Beware of commercial sweets, ice-cream and cereals with natural colouring that could be high in fruit flavours (salicylates).

Flavours

It is safest to avoid any processed foods that contain flavours except for those on the Shopping List, and even then they should be used with caution. Vanilla is safe for some people but not all (see Checklist of Common Mistakes on www.fedup.com.au). The reaction is dose-related so you can reduce the dose by omitting vanilla from home cooking. You can use salt, sugar, light brown sugar, golden syrup and maple syrup for flavouring – as well as good-quality fresh natural ingredients.

Dairy foods

Milk

You can use calcium-fortified soymilk, oat milk, ricemilk or pear syrup on cereals. None of the milk substitutes taste the same as cows' milk at first. They are all different so it is worth trying more than one. Don't expect a difficult child to like a new taste straight off. Make sure the milk substitute is chilled. Serve it with cereal or flavour (see Smoothies, p. 213) rather than plain. Pass the sugar bowl and suggest, 'You'll probably need to put sugar on your cereal if you're using soymilk.' You can cut that out later. Be lavish in your praise for even the tiniest sip. Some children will never learn to like soymilk. If you avoid dairy foods completely and use an unfortified drink, consult your dietitian about calcium supplements.

You will also need to avoid dairy foods in processed products. Read the labels. It is easy to bake your own biscuits and cakes using soymilk. (See warnings about soymilk, ricemilk, allergies and infant feeding on p. 195.)

A2 milk

A2 milk contains the original type of A2 protein that was in all dairy herds until there was a mutation in the European herd thousands of years ago. It is now available in Australia from specially bred Jersey cows (see www.A2Australia.com.au) and in the UK in buffalo milk. Yak, camel, goat and other milks often said to be better for 'allergies' are naturally high in A2 proteins. However, experts warn that A2 isn't suitable for young children with severe milk allergies. A2 doesn't seem to work as well as dairy-free for children with dairy-related behaviour problems, but for some people including me it is a godsend. My rhinitis appears to be entirely related to A1 but not A2 milk and for the last two years I have enjoyed unlimited A2 milk after 12 years on soymilk. There may be some compelling health reasons for switching to A2 milk, including reduced risk of heart disease and diabetes type 1. See A2 milk factsheet on www.fedup.com.au.

Lactose-free milk

Lactose intolerance is the inability to digest lactose, a type of sugar found in milk, due to temporary or permanent deficiency of the enzyme lactase. Symptoms include bloating, diarrhoea and abdominal cramps. Lactose intolerance is relatively rare in Westernised countries with a long history of dairy farming, although common in Africa, Asia and other non-Westernised countries. Short-term lactose intolerance can be induced by gastrointestinal infections but 'lactose intolerance' in babies may actually be cows' milk protein intolerance, see www.breastfeeding.asn.au/bfinfo/ lactose.html. A long period of complete dairy avoidance may result in loss of lactase and hence the ability to break down or tolerate lactose. Lactose-free milk is helpful for lactose intolerance but not for behavioural and other conditions associated with dairy foods.

Yoghurt

Fresh mild yoghurt is best for amine responders. Too much vanilla flavour (salicylates) can be a problem (see Checklist of Common Mistakes on www.fedup.com.au). You can buy or make your own yoghurt from milk, soy or A2 milk, see also probiotics (p. 145).

Butter

Look for a dairy-free, additive-free margarine like Nuttelex.

Mock cream
See p. 288

Non-dairy ice-cream

Vanilla tofu ice-cream usually contains coconut oil or similar and is therefore regarded as moderate in salicylates, so it's not suitable for your supervised elimination diet (see alternative, p. 278). Soy cheese would be acceptable if it didn't contain annatto colouring (160b).

Failsafe margarine

Choose margarine made with canola, sunflower or safflower oil, avoid preservatives 200–203, avoid antioxidants 310–312, 319–321, colours 102, 110, 160b (160a is failsafe). Choose milk-free if necessary. In Australia there are several failsafe margarines and at least one failsafe dairy-free margarine (Nuttelex, see Shopping List).

Failsafe oils

Sunflower, safflower and canola oils are failsafe but should not be cold-pressed (olive and other oils are too high in salicylates). Cold-pressed rice bran oil is suitable for most but not all readers – anyone who is sensitive to the wholegrain of wheat in products such as wholemeal bread and Weet-Bix should avoid daily use of rice bran oil (see Checklist of Common Mistakes on www.fedup.com.au). Avoid synthetic antioxidants (310–312, 319–320) in a few Australian supermarket cooking oils, nearly all New Zealand cooking oils, and virtually all commercially fried products. When any kind of vegetable oil is used in a product such as biscuits, frozen chips or soymilk, antioxidants in the oil need not appear on the label if the amount of oil is less than five per cent (due to the five per cent labelling loophole, see p. 103). In that case, to avoid these antioxidants you need to phone the manufacturer or stick to products on the Shopping List (see Checklist of Common Mistakes and the Product Updates on www.fedup.com.au or subscribe to our newsletter as the levels of unlisted antioxidants in oils changes constantly).

Crumbs

Commercial breadcrumbs usually contain the bread preservative (282). Commercial rice crumbs are an excellent alternative (see Shopping List), make your own breadcrumbs, or use crushed Rice Bubbles.

Preservative-free bread

As well as avoiding calcium propionate (282) you need to avoid vinegar, unlisted antioxidants (319–321, TBHQ, BHA and BHT) and non-failsafe items such as raisins, dried fruit or honey. In Australia we recommend the plain Brumby's and Bakers Delight breads, Laucke's premixes for your breadmaker, and there are others (see Shopping List, and the Product Updates on the website, or read labels and quiz your baker about vegetable oils). You can ask to read labels on premix packets and phone manufacturers of vegetable oils. Or make your own (p. 224).

Wholemeal bread, Weet-bix and other whole grains

Some people including children with behaviour problems can manage refined white flour, white bread and other refined products but not wholemeal bread and cereals such as Weet-Bix, Vitabrits, Weeties. They may even have problems with brown rice rather than white rice (see Checklist of Common Mistakes in www.fedup.com.au).

Wheat or gluten

See gluten-free section (p. 293). People who are avoiding wheat but not gluten can eat rye (see Shopping List for rye breads and crispbreads) and barley.

Fibre – psyllium

Psyllium is considered to be the safest and gentlest water-soluble fibre (p. 204). It can be mixed into cereals, yoghurt, soups or stews or stirred into a glass of water and consumed immediately or cooked into foods. See psyllium-enriched muffins (p. 217) and rolled oat bars (p. 289).

Doses: Some suppliers suggest starting with one tsp per day and building up slowly to 5 grams (approx 2 metric tsp) once or twice a day mixed with a glass of water; for children 8–12 years 2.5 grams (1 metric tsp) once a day; under 8, consult your dietitian. As treatment for constipation, allow 2–3 days for effects.

Cautions: Because it works by absorbing fluid from the bowel to form a kind of gel, each dose must be taken with the equivalent of a glass (150 ml) of water to prevent severe and life-threatening intestinal blockage. Flavoured psyllium is not failsafe. There have been some reports of allergies in people frequently exposed to psyllium.

Eggs

People who are allergic to eggs can use commercial egg replacer or 1 tbsp of oil per egg in baking recipes such as pancakes, muffins and cakes.

Dried fruit

Drying concentrates food chemicals so even dried mango is loaded with salicylates. If you have a home dehydrator you can dry very soft ripe pears (see p. 226) or bananas, if you don't react to amines (commercially dried pears include the skin, so they're very high in salicylates). We take dried pears bushwalking. You can also dry failsafe mince (p. 234) but beware of an amine build-up. See Product Updates on www.fedup.com.au for commercial sources of unsulphited dried fruit.

What to cook when you don't feel like cooking

We all have nights when we'd rather phone for a pizza. There is an alternative. Every time I cook, for example Darani's amazing chicken noodle stew (p. 231) or failsafe mince I cook double and freeze the extra. That way I can serve a frozen dinner on rice or instant noodles topped with failsafe mince

(p. 234) and frozen peas in ten minutes. If you have any vegetable soup in the fridge or freezer, you can quickly reheat a mug each in the microwave for extra nutrition. Toasted sandwiches are another option.

Green peas

Peas are not suitable for your strict elimination diet because they contain small amounts of glutamates that affect some sensitive people, however they are fine for the majority. It's good to try green peas as your first challenge because then you will probably have an easy vegetable that everyone loves. Most children will eat peas still frozen from the packet, or snack on home-grown peas from the garden.

Alcohol

Most alcoholic drinks are very high in problem-causing food chemicals. But you don't have to give up using alcohol in drinks or cooking. Simply substitute whisky with soda, gin with preservative-free tonic or vodka with Magic readymix.

Toothpaste

Anything that goes in your mouth, on your skin or up your nose can cause a problem. Avoid coloured and flavoured toothpastes (salicylates in flavour). Use unflavoured toothpaste (see Shopping List), a wet toothbrush or, even better, a battery-operated toothbrush as they don't need toothpaste.

Canned foods

Some of these recipes call for canned foods such as beans or pears. In the long term you may want to avoid a chemical called Bisphenol-A used to coat the inside of some food cans, especially if you are pregnant (see Notes). Japanese food manufacturers are currently reformulating the lacquer lining of metal cans and hopefully that will happen here, but until then you can reduce your use of canned food by cooking your own beans and pears. You can stew and freeze batches of pears at the end of the season (autumn) when they are very cheap and very ripe.

Yeast

Baker's yeast in bread and bakery products is failsafe. Brewer's yeast, sold as a supplement in health food stores, and used in food products such as beer, wine and Vegemite, is not failsafe (contains salicylates, amines and natural MSG). It is counterproductive to try to combine failsafe eating with a candida diet which excludes yeast and sugar. People who are failsafe 'but not 100 per cent' and swear they react to sugar have almost certainly failed to reduce their salicylate level enough.

The fridge list

Breakfast
Rolled oats, porridge (p. 211)
Rice Bubbles, Weet-Bix (limit to 2 every second day at first)
Milk, A2 milk, soymilk, ricemilk
Eggs (boiled, scrambled, poached, French toast) (p. 259)
Toast with butter only; or with pear jam, golden syrup,
    cashew spread (p. 272)
Pancakes with pure maple syrup (p. 223)
Pear smoothie (p. 213)

Lunch
Sandwiches, rolls or wraps, e.g. chicken, egg and lettuce
Crunchy chicken (p. 241)
Fried rice (p. 243)
Hard-boiled egg, omelette, leftover frittata (p. 260)
Failsafe salad with beans and pasta (p. 257)
Baked potato with cream cheese and chives
Chicken pasta (p. 264)
Homemade pie or sausage roll (p. 224)
Chicken and/or vegetable soup/stew (p. 231)

Main meal
Homemade chicken nuggets and chips (p. 241)
Failsafe burger/pizza/frittata (p. 232)
Spaghetti with garlic mince topping (p. 263)
Ten-minute stir-fry (chicken, beef, lamb, egg, vegetables)
    (p. 235)
Homemade fish fingers or pan-fried fresh fish (p. 246)
Grilled lamb/steak/chicken/failsafe sausages with
    vegetables (p. 245)
Roast chicken/beef/lamb with vegetables (p. 241)
Creamy cashew chicken (p. 245) or Irish stew (p. 238)

Drinks

Water – filtered, bottled, spring, mineral, soda, tap (if no nasty taste) • decaf coffee • unflavoured milk, A2 milk, soymilk, ricemilk, So Good Soyaccino soymilk • Magic cordial (p. 227).

Snacks

Fresh ripe peeled pear or equivalent (limit 2 per day) • Diced Pear Fruit Cups in syrup, can be frozen (see Shopping List) • plain or buttered wheat crackers such as Saladas • homemade muffins • Brumby's white iced finger buns • plain rice cakes with failsafe hummus (p. 253) or butter/margarine and homemade pear jam (p. 271) • trail mix made from unsulphited dried pears, Chic Nuts and raw cashews (see Shopping List) • homemade icypoles (p. 228) • homemade chicken noodle soup (p. 231) • homemade scones or pikelets (p. 223) • homemade potato wedges (p. 226) • sandwiches • beans on toast (p. 223) • anything from the lunch or main meals menu, e.g. pasta • plain or vanilla yoghurt (see Shopping List) • plate of crunchy failsafe salad vegetables, e.g. celery sticks filled with homemade cashew paste (p. 272) or failsafe hummus (p. 253) • homemade rolled oat bars (p. 289) or other biscuits • toast and homemade pear jam or other spreads • Kettle plain chips.

Treats and lollies

See Sweet Treats (p. 301)

Vitamins

See Vitamin icypole recipe (p. 229)

Toothpaste

See Shopping List

Week's menu plan

Write down what you eat now and look for similar, acceptable alternatives from the breakfast, lunch and dinner suggestions on the Fridge List, p. 208.

Cook extra

Long term failsafe cooks recommend preparing batches of soup, stews, pasta toppings, muffins and roasts for lunch fillings on the weekend. Extras can be frozen for quick meals during the week. See some examples below.

Dinner

For confirmed vegetable-haters, serve permitted salad vegetables in lunches and vegetable soup before the main meal.

Monday	Chicken and chips or stir-fry on noodles
Tuesday	Grilled meat and three veg or Irish stew on rice
Wednesday	Failsafe mince with noodles, pasta, rice or mashed potato
Thursday	Fresh fish with oven fries or mashed potato, lettuce, celery and parsley
Friday	Homemade hamburgers or pasta with previously prepared topping
Saturday	Roast chicken or lamb with vegetables
Sunday	Frittata or stir-fry using leftover chicken

Breakfast

Cereals

There are some suitable commercial cereals (see Shopping List). Always read the label – you need to avoid any cereals with corn, colours, fruit or honey.

Fibre is considered to be part of a healthy diet, but some sources can cause problems for people with irritable bowel symptoms.

If you have irritable bowel symptoms make sure your rolled oats are well-cooked and/or use psyllium for extra fibre (see p. 204). Some people including children with behaviour problems are affected by a natural chemical in the wholegrain of wheat. They do better on white bread rather than wholemeal, and on Rice Bubbles rather than wholegrain cereals such as Weet-Bix or Weeties (see Checklist of Common Mistakes on www.fedup.com.au). Homemade porridge is a healthy high-fibre alternative.

Fibre grams per 100 grams

Rice Bubbles	1
Rolled Oats	10
Weet-Bix	10
All-Bran	30
Psyllium husks	100

Five-minute oats

Rolled oats free of wheat contamination are now available (see Shopping List).

½ cup plain rolled oats per person
1 cup water per person

For a creamy texture, make cooktop porridge by placing rolled oats in a small saucepan with cold water and bring to the boil. Reduce heat and simmer for five minutes, stirring constantly while the porridge thickens.
Serve with milk, soymilk, pears, canned pear syrup, brown sugar or rhubarb (salicylates). For the quickest option, use quick-cook oats and make porridge in the microwave according to directions on the pack.

Muesli

2 cups rolled oats
½ cup oat bran
2 cups of a commercial cereal such as Rice Bubbles
(optional)
½ cup chopped raw cashew nuts

Mix ingredients together and store in an airtight container.
Serve with milk or milk substitutes and chopped fresh or
canned pears; or fruit like Golden Delicious apples
(salicylates) or bananas (amines, not suitable for supervised
elimination diet).

Toasted muesli

This is a breakfast to rival popular commercial cereals. Most
children find it irresistible because of the sugar content, which
you can slowly reduce once you're away from the processed
foods.

1½ cups rolled oats
2 tbsp brown sugar
2 tbsp white sugar
1 tbsp failsafe oil (p. 203)

Combine all ingredients in a large bowl and mix well. Stir
mixture in a hot frying pan for a few minutes until golden
brown and smelling delicious. Remove from heat
immediately to prevent burning. Serve with milk or soymilk
as a breakfast or with pear puree as a snack.

Rice (dairy-free, wheat-free)

Cooked brown or white rice with soymilk and real maple syrup.

Toast

Use preservative-free toast or croissants with butter, preservative-free cream cheese, golden syrup, pear jam, maple
butter or Magic spread (p. 271).

Fruit juice

All fruit and vegetable juices, whether commercial or homemade, are high in salicylates – and sometimes amines as well – and are likely to cause problems in food-sensitive people, except celery juice. Pear juice is moderate because it includes the skins. After your supervised elimination diet you can use your salicylate allowance on a small carrot to be juiced with the celery.

Fruit smoothies

Mangoes and bananas are not suitable for your supervised elimination diet.

1 cup milk, A2 milk, soymilk or ricemilk
1 peeled pear or ½ canned pear or ¼ cup frozen mango pulp (salicylates) and banana (amines)
carob powder (optional)

Blend until frothy. Serve in a tall glass with ice-blocks and a straw.

Papaya smoothie

Contains amines, not suitable for your supervised elimination diet. Papayas (or pawpaws) are exceptionally high in Vitamins A and C. We suspect the red variety may contain salicylates; stick with the more common yellow variety. Many children who won't eat them raw will enjoy this drink.

¾ cup milk, A2 milk, soymilk or ricemilk
¼ cup ripe yellow papaya
½ small ripe banana
2 tsp sugar

Blend until frothy. Serve in a tall glass.

Yoghurt drink

Called *lassi* in India, this drink is usually offered with meals and probably prevents flatulence due to dried beans.

1 glass ice-cold water
1–2 tbsp yoghurt or kefir (p. 145)
sugar or salt to taste

Mix well and serve.

Chocolate and carob drinks

Chocolate-flavoured drinks such as Milo and cocoa may be a problem, especially if there is a family history of migraine. Some children react to milk. This can be a slow, cumulative effect.

Carob can be used as a chocolate substitute but is sometimes disliked because of the practice of health food stores which sell carob confectionery with no added sugar. If you want to use carob as a chocolate substitute, you may need to add sugar.

1 cup milk, A2 milk, soymilk or ricemilk
1 tsp or less carob powder
sugar to taste

Blend until frothy.

Boiled eggs

Gently lower the required number of eggs into a saucepan of simmering water and adjust heat to retain simmer. Time required depends on the degree of firmness: soft boiled, 3–4 minutes; firm white, soft yolk, 4–7 minutes; hard-boiled, 8 minutes.

To make hard-boiled eggs easy to peel, cool quickly in ice-cold water.

Poached eggs

Have a saucepan of boiling, salted water ready. The salt is necessary to set the white quickly. Break the egg into a bowl and slip it carefully into the boiling water. Simmer gently until the white is set. Serve on hot buttered toast, garnished with parsley.

Scrambled eggs

1–2 eggs
1 tbsp milk, A2 milk, soymilk or ricemilk
salt to taste
1 tsp pure butter or failsafe margarine (p. 203)
chopped parsley
1 slice buttered toast

Beat egg a little, add milk and salt. Melt the butter in a
saucepan, pour in the egg mixture and cook gently till set,
stirring occasionally. Stir in parsley and serve at once on hot
toast. Eggs will become tough if overcooked.

French toast

4 slices failsafe bread (p. 204) or gluten-free bread (p. 295)
2 eggs, beaten
1 tbsp failsafe butter or oil (p. 203)

Soak bread in eggs. Melt butter in pan and cook bread on
both sides until golden. Serve with real maple syrup.

Plain omelette

1 or 2 eggs
1 tbsp water (optional)
failsafe oil (p. 203) or pure butter
chopped parsley
salt to taste

Beat eggs. Prepare a medium-hot frying pan with a little oil
or butter spread evenly over the pan with a paper towel.
Pour mixture into pan and cook over moderate heat until
brown on the bottom. Loosen with an egg slice, turn over
carefully and cook briefly, then fold over and serve at once,
garnished with parsley and sprinkled with salt.

Italian omelette (fluffy)

1 or 2 eggs
1 tbsp cold water per egg
failsafe oil (p. 203)
chopped parsley
salt to taste

Separate egg. Beat egg white until quite stiff. Add water to egg yolk and beat until thick. Carefully add beaten yolk to stiffly beaten white, folding in very lightly. Grease omelette pan with a little butter or oil, taking care to see the oil is spread evenly over the pan. Pour mixture into pan and leave until brown on the bottom. Fold over and serve at once. Garnish with parsley.

Margie's lunchbox pear muffins

This is my favourite recipe for baking – it's quick and easy, relatively low in fat and sugar, works equally well with gluten-free flours, and can be used with a variety of options.

1½ cups self-raising flour or gluten-free flour mix
½ cup sugar
1 egg, lightly beaten
⅔ cup milk, A2 milk, soymilk, ricemilk or syrup from
    canned pears
¼ cup failsafe oil (p. 203)
½ cup peeled, chopped pears (canned in sugar syrup, or
    fresh and soft)

Sift flour in a bowl and add remaining ingredients, stirring with a fork until mixed. Lightly grease a 12-cup muffin pan with failsafe oil and use an ice-cream scoop or spoon to three-quarter fill cups until three-quarters full. Bake at 180°C for 15–20 minutes.

Variation • **Carob chip:** add ½ cup carob chips, no added flavour • **Pear muffins:** add ½ cup chopped fresh or canned pears and use pear syrup instead of milk • **'Pear' muffins:** add chopped cooked choko and a little more sugar; the result tastes just like pear • **Apple muffins:** add 1 chopped Golden Delicious apple (salicylates) and 1 tbsp extra sugar • **Iced:** ice with white or lemon-flavoured icing (p. 289) • **Double chocolate chip** (amine challenge): add 2 tbsp cocoa and ½ cup Nestlé dark chocolate chips. Sprinkle some chips on top before baking • **Gluten-free:** use self-raising gluten-free flour (p. 173) instead of self-raising flour • **Gluten-free psyllium muffin:** add 2 tbsp psyllium hulls (flea-seed husks) and increase milk to ¾ cup • **Vegetable muffins:** use ½ tsp salt instead of the sugar and add finely diced safe vegetables such as chokoes, Brussels sprouts, potato and green beans as another good way of getting vegetables into children.

Snacks

Contrary to popular opinion, sugar doesn't cause bad behaviour. Sensitive children do better on foods with white sugar than on 'healthy' products with additives or salicylates. However, it is wise to limit sugar intake. Snacks such as muffins and rolled oat bars can be a nutritious part of a varied diet, whereas drinks and sweets consisting mainly of sugar are best saved for occasional treats.

- Fresh ripe peeled pear or equivalent (limit 2 per day)
- Diced Pear Fruit Cups in syrup, can be frozen (see Shopping List)
- plain or buttered wheat crackers such as Saladas or water crackers (be careful – any commercial biscuit with vegetable oil – except Arnott's – may contain unlisted antioxidants such as BHA 320, see Shopping List)
- plain rice cakes with any combination of butter, cream cheese, failsafe hummus (p. 253), cashew paste (p. 272) and homemade pear jam (p. 271)
- salad sandwich or roll (p. 219)

- freshly made plain roll when shopping
- homemade pear, carob or vegetable muffins (p. 217)
- pear or carob smoothie (p. 213)
- homemade rolled oat bars (p. 289) or similar
- plain or vanilla (no annatto) yoghurt, see Shopping List
- unsulphited dried pears, roasted chickpeas, raw cashews
- homemade icypoles (p. 228)
- raw vegetables, e.g. celery sticks, mung sprouts, carrot sticks when tolerated
- buttered toast (p. 212) or scrambled eggs or beans on toast
- Brumby's white iced finger buns
- homemade scones or pikelets (p. 223)
- homemade potato wedges (p. 226)
- hearty soups, e.g. homemade chicken noodle (p. 231) or vegetable soup (p. 229)
- pasta with thawed topping (p. 234)
- leftovers (quiche, pizza); for fussy eaters, teenagers or children whose appetite is suppressed by Ritalin, it is worth presenting hearty soups or easy meals when they say 'I'm hungry'. Meat leftovers should be eaten the day of cooking or frozen.
- pretzels (wheat or gluten free), plain chips
- for sweet treats, see p. 301

Lunches

You can ask the school canteen to offer permitted foods (p. 220) or you can send a packed lunch. Here are some suggestions for packing or eating at home:

- sandwiches, rolls or wraps, e.g. chicken or egg and lettuce (see below for other fillings)
- crunchy chicken nuggets (p. 241)
- fried rice (p. 243)
- hard-boiled egg, omelette, leftover frittata (p. 260)
- failsafe salad with beans and pasta (p. 257)
- vegetable muffins (p. 217)

- chicken pasta (p. 264)
- chicken or vegetable soups or stews (p. 229)
- homemade sausage roll (p. 224) or pies made in an automatic piemaker. Commercial meat pies are high in problem-causing food chemicals. You can make your own quickly by using commercial puff pastry. For fillings, try failsafe mince (p. 234), leftover chicken and mashed potato; egg, mashed potato and parsley
- toasted sandwiches in an automatic toasted sandwich-maker, using the same fillings as above, or leftover sausages with pear sauce or an egg
- cheese toasties made with mild cheese (for people who can manage amines) on rice cakes or bread toasted on one side, heated under the griller
- baked potato with preservative-free cream cheese and chives
- three-minute spaghetti (p. 264)
- omelette or scrambled egg on toast
- gluten-free pancakes (p. 295)

Sandwiches, rolls and toast

Fillings
Fresh or home-frozen chicken, lamb and beef with shredded lettuce, chopped shallots, mung bean sprouts, celery, grated cabbage and celery. Grated carrot, beetroot or other salicylate vegetables when tolerated (p. 165).

Spreads
• preservative-free cream cheese • egg spread, made by mashing together a warm boiled egg and some warm mashed potato with a little salt, parsley and mayonnaise (p. 267) • cashew butter made commercially or at home from blended raw cashews, salt and failsafe oil • kidney beans, lentils or any drained can of beans except broad beans, blended in a food processor with parsley or garlic • rice malt or malt extract,

made from malted grains, high in B vitamins and available in supermarkets • pear jam (p. 271) • Magic spread (p. 271) • golden syrup • Magic mayo (p. 268).

Howard's bean paste

Use red kidney beans from a can, drained and rinsed, or soak dried beans overnight in twice their volume of water. Rinse and discard water, cover again with water and add a little oil to stop foaming. Pressure-cook for 12 minutes or simmer for 60 minutes. Drain.

1 cup cooked red kidney beans
2 tsp failsafe oil
pinch of salt
¼ tsp citric acid
crushed clove of garlic (optional)
2 tbsp water

Mix in blender to a thick paste, adding a little water if too thick. Keep in fridge. Great in sandwiches, wraps, as a dip, a salad dressing, and on pizza.

Food at school

Schools vary in the amount of support they provide to children who are eating failsafe. The following are examples from supportive schools.

- The principal talked to the class about the importance of supporting the child, and made it clear – no teasing, no bullying, no lunch swapping.
- Teachers enforced the no lunch swapping rule.
- Teachers praised, gave gold stars or merit certificates to the child for sticking to his/her diet.
- Teachers bought Pascall's white marshmallows or non-food rewards to give children as motivators in class instead of coloured lollies and icypoles.
- Preschools provided permitted options (see p. 222) for children instead of a plate of fruit.

- A five-year-old was invited to eat his lunch with the assistant principal during the first week, to avoid lunch swapping – this was done in a positive and self-esteem building way.
- School canteens provided permitted options (see below).
- Schools sold water ice-cups as well as juice ice-cups – popular with all students.
- Schools provided permitted alternatives on all occasions where food was served, from class parties to school sausage sizzles and fetes, e.g. preservative-free sausages on preservative-free bread with permitted mayonnaise and shredded lettuce.
- Schools encouraged all children to eat healthy food and to avoid additives – the staff soon noticed the children were more manageable.
- A school excursion provided plain rotisseried chicken with hot chips and preservative-free bread for a picnic instead of going to a fast-food outlet.
- A school camp catered for several children by providing basic failsafe menus with options. Much to the teachers' surprise, 'the majority' of children improved.

The following failsafe items are on the canteen lists of several primary schools:

Sandwiches and rolls
Preservative-free cream cheese • egg • egg and lettuce • fresh chicken meat • chicken and lettuce • preservative-free bread • failsafe margarine.

Hot food
Fried rice (home-cooked).

Cold food
Hard boiled egg.

Sundries
Rice cakes with spread • plain water ice-cups • Dixie ice-cream cups • carob whirls • preservative-free iced finger buns • homemade cakes and biscuits such as Big Anzacs (p. 290).

Drinks
Plain milk (300 ml) • bottled spring water.

Preschool alternatives to a plate of fruit

A preschool teacher with a 'fruit-is-healthy-sugar-is-poison' mindset sabotaged an elimination diet by insisting 'there is nothing wrong with this child's behaviour, children have to have fruit', leaving the mother to cope with a difficult child who spent hours trying to get to sleep every night. You have to find an alternative that is acceptable to both the teacher and the child. It is not fair to the child to eat celery sticks while the others are tucking into watermelon and strawberries. Consider home-dried pears, pear puree or other icypoles, frozen pear-on-a-stick (p. 229), a muffin (p. 216), Sao or pikelet with Magic spread (p. 217), a Big Anzac (p. 290) and other homemade biscuits or a buttered iced finger bun cut in slices. Water is the best drink, but if the others are drinking grape juice, then Magic cordial (p. 227) is kinder.

Butter beans on toast

300 g can butter beans, or home-cooked beans except
    broad beans
30 g butter
2 tbsp chopped shallots

Drain and rinse beans. Heat butter in pan. Add beans and
shallots, stir-fry quickly. Serve on toast or rice. Serves two.

Pancakes

There are permitted wheat-based and gluten-free commercial
pancake premixes although most contain added flavours (see
Shopping List). Maple syrup must be pure with no preservative or added flavour.

1 cup self-raising flour or gluten-free flour
1 large egg
1 cup milk, A2 milk, soymilk or ricemilk
failsafe oil or pure butter for frying

Blend together the flour, egg and milk until smooth. The
batter will improve if allowed to stand for half an hour. Cook
in a hot, lightly oiled frying pan. Serve with butter and real
maple syrup, or savoury fillings.

Pikelets

1 cup self-raising flour
¼ cup sugar
salt
sodium bicarbonate
¾ cup milk, A2 milk, soymilk or ricemilk
1 large egg

Preheat frying pan to 180°C and oil lightly. Sift flour, sugar,
salt and bicarbonate in a basin. Make a well in the center of
dry ingredients, add milk and egg, beat well to make a

smooth batter. Drop tablespoons of mixture onto pan. Cook until bubbles rise to the surface, but do not break. Turn and cook on the other side until golden brown. Serve hot or cold, with butter or Magic spread. Makes approximately 24.

Emma's bread

This is a basic recipe for bread in an automatic breadmaker.

2½ cups plain flour
190 ml water
¼ cup milk or soymilk
1 tbsp failsafe oil
1 pinch ascorbic acid (Vitamin C) powder
1 pinch salt
1½ tsp dried yeast

Put all ingredients in breadmaker. Set the timer and wait for the wonderful aroma. The ascorbic acid helps to deliver well-risen bread every time. When finished, remove and cool before slicing. A good breadknife is essential. We have found a large knife with a scalloped edge is the best.

Wade's sausage rolls

This recipe was devised by a Darwin teenager. Kids love to make them.

500 g low-fat mince
3 chopped shallots
1 clove garlic, crushed (optional)
1 tbsp chopped parsley
salt to taste
commercial puff pastry ready-cut sheets

Preheat oven to 180°C. Mix mince with shallots, garlic, parsley and salt. Cut pastry sheets in half. Place a sausage shape of mince in the middle of the sheet. Roll over, prick top. Cut to required lengths. Bake for 20 minutes or until cooked.

Cornish pasties

1 medium potato
1 medium leek
1 slice of swede (or butternut pumpkin if tolerated)
3 sprigs parsley
250 g low-fat beef mince
2 tbsp peas (glutamates) or green beans
250 g short crust pastry (below)

Preheat oven to 200°C. Finely chop vegetables and parsley. Add mince and peas/beans and mix well. Roll out pastry and cut with saucer to form rounds. Put about 1 tbsp of the mixture on half of each round of pastry. Wet the edges and gently fold over. Using a fork, press around edges and prick tops several times. Brush with milk. Bake on greased oven tray for about 30 minutes, until cooked and brown.

Short crust pastry

You can make your own with this recipe or there are commercial pastry mixes available, including gluten-free. For a sweet pastry, add 4 tbsp sugar.

2 cups self-raising flour (or gluten-free self-raising flour)
¼ tsp salt
1 cup butter or failsafe margarine (p. 203)
cold water to mix

Sift flour and salt. Rub butter into flour with fingertips until mixture resembles breadcrumbs. Mix into a stiff dough with a little water (if too much water is used, pastry will be tough). Turn onto a floured board and knead a little. Do not handle more than necessary. If possible chill in refrigerator for 30 minutes before use. Roll out as required on a floured board. If cooking unfilled, bake at 200°C for about 10 or 15 minutes until golden brown. If filled, bake for about 30 minutes, depending on filling. Freeze left-over pastry.

Potato wedges

These are low in fat and delicious.

1 large potato per person
1 tsp failsafe oil (p. 203) per person
salt to taste

Preheat oven to 200°C. Peel potatoes and cut into wedges (eighths), storing in a bowl of cold water until finished. Pat dry with a clean tea-towel or kitchen paper, and toss in a bowl with the oil until coated. Place a single layer on a lightly oiled oven tray, bake for 20 minutes. Turn, bake a further 20–30 minutes. Sprinkle with salt to serve.

Home-dried pears

Make sure pears are very soft and ripe. Pears which are like hard little rocks will cause you problems. See Product Updates on the website for commercial dried pears.

2 cans (each 825 g) pears in syrup, or 1 kg peeled, ripe, juicy pears

Cut pears in halves, core, and slice across, making slices 3–4 mm thick. This quantity will fill three trays. Run dehydrator at 55°C until pears are thoroughly dried (12–24 hours). Eat sparingly.

Drinks and icypoles

The best drink is water. I am amazed by the number of adults and children who won't drink water because 'I don't like it.' I admit, tap water can taste terrible, but consider buying a water filter. Otherwise you can buy spring water, mineral water or soda water.

Fruit juice

(See p. 213.)

Pear and maple cordial

Use the sugar syrup from canned pears as a cordial. Or you can use a small amount of pure maple syrup. Dilute with chilled water or soda water.

Octopus

The quantities are per blender load, about two serves. You will need to buy or make a bag of crushed ice.

1 cup crushed ice
1 cup or more of tinned pears in syrup, drained
dash of pear syrup
dash of cold water
2 tsp citric acid
2–3 tsp sugar

Whiz in blender. You might like to adjust quantities to suit individual tastes.

Vegetable juice

All vegetable juices, whether commercial or homemade, are very high in natural food chemicals and are likely to cause problems in food-sensitive people, except for celery juice, which is low in chemicals. If you can tolerate it, you can spend your salicylate allowance on a small carrot to be juiced with the celery. Not suitable for your supervised elimination diet.

Fruit smoothies

(See p. 213.)

Chocolate and carob drinks

(See p. 214.)

Magic cordial

Our grandmothers called this 'poor man's lemonade'. A failsafe three-year-old calls it magic because it looks like water and tastes like lemon cordial. The following recipe is for the syrup, which can then be diluted to taste. Like all sweet-ened drinks, this should be limited.

1 cup sugar
1 cup boiling water
½–1 tsp citric acid

Combine water and sugar and stir until sugar is dissolved. Add citric acid. Allow to cool and store in the refrigerator. Dilute to taste with water or soda water before drinking.

Magic readymix
1 cup caster sugar
1 tsp citric acid

Put ingredients in a clean container and shake until well mixed. Use 3 tsp (more or less to taste) in a cup of hot water for a hot 'lemon' drink, or mix with cold water or soda water for a 'lemonade'. Carry in a small container for use when out.

Commercial soft drinks
Preservative-free tonic and preservative-free lemonade if you can find it (see Product Updates on www.fedup.com.au), limited to less than one small glass per week because the 'natural flavour' listed is lemon juice, and therefore contains salicylates and amines.

Gin, whisky and unflavoured vodka are failsafe, for drinking and cooking.

Icypoles
Try diluted Magic cordial (p. 227). You can also dilute pear syrup half-and-half with water, and try pureed pears or plain yoghurt with added sugar. More water makes the icypole harder, more sugar makes it softer. The best trick of all is water icypoles, quick, cheap and healthy, and children love them.

Variation • **Vitamin icypole:** dissolve vitamin tablet in the icypole mix above, divide between at least two icypoles since the dose for children is half an adult tablet per day. The cold of the ice numbs the tastebuds and makes medicine easier to take. See the 'Supplements' factsheet on www.fedup.com.au for permitted vitamins.

Pear-on-a-stick
Skewer a peeled pear or a canned pear half on a paddlepop stick, wrap in foil and freeze.

Soups and stews

Kerry's vegetable-hater soup
Kerry says, 'I've never liked vegetables, but when they're cooked like this they don't taste like vegetables.'

½ cup barley (contains gluten) or rice (if gluten-free)
3 cups water
1 leek
2 Brussels sprouts
⅛ cabbage
1 cup green beans
1 medium potato

Put barley and water in a saucepan and bring to the boil. Simmer for 30 minutes. Chop all vegetables in food processor. Add to soup. Simmer until tender. Add more water if necessary. Serves four.

Red soup
Brussels sprouts are high in vitamins, minerals and chemicals which protect against cancer, but some children hate them. Here is a way to eat sprouts without knowing. For children who dislike textures, puree to a creamy consistency with a wand blender.

1 cup (half a 375 g packet) of red lentils – these cook much
more quickly than brown lentils
2 tbsp white rice
10 cups water or homemade chicken stock (p. 242)
2 swedes, peeled and cubed
1 cup celery, chopped
1 cup leeks or shallots, sliced
2 cups cabbage, chopped
8 Brussels sprouts, sliced

Rinse lentils. Place lentils and rice in water/stock and bring
to the boil. Prepare and add vegetables. Reduce heat and
simmer gently until cooked, about 40 minutes. Serves eight.

Potato and leek soup
2 cups leek, chopped
2 tbsp failsafe oil
2 medium potatoes, peeled and finely diced
2½ cups homemade chicken stock (p. 242)
chives or parsley, chopped

Cook leek in oil on high for 6 minutes while peeling and
finely dicing potatoes. Add potatoes, stir and cook on high
for 8 minutes. Puree and add stock. Reheat for 2 minutes.
Sprinkle with snipped chives or parsley. Serves four.

Noodle soup
1 tbsp butter
½ medium leek, chopped
8 cups homemade chicken stock (p. 242)
¼ small cabbage, shredded
½ cup green peas (glutamates)
½ cup green beans, chopped
2 blocks colour-free, two-minute noodles (or rice noodles if
gluten-free)
salt to taste

Melt butter in large pan and stir-fry leek on low heat until soft. Add chicken stock, cabbage, peas and beans, stir through and bring to the boil. Add broken noodles and simmer until noodles are cooked. Season to taste. Serves ten.

Variation • add 2 lightly beaten eggs to soup just before serving.

Darani's amazing chicken noodle stew

Three-year-old Ethan ate this nearly every day during his elimination diet and nutritionists were surprised by how much it met or exceeded recommended daily intakes for essential nutrients.

1 whole free-range chicken
1 leek (halved lengthways)
1 tsp salt
1 cup red lentils
12 Brussels sprouts or ½ cabbage
1 swede
4–6 sticks celery
4–6 shallots
1 cup frozen green beans
375 g pkt noodles or rice noodles for gluten-free

Place chicken in pot with leek and enough water to cover, add salt, bring to the boil and simmer until cooked through, about 45 minutes. Remove chicken and allow to cool a little. Strain stock, return to pot and add red lentils then washed and finely chopped vegetables. Gently simmer until well cooked, about one hour. Meanwhile, remove skin and bones from chicken, finely chop or process and return to pot with vegetables. Add noodles and cook for a further 10–15 minutes. This usually makes enough to fill about 8 rectangular takeaway containers (2 serves in each), which can then be frozen and used as needed. This stew can be watered down to a soup if preferred. It can also be blended for fussy eaters.

Meat

Fresh beef, lamb, veal and rabbit are low in problem-causing food chemicals but cooking and storing methods can increase amines. It is best to buy fresh meat (p. 128), cook it that day, or freeze and use within four weeks. Browning, charring, or grilling meat will increase amine content. Aim for medium-rare. Delicious-tasting meat juices and gravy made from meat juices are high in amines. Marinades must be made of permitted ingredients. Any commercial marinade is likely to be very high in salicylates, amines and MSG, as are commercial sauces and gravies.

Failsafe rissoles

Fast-food hamburgers are high in additives, but you can make your own. I have heard whole families at a barbecue exclaiming about how surprisingly delicious these hamburgers are!

600 g preservative-free mince
3 shallots or 1 large leek, finely chopped
3 celery stalks, chopped
salt to taste
1 egg, beaten

Mix all ingredients in a large bowl. Shape into patties and grill or fry. Serve in a preservative-free hamburger bun with shredded lettuce and mayonnaise (see p. 267), or as rissoles with cooked vegetables and potato wedges (p. 226).

Hint • Cooking rissoles and sausages on the barbecue is a good way to get fathers to share the cooking, but make sure the meat is not charred, as this increases the amine content.

Failsafe sausages

Failsafe chicken sausages won a prize in the regional Sausage King Competition in South Australia. You can ask a butcher to make these special sausages for you. Permitted ingredients are: sausage casings, flour or rice flour, fresh minced beef, lamb, chicken or veal, salt, garlic, shallots, chives or parsley. Here's a recipe for your butcher for 10 kg sausages:

650 g brown rice flour (2 kg for 30 kg)
3 leeks (10 leeks for 30 kg)
3 cloves of garlic (10 for 30 kg) or less to taste
½ cup salt (1½ cups for 30 kg)
Make up to 10 kg with fresh minced beef or chicken
(no skin)

Serve with • grilled with mashed potato, mashed swede and green beans • barbecued with mayonnaise or pear ketchup, wrapped in a slice of preservative-free bread • fried with leek gravy, mashed potatoes and green beans.

Sausage on a stick

1 small swede, peeled and roughly diced
1 large stalk celery, roughly cut
1 choko, peeled and roughly diced
500 g chicken or lamb mince
1 egg
salt to taste

In a food processor, whiz the vegetables. Add egg and salt then gradually add the meat until thoroughly mixed. Shape mix into sausages, roll in rice crumbs, insert skewers (cut off

ends for safety) and bake or grill, turning, for about
15 minutes until thoroughly cooked. You can add a little
rice flour to the mix if it's too soft.

Variation • **Mini meatloaves:** Spoon into greased muffin tray
and bake for 30 minutes at 160°C.

Two-minute noodles

Noodles are permitted if they are colour-free. The flavour
sachets with commercial two-minute noodles are very high in
flavour enhancers. You can make your own failsafe mince
topping instead.

Failsafe mince topping

This recipe can be used as a topping on pasta, pizza, rice,
toast, and mashed potato (as a quick cottage pie), or in jaffles
and pies.

2 shallots or 1 leek, finely chopped
1 clove or more of garlic, crushed
1 tbsp failsafe oil (p. 203)
500 g preservative-free low-fat beef or lamb mince
salt to taste
1 tsp parsley, chopped
2 tbsp cornflour dissolved in 2 cups of water or homemade
    chicken stock (p. 242)
1 can (420 g) red kidney beans (optional)

In a heavy-based frying pan or large saucepan stir-fry
chopped shallots/leek and garlic in failsafe oil, then remove
from pan. Add mince to pan, stir until cooked. Drain fat if
necessary. Add shallots, garlic, parsley, salt and cornflour
mixture, stir until thickened. Add kidney beans if desired.
Suitable for making a double batch and freezing in small
containers if used within four weeks.

Cottage pie

This is a traditional recipe. For a quick version you can simply serve the meat on the mashed potato.

500 g failsafe mince (p. 234)
2 cups potato, mashed
butter or failsafe margarine (p. 203)
1 tsp parsley, chopped

Spoon failsafe mince into a pie dish. Top with mashed potato, dotted with butter. Bake at 180°C until top is golden, approximately 20 minutes. Garnish with parsley. Serve with cooked permitted vegetables.

Stir-fry

Chinese restaurant food is likely to be high in natural and artificial MSG and other problem chemicals, but you can cook your own additive-free stir-fry. Serve on steamed rice. This is a nutritious meal because it is relatively high in vegetables and grains, and low in meat and fats. Some restaurants will prepare this if given advance notice.

Use permitted vegetables such as garlic, green beans, cabbage, shallots, leeks, and mung bean sprouts. If you can tolerate them, add vegetables like carrots, snow peas and Chinese vegetables (not suitable for your supervised elimination diet). My favourite is pak choy. Cook diced chicken or beef in failsafe oil like canola and thicken with a water/cornflour blend. Salt, garlic, citric acid and pear syrup (from canned pears) can be used to add flavour. No soy sauce is permitted because even natural soy sauce is very high in natural MSG, but golden syrup can give the same kind of taste.

Basic beef stir-fry

400 g of lean beef, cut into long thin strips
4 cups permitted vegetables cut into same-size pieces
1 tbsp golden syrup

1 tbsp cornflour or arrowroot dissolved in 1 cup water
(optional)
salt to taste

Place a small amount of failsafe oil (p. 203) in a frying pan
and fry the meat. Remove meat from pan and wipe pan
clean with paper towel. Put another small amount of oil in
pan and stir-fry vegetables until cooked but still crunchy.
Add meat, stir in golden syrup. Thicken with the arrowroot or
cornflour mixture if you want. Add salt to taste. Serve on a
bed of noodles or rice. Serves four.

Meat loaf

500 g lean beef mince
1 small leek, sliced
1 cup rolled oats
½ cup chopped celery
1 egg
2 tbsp chopped parsley
sea salt to taste

Preheat oven to 190°C. Mix ingredients together. Bake in a
lightly oiled 12 × 20 cm meatloaf tin in moderate oven for
about 1 hour, or microwave on MEDIUM/HIGH for 20–25
minutes. Serve with pear ketchup, pear puree or leek sauce
(p. 263). Leftovers can be sliced and frozen for use in
sandwiches and jaffles.

Variation • for a more elegant meatloaf, mix ingredients,
slice pears from a 425 g can, and reserve the syrup.
Arrange pear slices in the base of the tin and press meat
firmly into meatloaf tin on top of pears. Invert on greased
baking tray and cook upside down for 30 minutes.
Unmould, baste with pear syrup and cook for a further
15 minutes. Remove from oven, baste and serve.

Mince and potato casserole

This is an excellent recipe and you can hide vegetables in it too.

2 tbsp failsafe oil (p. 203)
500 g lean beef mince
1 small leek, sliced
1 cup cabbage, finely chopped
1 clove of garlic, crushed (optional)
salt to taste
4 medium potatoes, sliced
butter or failsafe margarine (p. 203)

Fry mince in oil until browned. Add leek, cabbage, garlic and salt. Place one-third of mixture on the bottom of a greased casserole, cover with half the potato slices. Add remaining meat and cover with remaining potatoes, dotted with butter. Cook uncovered at 180°C for about 1 hour.

Kebabs

1 kg rump steak or diced lamb
⅔ cup failsafe oil (p. 203)

Trim steak and cut meat into 2 cm cubes. Moisten with oil. Thread meat cubes onto skewers. Grill, turning and basting for about 5 minutes. Makes 16–20.

Variation • thread alternate meat cubes and chunks of leek on skewers • brush kebabs with a mixture of oil and golden syrup for a soy sauce flavour.

Grilled or pan-fried steak

1 beef or lamb steak per person
2 tsp failsafe oil

Preheat griller. Grill steaks for 4 minutes on each side for medium. Longer cooking will increase amines. For pan-fried steaks, heat oil in a large non-stick frying pan over medium-high heat. Cook steaks for 2–3 minutes each side for medium-rare. Serve immediately.

Variation • for garlic topping, combine 1 clove garlic, crushed, 3 tablespoons light cream cheese, 3 tablespoons preservative-free cottage cheese or ricotta, 2 tablespoons chopped chives or shallot tops and salt to taste. Pour over steaks.

Irish stew

500 g diced lamb
water
salt to taste
4 potatoes, peeled
1 large leek
1 carrot (optional, salicylates) or other permitted vegetables
1 cup green beans, sliced

Put meat into a medium saucepan. Add enough water to cover the meat. Sprinkle salt over. Cut potatoes, leek and carrot into thick slices and arrange on top of meat. Vegetables do not have to be covered by liquid as they will steam. Bring to the boil and simmer gently until meat is tender or for 1 hour. Add beans in last 10 minutes. Serve on steamed rice or couscous (contains gluten).

Quick beef stroganoff

2 tsp failsafe oil
375 g lean boneless sirloin or fillet
    steak, trimmed and cut into strips
⅓ cup leek or shallots, chopped
1 clove garlic, crushed
½ cup homemade chicken stock
125 g wide colour-free egg noodles
¼ cup light sour cream
¼ cup natural reduced-fat yoghurt

1 tbsp fresh chives or parsley, chopped

Heat water in saucepan for cooking noodles. Heat oil over medium heat in a large heavy-based frying pan. Add beef strips, fry until browned, about 2 minutes. Remove from pan. Stir leek/shallots and garlic in frying pan until tender, add stock and simmer for 2 minutes. Cook noodles according to directions on packet. In a small bowl, combine sour cream and yoghurt. Return the beef and meat juices to frying pan, add sour cream mixture, stirring gently over low heat. Serve on noodles, sprinkled with chives or parsley. Serves four.

Roast lamb or beef

Roasts are easy, delicious, can be a family or social occasion, and can provide you with enough meat for an extra meal or school lunches. We do chicken, lamb and beef roasts but pork is too high in amines to be acceptable. Gravy is not failsafe even if the ingredients in the premix sound okay or you make it yourself, because of amines in the meat juices.

1 leg of lamb or roast of beef
potatoes, peeled and halved
leeks, washed, trimmed, cut into lengths and wrapped in
    a foil parcel
chokoes, peeled, quartered and sprinkled with salt
extra vegetables (see variation)

Preheat oven to 180–200°C. Trim excess fat and put meat in a lightly oiled roasting pan. Allow cooking time of 30–35 minutes per 500 g of meat. Prepare vegetables. Allow 1 hour for vegetables, turning once during cooking. When the meat is cooked it will be easier to carve if you allow it to stand for 15 minutes, keeping warm on a serving dish. Vegetables can be drained on kitchen paper and kept warm in the oven with the door open. Serve with leek sauce (p. 263), pear puree or Brussels sprout puree, green beans (salicylates) or green peas (glutamates) if tolerated.

Variation • extra vegetables: butternut pumpkin, sweet potatoes if tolerated (not suitable for your supervised elimination diet).

Herbed rack of lamb

2 racks of lamb with 6 cutlets in each
2 tbsp chopped chives and parsley
1 tbsp failsafe oil (p. 203)
4 tbsp pear syrup (from canned pears)
⅛ tsp citric acid dissolved in ¼ cup water

Preheat oven to 190°C. Trim fat from the racks of lamb, leaving a thin layer to prevent drying out. Combine parsley, chives, oil, pear syrup and citric acid mix in a large dish. Place racks of lamb, meat side down, in the marinade and brush exposed parts of racks with marinade. Cover and marinate in the refrigerator for 30 minutes. In a roasting pan, stand the racks of lamb upright with trimmed sides on the outside, and interlace the bones to form an arch. You might have to tie together with white kitchen string, which is removed before serving. Roast in preheated oven for 1 hour, brushing occasionally with marinade. Serve with roast potatoes and pumpkin (salicylates) and green beans. Carve down between the bones to serve. Serves four.

Chicken

Fresh chicken is one of the safest foods, except for the skin, which contains amines. Plain takeaway BBQ or rotisseried chicken used to be failsafe but most are now pre-seasoned and stuffed. Avoiding the stuffing or seasoning does not help because chemicals permeate the meat and cause reactions. Unless you can·find a plain chicken, you will have to cook your own.

Crunchy chicken

10 chicken thigh fillets
1 tsp salt
self-raising flour or gluten-free cornflour or failsafe
    ricecrumbs
failsafe oil (p. 203)

Place chicken fillets in a bowl and stir with salt. Add flour
and stir until well-coated. Last, stir with sufficient failsafe oil
to make sure all chicken pieces are moist. Bake at 180°C
for 1 hour.

Variation • **Nuggets:** cut chicken fillets into nugget-sized
pieces, coat as directed and shallow fry in failsafe oil until
crisp and golden brown. Serve with chips, vegetables or
on hamburger buns with lettuce and mayonnaise.

Roast chicken

Roasts are easy and delicious. Leftovers should be frozen and
can be used as sandwich fillings (see p. 242 to make chicken
stock from your roast).

1 chicken
1 tbsp failsafe oil
1 small leek, chopped (including
    the green bits)
potatoes, peeled
pumpkin, peeled (if tolerated)
parsnips, peeled (if tolerated)

Preheat oven to 180–200°C. Trim excess fat off chicken
and put in a roasting pan with oil. Stuff the cavity with
chopped leek. Allow 30 minutes per 500 grams of chicken.
Cut vegetables into similar-size pieces. (Remember
pumpkin and parsnip are moderate in salicylates and
cannot be used on your supervised elimination diet.)
Allow 1 hour for vegetables, turning once during cooking.

When the chicken is cooked, it will be easier to carve if you allow it to stand for 15 minutes, keeping warm on a serving dish. Serve with gravy (p. 268) or you can use pear puree or Brussels sprout puree made with butter or cream (p. 254). Serve with green beans, Brussels sprouts or green peas if tolerated. Leftover chicken should be frozen the day of cooking and eaten within 4 weeks.

Chicken stock

There are two ways of preparing chicken stock. To reduce amine build-up, cook for the shortest time you can and do not include skin.

- When you have finished with your roast chicken, you can put the bones and neck in a saucepan with water, leek, parsley, celery and salt, and simmer for one hour. Strain, cool and skim off fat. Store in refrigerator or freezer.

- Another way of making stock gives you more concentrated stock and leaves you with a cooked chicken. In a large saucepan, cover the skinned chicken with water and add a chunk of leek, celery, parsley and salt. Simmer for one to two hours, depending on the size, then strain off the juice. When it cools you have a bowl of good stock and a pleasantly moist chicken suitable to eat cold, in salads, to slice and freeze for school lunches, or for recipes requiring cooked, diced chicken such as the chicken fried rice, below.

Free-flow chicken

You can chop leftover chicken into small pieces, spread in a thin layer on a sheet of foil and cover with foil. Frozen chicken pieces can be used on sandwiches without thawing. They are also useful for stir-fries, fried rice, jaffle fillings or tossed with rice and salad for a quick lunch.

Chicken fried rice

2 tbsp failsafe oil (p. 203)
2 eggs
500 g cooked rice, cold
200 g cooked, diced chicken
2 tbsp shallots, chopped
2 sticks celery, chopped
½ cup bamboo shoots (optional)
½ cup mung bean sprouts (optional)
½ cup cooked fresh or uncooked frozen peas (glutamates)
125 g corn kernels (salicylates)
1 tbsp golden syrup

Heat small amount of oil in a large pan or wok and cook
eggs as a plain omelette, remove from pan and keep
covered. Add remaining oil and quickly fry rice. Add all
other ingredients except golden syrup. Stir continually to
ensure even cooking without burning. Cut omelette into
small strips and add to rice. Lastly, add golden syrup
(optional). Be careful not to overcook. Vegetables should
still be slightly crunchy. Serves two as a main course.

Chicken satay

Arrange cubes of chicken (no skin) on satay sticks, brush
with a mixture of golden syrup and failsafe oil, and grill.

Chicken and leek stir-fry

250 g diced, cooked chicken
4 cups chopped leeks, garlic, green beans, cabbage,
    Brussels sprouts, shallots, mung bean sprouts or – not
    suitable for your supervised elimination diet – salicylate-
    containing vegetables like carrots, snow peas, corn
    kernels and Chinese greens.
1 tbsp cornflour or arrowroot dissolved in 1 cup water or
    chicken stock (optional)
salt, citric acid, pear syrup or golden syrup for flavour
failsafe oil

Place a small amount of failsafe oil (p. 203) in a frying pan.
Add all vegetables to pan and stir-fry until they are cooked
but still crunchy. Thicken with arrowroot or cornflour mixture
and flavour with salt, citric acid, pear syrup, or golden syrup
if liked. Serve on a bed of noodles or rice. Serves four.

Chicken in yoghurt sauce

500 g chicken fillets, cut into
    pieces
200 ml fresh natural yoghurt
1–2 tbsp failsafe oil
1–2 cloves garlic, crushed
chopped chives

Place fillets in a casserole dish. Combine remaining
ingredients, spoon over chicken. Bake at 180°C for about
30 minutes. Turn halfway through cooking. Serves four.

Easy chicken fillets

4 single skinless chicken breast fillets
1 medium leek, white part sliced, green part washed
salt to taste

Arrange fillets on a bed of green leek, top with leek slices,
microwave on medium–high for 10–15 minutes or until
cooked. Sprinkle with salt. Serve with mashed potato,
swede and green beans.

Variation • with leek sauce: pour 1 cup pear syrup over
chicken before cooking. After cooking, drain juices into a
bowl. Blend 1 tablespoon cornflour with a little cold water
and stir into juices. Microwave on high for 1–2 minutes, stir
until thickened. Serve chicken on a bed of rice with a little of
the sauce. • in a slow cooker: arrange chicken as above
and cook in slow cooker for 4–6 hours. This is a good way
to cater for family members who are coming home from
after-school activities at different times, although it is not
recommended for amine responders.

Chicken fillets, grilled or BBQ

4 single chicken breasts, skinned

Marinade

2 tbsp parsley, finely chopped
2 cloves garlic, crushed
⅓ cup Magic cordial (p. 227) with 1 tbsp golden syrup,
stirred in 3 tbsp failsafe oil
salt to taste

Trim fat from chicken breasts. Combine remaining
ingredients in a large, shallow dish. Add chicken to
marinade and coat well. Cover and leave in fridge for at
least 1 hour, turning after 30 minutes. Prepare a medium–hot
barbecue or preheat grill. Spray barbecue rack or grill rack
with failsafe oil. Remove chicken from marinade and
barbecue or grill for 5 minutes, brushing frequently with
marinade. Turn the chicken and cook for a further 10–15
minutes, or until cooked, brushing frequently with marinade.
Test the chicken with a skewer. The juices should be clear
when the chicken is cooked. Avoid charring as it increases
amines. Serves four.

Creamy cashew chicken

Great for special dinners, this may just be the most delicious
recipe in the book (contains dairy).

500 g chicken thighs or breast, cut into bite-size pieces
1 tbsp failsafe oil (p. 203)
½ cup raw cashews
½ cup light cream
125 g light preservative-free cream cheese
2 cloves garlic, peeled
½ cup peeled pears, canned or fresh
salt to taste

Pan-fry chicken in oil until lightly cooked. Put all other ingredients in a food processor and whiz until creamy. Pour over chicken and cook gently for five minutes. Serve on rice with green peas or beans.

Fish

Fresh seafood can be okay if eaten within 12 hours of being caught – 24 hours at most – or frozen within 12 hours and eaten within two weeks (one week for people who are extra sensitive). Fish must be white fleshed, not pink like salmon, tuna or trout, and prawns are always high in amines no matter how fresh they are. Other seafood like calamari, lobsters, oysters, mussels, scallops, crab and marron (freshwater crayfish farmed in Western Australia) are permitted when fresh. Amines develop with age, freezing, and processing such as canning and smoking.

Fish and chips
This is one takeaway which may be relatively safe, so long as the fish is fresh. Mixes for crumbing and batter may contain colours and preservatives, so grilled fish is safer. Hot chips will probably be cooked in oil containing preservatives such as BHA (320) or BHT (321), which can cause problems, usually the next day, so minimise your intake.

Crumbed fish
Children love crumbed food. You can use this method for fish, crumbed cutlets and veal schnitzel. These are good hot or cold and can be used in lunchboxes. Commercial breadcrumbs all contain preservative (282) and possibly spices or flavour enhancers.

Wipe the fish and cut into neat pieces. Dust the fish with flour or gluten-free cornflour. Dip into beaten egg and coat with additive-free breadcrumbs, or failsafe ricecrumbs. Heat oil in pan. Gently place fish in pan and cook over moderate heat until fish is cooked and crumbs are golden brown.

> Due to mercury contamination, Food Standards Australia New Zealand (FSANZ) advise pregnant women, women planning pregnancy and young children to limit their intake of shark (flake), broadbill, marlin and swordfish to no more than one serve per fortnight, with no other fish to be consumed during that fortnight. For orange roughy (also sold as sea perch) and catfish, the advice is to consume no more than one serve per week, with no other fish being consumed during that week (www.foodstandards.gov.au).

Grilled fish

Preheat the grill and grease the grill rack. Cut small whole fish across in deep gashes to allow the heat to penetrate. Brush cutlets with melted butter or oil before cooking. Cook the fish until the flesh leaves the bones easily. Serve at once with parsley sauce.

Grilled fish with garlic

2 fillets of fresh white fish, about 500 g each
2 tbsp failsafe oil
2 tbsp additive-free breadcrumbs
salt to taste
2 tsp garlic, minced
2 tsp parsley, minced
1 tsp water combined with 1 pinch citric acid

Preheat griller. Place fish in lightly oiled baking dish. Brush with half the oil and sprinkle with crumbs and salt. Place the fish about 10 cm from heat and cook for 10 minutes. Heat remaining oil in small pan briefly with the garlic and pour over fish. Sprinkle with parsley and citric acid mix.

Vegetables and vegetarian meals

Vegetables protect against heart disease and cancer. High in nutrients and fibre and low in fat, vegetables are often hated by fussy eaters. This is a form of learning delay, as a taste for vegetables has to be learned. The way to do it is offer a tiny piece of the vegetable (⅛ teaspoon) every few days at least twenty times, with a reward such as dessert for eating. Textures are often a problem. There is nothing wrong with blending or mashing vegetables to a creamy and anonymous consistency. Although being a full-time vegetarian on failsafe is difficult, you can easily include vegetarian meals in your menu. Make sure that vegetarian meals contain complete protein. Eggs are a source of complete protein, so too is a combination of dairy products or dried beans such as lentils or kidney beans with rice or wheat products likes noodles or toast. A hearty soup can be an easy meal in itself, served with hot bread.

Quick vegetable and bean stir-fry

4 cups permitted vegetables cut into same-size pieces
failsafe oil (p. 203) for frying
1 can (300 g) kidney or other beans, drained
salt to taste
Put small amount of oil in pan and stir-fry vegetables such as leeks, shallots, garlic, mung bean sprouts, green beans and other vegetables as tolerated. Add kidney beans and salt. Serve on a bed of noodles or rice. Serves four.

Variation • pour a lightly beaten egg into a clearing in the pan. When nearly cooked, scrape off pan with egg slice and mix with other ingredients • top with grated mild cheese (contains dairy products and amines, tasty cheese contains natural MSG) if tolerated • as a sauce, top with Howard's bean paste (p. 220).

Vegetable parcels

4 cups permitted vegetables cut into same-size pieces
4 sheets commercial puff pastry

Preheat oven to 200°C. Cut pastry sheets in 10 cm squares. Place 1 tablespoon of vegetable mixture in the middle of each. Moisten the edges and fold in halves along the diagonal, making a triangle shape. Bake 15–20 minutes. Serve with salad and leek or hollandaise sauce or pear puree.

> Be careful as many commercial pastries contain additives. Read ingredients lists. Note that large and catering packs are more likely to contain nasty preservatives or antioxidants.

Baked potatoes

4 large potatoes
failsafe oil (p. 203)

Topping

2 shallots, chopped
½ cup preservative-free cottage cheese or ricotta
4 tsp fresh natural yoghurt (optional)
parsley garnish
Preheat the oven to 200°C. Peel potatoes and wrap in foil. Bake for 50 minutes or until tender. Remove foil. With a sharp knife, cut a cross on the top of each potato, gently squeeze until the top opens out. Brush with oil and return to oven for 10 minutes. Serve immediately with topping.

Cabbage and sour cream bake

¼ cabbage, finely shredded
½ cup sour cream
1 egg
1 tbsp butter
salt to taste

Preheat oven to 180°C. Cook cabbage in boiling, salted water or microwave until tender but still crisp. Mix sour cream and egg. Drain cabbage and fold butter through it, then pour cream mixture over and blend well. Add salt. Pour into a buttered casserole dish and bake until browned on top. This dish can be prepared in advance and reheated in the oven before serving.

Variation • for stove-top cooking, cook cabbage in butter for 10 minutes. Add egg beaten with salt and stir constantly until egg is cooked and cabbage tender. Stir through sour cream, heat gently and serve.

Rosti potato cakes

3 medium potatoes, peeled and grated
½ cup shallots or leeks, finely chopped
2–3 tbsp butter or failsafe margarine (p. 203), soft

Mix ingredients, form into cakes and fry in hot failsafe oil.

Variation • these are another way of camouflaging very finely chopped or grated vegetables such as Brussels sprouts, cabbage, leeks and green beans for fussy eaters. Adding a beaten egg and a tablespoon of flour will help to hold them together.

Potato pancakes (wheat-free)

2 large uncooked potatoes, peeled and chopped
3 eggs
¼ tsp citric acid

100 g gluten-free flour
pinch salt
garlic or parsley (optional)

Blend ingredients to the consistency of smooth cream. Cook as for pancakes. These can be served as savoury with chopped chives and vegetables, or sweet, with pear purée.

Colcannon (Irish mashed potato and cabbage)
6 large potatoes (about 2 kg)
⅓ cup hot milk or water
knob butter
¼ cabbage, shredded
4 shallots, chopped
extra butter or failsafe oil (p. 203)
salt

Peel potatoes and chop into 4 even pieces. Cover with milk/water and simmer in a saucepan or microwave until tender. Drain, reserving liquid. Mash well. Add liquid and butter and beat until the butter has melted and the potatoes are creamy. Heat butter or oil in pan, add cabbage and shallots. Cover and cook for 2 minutes. Mix into mashed potato or pile on top. Sprinkle with salt. Serve immediately.

Potato gratin
4 large potatoes, peeled
300 ml cream or yoghurt or preservative-free cream cheese
    mixed with a little water
1 cup mozzarella cheese, grated (optional, amines)

Preheat oven to 180°C. Brush a deep, ovenproof dish with melted butter or oil. Cut potatoes into very thin slices. Layer slices into dish. Pour over combined cream or yoghurt and mozzarella. Cover and bake for 30 minutes. Uncover and bake for a further 40 minutes or until potatoes are tender and golden brown.

Hash browns

1 cup leftover mashed potato
½ cup leftover cooked cabbage
failsafe oil for cooking (p. 203)
1 egg, beaten

Mix potato and cabbage together. Preheat frying pan with oil and add potato mixture. Shape into a rissole, pour egg around. Turn over halfway through cooking. Serve with lettuce and chopped chives.

Barley vegetable casserole (contains gluten)

⅔ cup pearl barley
2½ cups chicken stock (p. 242) or water
1 tbsp failsafe oil (p. 203)
1 clove garlic, crushed
2 sticks celery, chopped
2 Brussels sprouts or carrots (salicylates), chopped
1 cup green beans or peas (glutamates)

Soak barley overnight in stock. Bring to boil and simmer for 1 hour. Drain barley and reserve liquid. Fry garlic and vegetables in the oil over low heat for 8 minutes, stirring so they don't burn. Add stock from barley and simmer for 20 minutes until vegetables are tender and liquid has almost evaporated. Add the barley and reheat. Serves four.

Vegetable pie

1½ cups cooked rice (can be frozen and thawed)
1 tbsp butter or failsafe margarine (p. 203)
2 eggs
1 cup grated mozzarella (if tolerated – dairy food, high in amines)
½ cup leek, sliced
1 cup celery, chopped
1 tbsp failsafe oil (p. 203)
1 cup cabbage, shredded finely

1 cup thinly sliced potato or corn kernels (salicylates)
½ cup yoghurt and cottage cheese, combined to creamy
    consistency (or soy yoghurt and tofu for dairy-free)
2 eggs, extra
salt to taste
failsafe breadcrumbs (p. 204)
butter or failsafe margarine (p. 203) extra

Preheat oven to 190°C. Add butter and lightly beaten eggs
to rice while still hot. Press into 23 cm pie plate and sprinkle
with half the grated cheese. Fry leek and celery in oil until
tender. Place in pie, sprinkle with remaining cheese. Layer
cabbage and potato into pie. Combine yoghurt mix, eggs
and salt and pour into pie. Top with crumbs dotted with
butter. Bake for 40 minutes or until pie is set.

Lentil pie 2

1½ cups brown or green lentils
2 medium potatoes
failsafe oil for frying
½ cup chopped leek or shallots
½ cup chopped celery
2 tbsp chopped parsley
2 tbsp rice crumbs

Cover lentils with cold water, simmer for about 50 minutes
then mash. Preheat oven to 180°C. Peel potatoes, cook until
tender and mash with milk. In a hot frying pan, stir-fry leek
and celery quickly until tender. Thickly butter a 30 cm pie
dish and sprinkle rice crumbs evenly. Combine lentils,
potato, parsley and celery mixture and place in dish. Bake
for 25 minutes or until brown. Nice served with pear ketchup
(p. 270) and yoghurt.

Failsafe hummus

440 g can chickpeas (garbanzos), drained and rinsed
2 cloves of garlic, crushed

3 tbsp failsafe oil (p. 203)
⅛ tsp citric acid
1 tbsp parsley, chopped
salt to taste

Combine ingredients in a food processor and blend until
smooth. Use as a spread on sandwiches and rice cakes or
as a dip with preservative-free bread and salad.

Asparagus

250 g fresh asparagus (salicylates)

Rinse asparagus, cut off tough ends. Cut stalks in half.
Place in a steamer above a pan of boiling water and steam
for 10–15 minutes, or cook in microwave. Drain well. Serve
on pasta or rice with melted butter mixed with a pinch of
citrus acid, or hollandaise sauce (p. 263). Or wrapped in
crepes. Not suitable for your supervised elimination diet.

Swedes

Swedes are a source of Vitamin C and add colour to a meal.
They are at their best when cooked until very tender. You can
mash thoroughly with butter, or mash swede and potato
together. In Southland, New Zealand, you can buy them
chipped like potatoes.

Brussels sprouts

Another often disliked vegetable, nutritionally these baby
cabbages have everything going for them. Hide them in soups,
stews or mashed potato. For a green sauce that goes well with
roasts, burgers and sausages, boil sprouts until tender then
puree in a food processor with a one or two tablespoons each
of butter and cream.

Chokoes

Choko vines grow like weeds and produce green, rather watery vegetables which can be ruined by overcooking. Try them peeled and quartered, steamed or microwaved and served with a dob of butter. Chokoes also go well sliced in stir-fries or as cold, cooked leftovers in salads and sandwiches. Also useful when introducing solids to babies.

Beetroot

Beetroot (salicylates) is rich in potassium folate and Vitamin C, but canned beetroot often contains spices which increase the salicylate content. Good grated in salads.

1 large beetroot
2 tbsp sugar dissolved in a little boiling water
salt to taste
½ cup water and ½ tsp citric acid

Cook beetroot in boiling water until tender. This can vary from 20–60 minutes, depending on the age and size of the vegetable. Mix other ingredients, pour over beetroot and serve cold. Not suitable for your supervised elimination diet.

Salads

On your supervised elimination diet, for vegetables you are stuck with such salad vegetables as celery, iceberg lettuce, mung bean sprouts, shallots, chives, shredded cabbage, red cabbage, cooked potatoes and cooked green beans, chickpeas and other beans except broad beans. If you can tolerate some salicylates, you can add asparagus, beetroot, carrot, Chinese greens, lettuce other than iceberg, snow peas and snow pea sprouts – not suitable for your supervised elimination diet.

Coleslaw

¼ cabbage, shredded
¼ red cabbage, shredded
2–4 celery stalks, chopped
1 fresh pear, peeled and chopped
125 g chopped raw cashews (optional)
2 tbsp chopped shallots or chives
1 carrot, grated (salicylates)

Toss ingredients together in a salad bowl and moisten with a dressing of your choice (p. 267). Coleslaw improves if made 2 hours before serving.

Tossed salad

1 lettuce, torn into pieces
3 cups chopped vegetables such as celery, parsley, chives, mung bean sprouts, cold cooked green beans. Plus (not suitable for your supervised elimination diet) choose
    1 cup from asparagus, beetroot, carrot, Chinese greens, lettuce other than iceberg, snow peas and snow pea sprouts.
1 clove of garlic
salt to taste
¼ cup salad dressing (p. 267)

Rub salad bowl with cut garlic. Add salad vegetables, pour over salad dressing and toss until coated lightly.

Potato salad

2 large potatoes, about 500 g
1 cup Mighty mayo (p. 268)
salt to taste
1 stick celery, finely chopped
1 tbsp shallots or chives, finely chopped
1 tbsp chopped parsley
1–2 hard-boiled eggs, finely sliced (optional)

Peel potatoes and cook until tender. Cut into cubes and while still warm, mix in mayonnaise, taking care not to break potatoes. When cool, add other ingredients and chill well.

Rice salad

¼ cup Mighty mayo (p. 268)
1 cup rice cooked in 2½ cups of homemade chicken stock
    (p. 242)
2 hard-boiled eggs, sliced
1 cup celery, sliced
1 shallot, chopped
1 lettuce

Pour dressing over hot rice, toss and set aside to cool. Add remaining ingredients, toss gently and chill. Serve on a bed of shredded lettuce.

Bean and pasta salad

1 cup cooked chickpeas or cooked chopped green beans
1 cup cooked butter beans
1 cup chopped celery
1½ cups spaghetti springs, macaroni or gluten-free pasta,
    cooked
Mighty mayo (p. 268) or mayonnaise (p. 267)
salt to taste
1 tbsp chopped chives

Mix beans, celery and pasta together in salad bowl. Pour salad dressing over and toss. Add salt to taste and garnish with chives. Handy to carry in a lunch container.

'I like beans but they don't like me,' commented one father. To avoid post-bean flatulence, have a kefir drink (p. 145) with your meal.

Chicken and asparagus salad

3 skinless chicken breasts
½ cup homemade chicken stock (p. 242)
1 bunch asparagus, about 250 g (salicylates)
½ cup sliced celery
1 cup mung bean sprouts
1 iceberg lettuce

Trim chicken, place in a heavy-based frying pan with the stock. Cover and bring to a gentle boil. Reduce heat and simmer for 5 minutes. Turn chicken and simmer for another 5 minutes or until tender. Test with a skewer. Drain and cool. Make salad dressing (p. 267). Cut cooked chicken into strips and place in a bowl. Pour dressing over, toss until coated. Cover and refrigerate for at least 30 minutes for flavour to develop. Rinse asparagus, cut off tough ends. Cut stalks in half. Place in a steamer above a pan of boiling water and steam for 10–15 minutes. Plunge into a bowl of iced water. Drain well. Fold asparagus, mung bean sprouts and celery into chicken mixture. Add torn lettuce.
Serves four.

Warm salad

When offered in five-star restaurants, warm salads usually feature exotic greens. This recipe uses down-to-earth ingredients but retains the combination of the crisp salad with the warm meats, potatoes or eggs to make a light lunch or alternative to a heavy meal.

1 small iceberg lettuce, washed and shredded
1 stick celery, chopped
4 slices of bread, toasted and cut into squares as croutons
250 g cooked chicken, chopped
2 eggs

Dressing
½ cup mayonnaise (p. 267)
½ cup fresh plain yoghurt
1 tbsp parsley, finely chopped
1 tbsp chives, chopped
salt to taste

Stir the dressing ingredients to combine. Arrange a bed of lettuce and celery with croutons over. Add chicken, pour over well-mixed dressing and top with poached eggs. Serves two.

Variation • replace croutons with cooked brown rice or warm potatoes.

Eggs

Eggs are a highly nutritious package of vitamins, minerals and essential amino acids and an important failsafe source of Vitamin A. Expert recommendations vary between three and seven eggs a week, including those used in cooking. For a skinny, food intolerant child this limit does not apply. Check with your dietitian. One suggested that up to 4 eggs a day would be reasonable in such a case. People who are allergic to eggs can use commercial egg replacement or 1 tbsp of oil per egg in baking recipes such as pancakes, muffins and cakes.

Fresh eggs cook better and are low in amines. Test a whole egg in water. If it's fresh it sinks. The thicker the white, the fresher the egg.

Egg Foo Yung
5 eggs, well beaten
½ cup finely diced cooked chicken
1 cup leek or shallots, finely chopped
1 cup mung bean shoots
½ cup celery, diced
failsafe oil (p. 203) for frying

Combine all ingredients, divide into 4 portions and fry one at a time in hot oil. Serves four.

Chicken and leek frittata

3 leeks, chopped
3 tbsp failsafe oil
2 cups diced, cooked cold potatoes
2 cups other diced, failsafe cooked vegetables (e.g. celery, shallots, cabbage)
2–3 cups chopped leftover cooked chicken (optional)
4 eggs
2–3 tbsp fresh cream, milk or soymilk
½ cup grated mild or mozzarella cheese (optional, amines)

In a frying pan with a high domed lid or an oven-proof pan, cook leeks in oil over medium heat until transparent. Add potatoes, vegetables and chicken. Beat eggs in a bowl, add cream and cheese. Pour over potato and vegetable mixture. Allow to cook over a gentle heat until the sides and the bottom set then bake in a preheated moderate oven (or cover with lid and continue cooking) for 12–15 minutes. Leave the frittata to set in the pan for 5–10 minutes after cooking.

Quick quiche

2 cups of raw vegetables, e.g. cabbage, leek, shallots, peas and carrots (if permitted), finely chopped
1 tbsp failsafe oil (p. 203)
4 eggs
salt to taste
1 cup milk, A2 milk, soymilk or ricemilk
¼ cup yoghurt or soy yoghurt (optional)
1 tsp finely chopped parsley
1 sheet of commercial puff pastry or short-crust pastry (p. 225) or gluten-free pastry (p. 296)

Preheat oven to 200°C. Stir-fry vegetables in oil until transparent. Set aside. Beat eggs with a fork until light and fluffy. Add salt, milk, yoghurt and parsley and mix thoroughly. Spray 22 cm quiche pan with failsafe canola oil and line with pastry. Arrange vegetables over base. Spoon egg mixture gently into dish. Bake for 30 minutes or until golden brown.

Impossible quiche

¾ cup plain flour
½ cup wholemeal flour
1 tsp chives, chopped
1 cup leek, chopped
125 g pure butter or failsafe margarine (p. 203), softened
½ cup preservative-free cottage or ricotta cheese
4 eggs
2 cups milk

Mix ingredients together. The flour will settle and form a kind of crust. Pour into a greased pie dish and bake at 180°C for 1 hour.

Pizza and pasta

Tomato paste, parmesan cheese, and most pizza toppings like olives, pepperoni, ham and pineapple are high in natural problem-causing chemicals, but you don't have to avoid these kinds of foods altogether. If you don't react to amines or nitrates, you can order a pizza with egg, bacon and mozzarella cheese, no tomato sauce. Otherwise, here are some tasty home substitutes.

Pizza

Pizza is the kind of meal that can involve the whole family and fill the kitchen with delicious smells. If everyone has a task, the meal will be more fun. You can reduce the work by using a breadmaker and a food processor. Grate the cheese first then, without washing the processor, puree the beans and garlic.

Yeasted pizza base

1 tsp dried yeast
1 cup water
½ tsp sugar
1 tbsp failsafe oil (p. 203)
½ tsp salt
2½ cups plain flour

If you have a breadmaker throw all the ingredients in and press 'dough'. Otherwise dissolve the yeast in the water with the sugar. Mix with oil, salt and flour in a large bowl. Blend well and knead until smooth and elastic on a floured board. Let rise in a bowl in a warm place until doubled in volume (about 1½ hours). Punch down and knead again for a few minutes to make dough easy to handle.

To make two 30 cm pizzas, divide the dough in half, stretch out to about a 15 cm circle by hand, then roll out to 30 cm. Place on a greased pizza pan and bake at 220°C for 15 minutes.

Quick pizza dough (yeastless)

2 cups self-raising flour or gluten-free
    flour (p. 173)
pinch of salt
2 tbsp butter or failsafe margarine (p. 203)
enough milk or soymilk to make a workable
    dough (about ¾ cup)
failsafe oil (p. 203)

Sift the flour and salt into a mixing bowl. Rub in the butter. Add the milk gradually, mixing to a soft dough. Roll out to form a circle and place on a well-oiled oven tray. Brush with oil and bake at 220°C for 15 minutes. Remove from the oven. Cover with topping. Bake until golden, about 15 minutes.

Garlic meat topping

2 cloves of garlic, crushed
shallots, chopped
500 g low-fat mince
2 tbsp cornflour dissolved in 1½ cups water
failsafe oil (p. 203)
salt to taste

Stir-fry garlic and shallots in a little oil, remove from pan.
Fry mince in a little oil, stirring until cooked. Add garlic
and shallots to mince with cornflour mixture, reduce heat
and stir until thickened. Spoon over pizza base. Sprinkle
with salt.

Variations • **Cheese topping:** if you do not react to amines,
you can sprinkle over grated mozzarella cheese, bake until
golden, about 15 minutes at 220°C. • **Vegetarian topping:**
spread a layer of preservative-free cream cheese on base
(optional). In a food processor or blender, combine 2 tins of
partially drained red kidney beans with garlic to form a
smooth paste. Spread on pizza. • **Chicken topping:** spread
preservative-free cream cheese (light or regular) thickly on
base. Sprinkle with free-flow chicken (p. 242) mango slices
(salicylates) and parsley.

Garlic bread

garlic
butter (p. 203)
1 loaf of failsafe French bread (p. 204)

Preheat oven to 180°C. Crush garlic and mix into softened
butter. Cut each loaf crosswise into diagonal slices, without
cutting all the way through. Soften garlic butter and spread
each side of slices. Wrap loaf tightly in foil and bake on
baking tray for about 20 minutes, until heated through.
Serve immediately.

Pasta

Apart from takeaways, spaghetti bolognaise is the meal most often identified as causing children's behaviour problems, but that doesn't mean you have to give up pasta. Although the tomato sauce and tasty cheese must be avoided, there are other pasta toppings. There are now wheat-free noodles in the health food section of supermarkets and look for rice noodles, thick and thin, in the Asian section.

Three-minute spaghetti

Great as a quick meal (or snack) served with salad.

1 cup (100 g) uncooked three-minute spaghetti
knob butter or failsafe margarine (p. 203)
preservative-free cream cheese (optional)
garlic salt

Cook and drain spaghetti. Add butter, cream cheese and garlic salt and stir through. Serve hot. Serves one.

Chicken and pasta

This is my favourite quick meal. You can microwave chicken fillets with a leek for flavour, or use free-flow chicken from the freezer (p. 242).

cooked pasta or noodles
100 g chopped, cooked chicken per person
½ cup water
1 tbsp parsley, chopped
1 tbsp shallots, chopped
salt to taste
2 tbsp preservative-free cream cheese (or baby pear puree)

Prepare pasta as directed. Top with chicken pieces. Add parsley and shallots to water. Microwave on high for 1 minute. Stir in salt and cream cheese and pour over pasta. Serve with green beans.

Macaroni 'cheese'

1 cup uncooked wheat or gluten-free macaroni per person
1 cup basic white sauce (p. 263) per person, made
    dairy-free if necessary
1 tbsp preservative-free light cream cheese per person
    unless dairy-free
parsley garnish

Cook macaroni as directed, drain. Make white sauce with
extra 1 tsp salt and stir in cream cheese. You can stir in one
beaten egg per person for extra nutrition. Pour sauce over
macaroni, garnish with parsley. Serve with peas
(glutamates) or other green vegetables.

Spaghetti Caesar

6 eggs
4 tbsp cream or fresh natural yoghurt
salt to taste
2 cups cooked spaghetti
1 tbsp finely chopped parsley
chopped chives

Blend together eggs, cream and salt. Pour egg
mixture over spaghetti and cook over low heat
until egg mixture is slightly set and clinging to spaghetti.
Add parsley and gently stir through. Top with chives.
Serves four.

Creamy celery pasta sauce

1 cup preservative-free cottage or ricotta cheese
½ cup yoghurt
2 tbsp butter or failsafe oil (p. 203)
4 stalks celery, chopped with leaves
2 tbsp fresh parsley, chopped
1–2 leeks, sliced
salt to taste

Blend cottage cheese and yoghurt together until smooth. Heat butter or oil in frying pan and stir-fry celery, parsley and leeks until just tender. Add salt, remove from heat and add cottage cheese mix. Serve over pasta.

Farmhouse lasagne

9 lasagne sheets, preservative-free
failsafe oil (p. 203) for frying
1 cup celery, finely chopped
1 cup leek, finely sliced
1 clove garlic, crushed (optional)
1 cup shredded cabbage
500 g preservative-free cottage cheese
2 cups garlic meat sauce (p. 263)
1 cup grated mozzarella (amines)

Preheat oven to 180°C. Cook lasagne sheets according to directions. In a hot lightly-oiled pan, stir-fry leeks, celery and garlic until tender, add cabbage and stir-fry for 2 minutes. Remove from pan, mix well with cottage cheese. Spread one third of meat sauce in the bottom of a lightly oiled 32 × 23 cm baking dish. Place 3 lasagne sheets over sauce. Spread half of the leek mixture over sheets. Place 3 lasagne sheets on top. Spread with remaining leek mixture. Top with ½ cup meat sauce. Add last layer of lasagne sheets and remaining meat sauce. Sprinkle mozzarella over top. Bake for about 45 minutes. Serves six to eight.

Variation • for vegetarian lasagne, substitute 2 cups of cooked kidney beans, processed with 2 cloves garlic.

Dips, spreads, sauces, salad dressing and mayonnaise

Quick mayonnaise

400 g tin sweetened condensed milk
equal volume of water
3 tsp citric acid (or more to thicken)
1 tsp salt or to taste

Combine all ingredients in a glass screwtop jar and shake well to mix. Store in refrigerator.

Variation • use malt vinegar instead of water with citric acid if you don't react to amines.

Yoghurt dip/mayonnaise

1 pot fresh natural yoghurt
1–2 tbsp oil
1–2 cloves garlic, crushed
chopped chives

Combine. Use as a dip, sauce or mayonnaise.

Quick salad dressing (dairy-free, egg-free)

¼ cup failsafe oil
1 tsp citric acid dissolved in 1 tbsp of water, or 1 tbsp malt
    vinegar (if you don't react to amines)
1 clove garlic, chopped
salt to taste

Combine ingredients in a glass jar with a screwtop lid and shake.

Mighty mayo (aka Robin's dressing)

An easy-to-make, delicious dressing that really works.

¼ cup maize cornflour
1 tsp citric acid (or more to taste)
1 tsp salt
½ cup sugar
1¼ cups water
2 eggs
175 ml failsafe oil (p. 203)

Cook together cornflour, citric acid, salt, sugar and water.
When thickened, pour into blender and while whizzing add
eggs and drizzle in failsafe oil. Keeps well in refrigerator
for approximately 2 weeks.

Gravy

Gravy made from meat juices is very high in amines and not
suitable for your supervised elimination diet. As a gravy
substitute you can use leek sauce (p. 263), failsafe hummus
(p. 253), Brussels sprout puree (p. 254), pear puree, or pear
ketchup (p. 270).

¼ cup plain flour or gluten-free cornflour
30 g butter
1½ cups milk, A2 milk, soymilk or ricemilk
1½ cups water
salt to taste

Gently brown flour in a dry pan using medium heat. Remove
flour and melt butter in the pan. Return flour to the pan and
stir until smooth. Mix flour and water and add slowly to pan,
stirring all the time. Bring to the boil and allow to thicken.
Note that browning creates amines.

Golden marinade

3 tbsp golden syrup
3 tbsp failsafe oil (p. 203)
2 cloves of garlic, crushed
1 pinch citric acid
1 shallot, chopped
1 tsp finely chopped parsley
salt to taste

Combine all ingredients.

White sauce

1 tbsp pure butter or failsafe margarine (p. 203)
1 tbsp flour or gluten-free cornflour
1 cup milk, milk substitute or chicken stock (p. 242)
salt

Melt butter in pan. Add flour dissolved in liquid. Bring to the boil, stirring constantly and simmer until the sauce thickens, about 5 minutes. Stir in salt to taste.

Variation • **Parsley sauce:** add 2 tbsp finely chopped parsley • **Leek sauce:** add 1 medium-sized cooked and chopped leek • **Hollandaise sauce:** remove white sauce from heat, stir in a beaten egg yolk and ¼ tsp citric acid. Reheat but do not boil • **Cheese-tasting sauce:** 1 tsp of salt in this recipe will fool people into thinking it is a cheese sauce.

Creamy leek sauce

1 small leek, chopped
2 cups water
1 tbsp pure butter or failsafe margarine (p. 203)
1 tbsp flour
pinch salt
1 egg yolk
1–2 tbsp cream

Boil leek in water until tender. Add butter, flour and salt, stir while bringing to the boil and simmer for 5 minutes on low heat. Remove pan from heat, fold in egg yolk and cream.

Whisky cream sauce

1 tbsp whisky
¼ cup sugar
2 egg yolks
300 ml cream

Combine whisky and sugar and allow to stand for 1 hour. Beat egg yolks until thick and creamy and add gradually to whisky mixture, beating well. Cover and stand for 1 hour. Just before serving, whip cream and gently stir into sauce.

Birgit's pear ketchup

Use instead of tomato sauce.

1 large tin (825 g) of pears and syrup
½ cup brown sugar
2 tsp citric acid
1 tsp salt

Drain and dice pears. Put syrup in a saucepan and simmer until reduced to half. Add pears and remaining ingredients. Simmer about 15 minutes or until mixture thickens. Allow to cool. Puree in blender. Store in an airtight container in fridge.

Variation • puree for ketchup or leave as is for chutney. Spoon into containers and store in the refrigerator or freezer. Warning: if tinned pears are not soft and ripe, they may contain salicylates. Limit use of this sauce at first.
• Add chopped leeks, shallots and minced garlic to diced pears.

Magic spread

This is one of my favourites for camping and bushwalking, carried in a plastic tube from a camping store. It is good on bread and crackers, keeps much better than plain butter and everyone loves the flavour.

90 g butter or failsafe margarine (p. 203)
1½ cups sugar
3 eggs (avoid omega-enriched which taste
    fishy in this recipe)
2 tsp citric acid in ½ cup warm water

Melt butter in the microwave on high for 90 seconds. Beat together sugar, eggs and citric acid in water. Stir into melted butter, mixing well. Cook on high, stirring well every 30 seconds until the mixture thickens (about 3 minutes). Makes about 2 cups. Keeps about 2 weeks in a glass jar in the refrigerator. Also a delicious topping for yoghurt, ice-cream and cheesecake.

Birgit's pear jam

All jams except pear jam are very high in salicylates because food chemicals become concentrated as the fruit is boiled down. If pears used are not soft and ripe, your jam will contain some salicylates. Traditional jam-making requires the pectin in lemon juice. We can't use lemons but fortunately commercially prepared pectin powder called Jamsetta is available to assist setting. You can buy it in supermarkets. Jam-making generally requires roughly equal quantities of sugar and fruit.

1 kg ripe pears, peeled and cut into small pieces (should
    be about 750 g), or 2 large (825 g) tins soft pears,
    drained
750 g sugar
1 tsp citric acid
1 packet of Jamsetta (50 g)

Puree pears. Put in a large saucepan and heat gently. Add sugar and citric, then Jamsetta, stirring with a wooden spoon until sugar is dissolved. Bring to the boil and boil rapidly for five minutes, stirring occasionally. Allow to cool. Pour into sterilised glass jars or plastic storage containers. Store in refrigerator or freezer.

Deborah's cashew paste

1 cup (140 g) raw cashews
1–2 tsp salt
failsafe canola or sunflower oil for mixing (about 2–3 tsp)

Put cashews in blender, add salt, blend briefly. Add oil a little at a time and blend until the desired consistency is reached. To compete with commercial peanut pastes, add plenty of salt. You can reduce quantity later when children have been weaned off processed foods. Use as a sandwich spread alone or with golden syrup. Delicious on rice cakes.

Variation • Add half a tin (200 g) of drained chickpeas for a different texture • **Carob cashew spread:** omit the salt but use 1 tbsp carob powder, 1 tbsp caster sugar and about 1½ tbsp oil for a Nutella taste-alike. Store in an airtight jar.

Vegemite substitute

The mother who developed this spread commented 'the kids love it and eat it all up the day it is made'.

100 g minced beef
100 g assorted failsafe vegetables
water as needed
salt to taste

Put meat and vegetables in a pot just covered with water, bring to the boil and simmer until cooked, add salt to taste. Blend until smooth and use as a spread. Serve the day it is cooked or freeze leftovers immediately in small batches (e.g. ice-cube trays) and use the day it is thawed.

Desserts and celebrations

For salicylate responders who don't react to amines, you can adapt any dessert recipes containing chocolate or bananas or buy commercial additive-free chocolate desserts. For amine responders who don't react to salicylates, fruits like cherries, watermelon and strawberries are okay, but be careful, don't assume that all fruit and vegetables are now suitable. Common fruit like oranges, grapes, dates and sultanas contain both amines and salicylates and some contain natural MSG as well. Remember that cakes can be served as dessert.

Pear mousse

2 cups stewed or canned pears
¼ cup caster sugar
1 tsp citric acid, dissolved in
     1 tbsp water
1 tbsp gelatine, dissolved in
     4 tbsp water
1–2 egg whites, beaten until stiff
⅔ cup (150 ml) cream, whipped

Puree fruit in blender, combine ingredients in order above, and refrigerate.

Variation • Use Golden or Red Delicious apples, mango, rhubarb (salicylates), or pawpaw (amines). Not suitable for your supervised elimination diet.

Pear fool

For a simple dessert, mix equal quantities of pears or other sweetened pureed fruit (salicylates) and creamy yoghurt.

Golden pears or apples

1 pear or Golden Delicious apple (salicylates) per person
golden syrup

Peel and core pears or apples. Microwave on high for 2 minutes per piece of fruit. Place in a bowl with juices from cooking. Drizzle with golden syrup. Serve with ice-cream or yoghurt.

Howard's pear crumble
One of the most popular recipes in our house.

3–4 cups of stewed, fresh or canned pears, peeled and diced

Topping
¼ cup butter or failsafe margarine (p. 203)
1½ cups rolled oats (gluten-free if required)
¼ cup brown sugar

Preheat oven to 180°C. Drain juice, sweeten if necessary, and place fruit in the bottom of a pie dish. To make the topping, melt the butter in a pan, then stir in oats and sugar. Spread over fruit. Bake for 30 minutes or until topping is golden.

Variation • Use Golden Delicious apples and/or stewed rhubarb (salicylates).

Golden banana
1 banana (amines) per person
pure maple syrup

Peel and slice banana. Microwave for 1 minute. Pour maple syrup over. Serve with yoghurt or ice-cream.

Stewed rhubarb
Rhubarb (salicylates) is easily grown in your home garden. It has a tart flavour and will not appeal to children as readily as sweeter fruits. It is worth adding sugar to get them to like this nutritious fruit, which contains good quantities of fibre, iron and vitamins A and C.

1 kg rhubarb
1 cup sugar or to taste
½ cup water

Wash stalks, discard the leaves (which are very poisonous)
and chop rhubarb into small pieces. Add sugar and water
and simmer on the lowest heat until tender. Serve on cereal,
or with ice-cream or yoghurt for dessert.

Rhubarb crème brûlée

A delicious special-occasion dessert. If you don't have a
blowtorch, cooking the toffee on top can be tricky.

½ cup rhubarb cooked with sugar (salicylates)
300 ml cream (35 per cent fat)
4 egg yolks
2 tbsp caster sugar
1 tsp cornflour
4 tbsp extra caster sugar for topping

Spoon rhubarb into four small ramekins. Preheat oven to
180°C. Bring the cream to scalding point without boiling.
Beat the egg yolks with sugar and cornflour until creamy,
stir in the warm cream. Place the mixture back into a double
saucepan or a bowl over simmering water and gently heat,
stirring until the custard just coats the back of the spoon. Be
careful not to curdle the custard. Divide the custard by
pouring gently over the rhubarb. Place the ramekins in an
ovenproof dish, pour boiling water around them until half-
submerged. Place in the oven for 12 minutes, remove gently
and allow to cool. Refrigerate. To finish the brûlée, sprinkle
the top of the custard with a uniform 3 mm of caster sugar.
Place ramekins under a blazing hot grill, as close as
possible, until the sugar melts and caramelises – be very
careful not to burn! Allow to cool before serving, when the
top should be hard and crackly. Serves four.

Fresh persimmons

Originally from Japan, persimmons (salicylates) look like orange tomatoes. They are only ready to eat when they are very soft all over. I can remember rows of persimmons ripening on the windowsill when I was a child. The texture and colour of a ripe persimmon is like apricot jam, with a more subtle flavour. Remove the stem, cut in half and scoop the flesh out with a spoon.

Fresh tamarilloes

An excellent source of Vitamin C, tamarilloes (salicylates) are shiny red egg-shaped fruits with colourful red flesh and edible black seeds. They are ready to eat when soft. Cut in half and scoop out the flesh with a spoon, or use pulp to decorate cheesecakes or pavlova (see below). Tamarilloes may also be stewed gently with sugar and served with yoghurt or ice-cream.

Mini pavs

A luxurious and easy dessert that can be gluten-free and dairy-free. I like these with stewed rhubarb.

2 egg whites
6 tbsp caster sugar
1 pinch citric acid

Preheat oven to 180°C. Combine all ingredients. Beat for 10 minutes until glossy then spoon onto a greased oven tray in 4 rounds. Put in oven and turn oven down to 120°C. Cook for 15 minutes. Allow to cool in oven. Topping suggestions are sliced or pureed pears; salicylate fruits like sliced or pulped tamarillo, stewed rhubarb, mango; banana (amines); cream and ice-cream, dairy-free custard (p. 283) or yoghurt (p. 176). Serves four.

Pannacotta

This is simple dessert meaning 'cooked cream'.

½ cup sugar
1½ cups pure cream (35 per cent fat)
1½ cups milk, A2 milk or soymilk (not light)
2 drops pure vanilla (optional)
1 tbsp gelatine sprinkled over 1 tbsp cold water

Heat sugar, cream and milk but do not boil. Stir in the gelatine until thoroughly dissolved. Pour into wet moulds and refrigerate immediately until set, at least 4 hours. Serve with ripe pear, mango or poached tamarilloes.

Ice-cream

There are some suitable commercial ice-creams, but look out for effects from vanilla flavour and also avoid 160b colouring (some ice-creams labelled 'all natural – no artificial colours, flavours and preservatives' contain 160b and should be avoided). The *Failsafe Cookbook* has several delicious homemade recipes at various levels of fat. There are additive-free ice-cream cones but you need to read the label and watch out for unlisted antioxidants (p. 103).

Topping suggestions

Nestlé caramel Top 'n' Fill, real maple syrup, Magic spread (p. 271).

Homemade dairy ice-cream (15 per cent fat)

This is a traditional recipe that uses simple wholesome ingredients.

1 cup milk
1 egg
2 egg yolks
4 tbsp sugar
½ cup cream (35 per cent fat)

Boil milk. In a bowl, whisk egg, egg yolks and sugar into a froth, pour the milk on top and stir mixture over a low heat until it is reduced to a thick consistency. Whip cream with a beater and gently stir into the mixture, pour into a bowl and freeze. Lightly beat and freeze once more before serving to give it a soft creamy texture.

Dairy-free desserts

Commercial non-dairy ice-creams may contain salicylates and amines in vegetable oil and some people are affected by vanilla. You can make your own jellies, dairy-free cakes, fruit crumbles (p. 274) and pavlova (p. 276).

Maple ice-cream (7 per cent fat)

½ cup sugar
1 egg
2 tbsp failsafe oil (p. 203)
3 tbsp pure maple syrup
1½ cups soymilk or ricemilk (or A2 milk)

Mix all ingredients thoroughly with wand blender, chill and prepare according to your ice-cream maker's directions. Makes a soft ice-cream. You can substitute ⅔ cup of ripe pears for ⅔ cup of milk and leave out the maple syrup for a delicious pear ice-cream.

Dairy-free ice-cream (3 per cent fat)

This reduced-fat dairy-free ice-cream has an excellent texture when made in an ice-cream maker but you can still use the traditional beat–freeze–rebeat–refreeze method. As for any ice-cream, you must beat the mixture very well.

3 tsp gelatine
3 tbsp boiling water
⅔ cup golden syrup
3 egg yolks
3 cups soymilk (not light)

Sprinkle gelatine over boiling water to dissolve. Heat golden syrup in microwave or on stovetop for 40 seconds, or until nearly boiling. Whisk the egg yolks until pale and frothy. Gradually add golden syrup, continue to beat until mixture cools slightly. Stir in gelatine mixture. Add soymilk to golden syrup mixture and beat well. If using an ice-cream maker, refrigerate for 2 hours or store in freezer for one hour before processing.

Variation • Substitute ½ cup sugar dissolved in 50 ml of maple syrup and 50 ml water for golden syrup.

Pear sorbet
If you have an ice-cream maker, this low-fat pear sorbet is a winner.

½ cup sugar
1½ cups (400 ml) chilled water
1 cup pear puree, frozen
2 egg whites

Dissolve sugar in water. Blend frozen pear puree into sugar water. Beat egg whites until stiff and gently fold into pear mixture. Pour into ice-cream maker while it is running and process for 20 minutes. Best frozen before serving. Serves eight.

Variation • Mango puree (salicylates) is even better.

Pure fruit ice-cream
Make pure fruit ice-cream substitutes from pear puree, or mango pulp (salicylates) and banana (amines), frozen and then beaten in a food processor.

Jelly cups

3 tsp gelatine (1 extra in the tropics)
½ cup pear syrup or Magic cordial (p. 227)
1½ cups water

Dissolve gelatine in syrup and boil gently for a few minutes.
Add the water, stir well. Pour into tumblers or similar
individual serving containers and allow to cool. Serve alone
or with dairy-free ice-cream (p. 278).

Variation • Fold 2 cups of diced pear or mango (salicylates)
into the thickening jelly.

Birthdays and social occasions

There are two ways of handling your children's birthday
parties. You can provide totally failsafe alternatives such as
sausage rolls (p. 224), chicken nuggets (p. 241), additive-free
crisps (Kettle chips, or see p. 226) and failsafe treats, or a
combination of failsafe with other food that isn't too tempting
for the birthday child. To make birthdays look colourful, cook
a Fete cake (p. 285) or carob cake (p. 297) with white icing
(p. 289), or prepare an ice-cream cake (below) and decorate
with coloured plastic decorations, ribbons or paper streamers,
or use cochineal pink colouring (salicylates) in the icing.

For birthday parties away, slip in with a bottle of permitted
lemonade and a plate of food to share. Cupcakes (p. 286) are
good for this. Or join in the theme – for example, a Spot the
Dog birthday cake can be accompanied by a small white-iced
gluten-free failsafe cake in the shape of Spot's bone (see our
DVD cover). It also helps if your child arrives with a full
stomach. Parents have reported surviving birthday parties at
fast-food burger restaurants by allowing chicken nuggets,
chips and water, avoiding the cake and providing their own
lolly bag. You can just treat the whole party as a challenge, or
you could take your child's failsafe lemonade and failsafe
burger and have it presented in store wrapping like all the rest.

Ice-cream birthday cake

1 litre failsafe vanilla ice-cream
300 ml cream, whipped with 1 tbsp sugar
carob buttons, plastic decorations

Make sure ice-cream is firmly frozen. Remove from
container by dipping briefly into hot water and running a
knife around the edge. Cover with whipped cream.
Decorate and replace in freezer until well frozen. Do this the
day before your event.

Christmas cakes and puddings

Cakes and puddings containing dried fruit are exceptionally
high in problem-causing food chemicals. We use basic Fete
cake (p. 285) or carob cake (p. 297), iced with white icing,
decorated with a sprig of plastic holly and wrapped with red
or green paper frills. Dominion pudding, below, is a delicious
Christmas pudding alternative.

Dominion pudding

2 tbsp butter or failsafe margarine (p. 203)
½ cup sugar
1 egg
1 cup self-raising flour or gluten-free flour (p. 173)
½ cup milk or soymilk
4 tbsp golden syrup

Cream butter and sugar, add egg and beat well. Add sifted
flour alternately with milk. Place golden syrup in the bottom
of a greased bowl, pour batter over, tie brown paper or
baking paper over the top and steam in a covered
saucepan with 2 cm of water for 1¼ hours. Serve with a
failsafe version of the traditional brandy sauce (below),
cream, ice-cream or Narni's custard (p. 283).

Golden dumplings

A traditional recipe for a winter dessert.

Sauce

1 cup water
½ cup sugar
1 tbsp golden syrup
1 tbsp butter or failsafe margarine (p. 203)

Dumplings

1 cup self-raising flour
1 tbsp butter or failsafe margarine (p. 203)
1 egg, lightly beaten
cold milk

Place sauce ingredients in pan and heat. For dumplings, rub butter into flour, stir in egg and enough milk to make a fairly stiff dough. Roll into little balls and drop into the boiling syrup for about 5–10 minutes.

Bread and butter pudding

6–8 slices preservative-free bread
1½ tbsp (30 g) butter or failsafe margarine (p. 203)
3 eggs, lightly beaten
2¼ cups milk, A2 milk, soymilk or ricemilk
¼ cup maple syrup
2 tbsp caster sugar

Spread bread slices with butter. Arrange slices butter side up over base of lightly greased 23 cm ovenproof dish. Combine eggs, milk, syrup and sugar in a large bowl, pour mixture over bread. Press bread gently into egg mixture with spoon. Bake at 180°C for 30 minutes or until just set. Stand 10 minutes before serving. Serve warm or cold with cream or ice-cream.

Narni's custard

This is an easy-to-make low-fat alternative to ice-cream, as one reader reported: 'Feeling like something sweet, I made some soy custard. It was nice and satisfied my cravings.'

1 egg
2 tbsp cornflour (extra for thicker custard)
2–4 tbsp sugar (to taste)
3 cups milk or A2 milk, soymilk or ricemilk
1 tbsp maple syrup

In a large microwavable jug, beat ingredients together until sugar dissolves. Microwave for 5 minutes. Stir. Repeat in one-minute intervals until thickened, making sure it doesn't boil over. Thickens further as it cools.

Baked custard

2½ cups (600 ml) milk or soymilk
2 eggs
2 tbsp sugar
½ cup powdered milk or soymilk
¼ tsp salt

Whiz all ingredients in blender until smooth. Place in a casserole dish and stand in a tray of water. Bake at 180°C for approximately 1½ hours or stir over a low heat until it thickens.

Variation • Add 1 tbsp instant decaffeinated coffee • Line the casserole with caramel, made by boiling 1 cup sugar and ½ cup water until a light caramel colour. Do not stir.

No-bake lemon-topped cheesecake

1 packet plain sweet biscuits
50 g melted butter or failsafe margarine (p. 203)
350 g preservative-free cream cheese

1 tin sweetened condensed milk
1 tsp citric acid dissolved in 1 tbsp water
1 tbsp gelatine dissolved in ¼ cup boiling water
¾ cup whipped cream

Crush biscuits and mix with melted butter. Press into the sides and bottom of a 20 cm springform tin. Chill. Beat cream cheese until smooth and creamy. Gradually add condensed milk and citric acid mix. Mix well. Fold in whipped cream. Add gelatine and place mixture on biscuit crumb base. When set, decorate with failsafe fruit or lemon topping, below.

Lemon topping

⅔ cup sugar
2 tbsp cornflour
¾ cup boiling water
2 tsp butter
1 egg, beaten
2 tsp citric acid

Mix sugar and cornflour in a saucepan. Gradually add boiling water and blend thoroughly. Cook until thick, stirring to prevent lumps. Add butter and beaten egg. Cook for 2 minutes. Remove from heat, add citric acid. Continue stirring for a few minutes to allow mixture to cool slightly. Spread topping over cheesecake and refrigerate until topping sets.

Light cheesecake

This is an easy baked cheesecake.

200 g packet plain sweet biscuits
100 g butter or failsafe margarine (p. 203)
250 g light cream cheese
250 g preservative-free, low-fat cottage cheese
3 medium eggs

2 tbsp cornflour
¾ cup caster sugar
¼ cup light sour cream
¼ cup plain reduced-fat yoghurt

Preheat oven to 180°C. Crush biscuits and mix with melted butter. Press into the sides and bottom of a 20 cm springform tin. Chill. Beat cream cheese until smooth and creamy. Add remaining ingredients, mix until smooth. Pour filling into crust and bake 1 hour or until set. Allow to cool.

Cakes, biscuits and slices

The recipes in this section are essentially different combinations of flour, sugars, eggs and butter with flavourings like golden syrup, citric acid and fruit. You can adapt recipes from any recipe book by sticking to failsafe ingredients. Remember that cakes can be used as desserts, served with ice-cream or cream. This can be a dairy-free dessert by using soymilk in the cake and mock-cream topping (p. 288). Children like to know that they can have treats, but it is best to keep sugary snacks to a minimum.

Fete cake
This cake, and the Cool cupcakes variation below – formerly known as the basic plain cake – are always well-received and go like proverbial hot cakes. They make a good plate to take to a party or a school fete.

2 cups self-raising flour or gluten-free flour (p. 173)
¼ tsp salt
125 g butter or failsafe margarine (p. 203)
½ cup sugar
2 eggs, well beaten
½ cup milk

Grease a cake tin. Preheat oven to 180°C. Cream butter and sugar. Add beaten eggs gradually. Sift flour and salt and add to mixture alternately with milk. Put in tin and bake 40–45 minutes. Ice with white or other icing (p. 289).

Variation • **Cool cupcakes:** As for cake, but use paper patty cases. Makes 24. Bake for 12–15 minutes. Ice with pink or white icing (p. 289).

Jane's pear dessert cake
Everyone loves this soft, moist cake.

2 cups self-raising flour or gluten-
    free flour (p. 173)
4 tbsp cornflour (gluten-free if
    necessary)
4 large eggs
1 cup pear syrup from 800 g can of pears
2 cups sugar
8 tbsp soft butter or failsafe margarine (p. 203)
sliced canned pears for topping

Sift dry ingredients. Add eggs, syrup, sugar and butter, beat until well mixed. Pour into a large greased and lined cake tin (32 × 20 × 5 cm). Place sliced pears on top. Bake at 180°C for 1 hour. Serve warm. Leftovers can be used for school lunches.

Never-fail carob cake
For those who tolerate amines, this cake can be made with unflavoured cocoa and iced with chocolate. We often make it with one half chocolate, the other half carob, to accommodate everyone.

125 g butter or failsafe margarine (p. 203)
1 cup caster sugar
2 eggs

1 cup self-raising wheat flour or self-raising gluten-free flour
2 tbsp carob powder
½ cup milk or soymilk

Preheat oven to 180°C. Grease 20 cm ring pan. Combine all ingredients and beat thoroughly until smooth. Bake for 40 minutes, then allow to stand several minutes before turning out to cool. Ice with cream cheese frosting (p. 289).

Sticky gingerbread cake
(See p. 297.)

Mango roll
3 eggs, separated
½ cup caster sugar
¾ cup flour
2 tsp baking powder
2 tbsp hot milk
2 tbsp caster sugar for sprinkling

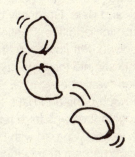

Filling
1 cup thickened cream
1 cup mashed mango or frozen mango pulp (salicylates)
1 tbsp icing sugar, sifted
1 tsp whisky

Grease and paper-line a Swiss roll tin. Beat egg whites until stiff. Gradually beat in sugar until mixture becomes thick and glossy. Beat in yolks one at a time. Sift flour and baking powder in a bowl and fold in to mixture with hot milk. Pour mixture into tin and smooth the surface. Bake at 220°C for 10 minutes. Turn cake out onto a sheet of greaseproof paper sprinkled with caster sugar mixture. Roll cake up and allow to cool. For the filling, whip cream until thick. Fold in mango, sugar and whisky, and chill. Unroll cake and spread with filling. Roll up, chill and top with cream before serving.

Classic sponge

Sponge cakes are tricky and apt to turn out like car tyres. I
wouldn't attempt this without a good mixer. Make sure your
oven is hot enough. This sponge can be gluten-free if you use
cornflour from corn rather than wheat.

3 eggs
½ cup caster sugar
½ cup cornflour
2 tbsp self-raising flour

Beat eggs on high speed in the mixer for 5 minutes or until
thick and pale. Gradually beat in caster sugar, beating well
after each addition. Continue beating until sugar has
dissolved. Sift flours together three times then quickly and
gently stir into the egg mixture. Do not overmix. Divide
batter evenly between two greased and floured 20 cm
sandwich pans and bake for 18–20 minutes at 180°C. Allow
to cool in the pans for a few minutes then turn out onto wire
rack to cool. Spread with Birgit's pear jam (p. 271) and
whipped cream or mock cream (below) and dust with icing
sugar.

Cornflour sponge (gluten-free)
(See p. 298.)

Mock cream
1½ tsp cornflour
½ cup milk
2 tbsp butter or failsafe margarine (p. 203)
2 tbsp sugar

Mix cornflour with milk to make a smooth paste. Put into a
saucepan and boil for 3 or 4 minutes. Remove from heat.
Mix butter and sugar to a cream. Slowly add the cold
cooked cornflour mixture. Beat well.

White icing

1 cup icing sugar (pure icing sugar for gluten-free)
2 tsp butter or failsafe margarine (p. 203), melted
1 tbsp water (approximately)

Sieve icing sugar and mix with butter. Gradually add water until you have a thick, spreadable paste.

Variation • **Coloured icing:** vitamise cabbage leaf with water and a little sodium bicarbonate (blue) or citric acid (red), or use cochineal 120 (some allergic responses, not kosher) or turmeric 100, or for special occasions use commercial natural colours (see Shopping List). Avoid annatto 160b • **Lemon:** Dissolve ½ tsp citric acid in the water • **Carob:** Dissolve 1 tbsp carob powder in the water • **Coffee:** Dissolve 1 tsp instant decaffeinated coffee powder in the water • **Quick caramel:** Use golden syrup instead of water • **Cream cheese:** substitute ½ cup of preservative-free cream cheese for half of the icing sugar.

Rolled oat bars

A healthy high-fibre alternative to commercial muesli bars. For gluten-free option, see gluten-free variation below.

1 cup white or wholemeal self-raising flour
2 cups rolled oats
150 g butter or failsafe margarine (p. 203)
½ cup sugar
1 tbsp golden syrup

Combine flour, oats and sugar in a bowl. Melt butter, add golden syrup and mix into dry ingredients. Press into slice tray and bake for 15–20 minutes at 160°C until brown. Cut into bars while still hot. Leave to cool before removing from tray. Makes 20.

Variation • For a **chewier, high-fibre** bar, add 1 cup chopped pears (canned or fresh) and 2 tbsp psyllium hulls (flea-seed husks) to mix • Can be made **gluten-free** using wheat-free oats and gluten-free flour, or see gluten-free slice (p. 292).

Big Anzacs

1 cup plain flour
2 cups rolled oats
¾ cup sugar
125 g butter or failsafe
    margarine
    (p. 203)
2 tbsp golden syrup
2 tsp sodium bicarbonate
2 tbsp boiling water

Mix together flour, oats and sugar. Melt butter and golden syrup together. Mix bicarbonate with boiling water and add to butter mixture. Pour into blended dry ingredients and stir to combine. Place large spoonfuls of mixture onto greased oven tray, leaving room to spread. Bake at 160°C for 20 minutes.

Rebecca's gingerless pigs

You won't know the ginger has been left out of these ginger-bread animals. Fun to make and good for a plate to take to a party. Icing is essential.

125 g butter or failsafe margarine (p. 203)
⅓ cup brown sugar
⅓ cup golden syrup
3 tsp sodium bicarbonate
1 egg
3 cups plain flour

Preheat oven to 180°C. Dissolve butter, sugar and golden syrup in the microwave or in a saucepan over low heat.

When lukewarm, stir in bicarbonate and egg. Place flour in bowl, make a well in the center and add other ingredients. Knead to form a dough, roll out on a floured surface and cut into shapes. Bake for 15 minutes. Ice with lemon citric icing (p. 289).

Butterscotch biscuits

These biscuits freeze well so you will probably want to double the recipe. The gluten-free option is also particularly success-ful, so I take one or two in a small container when having a decaf in a cafe.

125 g butter or failsafe margarine (p. 203)
½ cup brown sugar, firmly packed
1 tbsp golden syrup
1¼ cups self-raising flour, gluten-free if required

Beat butter, sugar and golden syrup in a small bowl. Stir in sifted flour. Roll into balls. Place about 5 cm apart on greased oven trays and flatten with a fork. Bake on greased trays for 15 (soft) to 20 minutes (very crunchy) at 180°C.

Afghans

200 g butter or failsafe margarine (p. 203)
⅓ cup sugar
1⅓ cup plain flour
2 tbsp carob
½ cup rolled oats

Cream butter and sugar. Add flour, carob and, lastly, rolled oats. Put spoonfuls on a greased oven tray (they don't spread) and bake about 15 minutes at 180°C. When cold, ice with carob icing and top with a raw cashew nut each. Good gluten-free – use wheat-free oats.

Pear crumble slice

1¼ cups rolled oats (gluten free if required)
1¾ cups plain flour (gluten free if required)
¼ cup brown sugar
185 g melted butter or failsafe margarine (p. 203)
1 small (420 g) tin soft pears or 1⅔ cup stewed or fresh pears

Preheat oven to 190°C. Combine rolled oats, flour and sugar in a mixing bowl. Add butter and mix thoroughly. Press ½ of mixture firmly into the base of a greased, lined 20cm × 30 cm lamington pan. Drain pears, sweeten and lightly mash if necessary, and spread evenly over rolled oat base. Sprinkle remaining rolled oat mixture over pear and press down with the back of a spoon. Bake for 35–40 minutes until topping is golden. Allow to cool in the pan before cutting into slices.

Highlander biscuits

125 g butter or failsafe margarine (p. 203)
¼ cup sugar
1 tbsp sweetened condensed milk
1½ cups self-raising flour

Cream butter, sugar and condensed milk together. Add flour. Cut off small pieces and roll into balls. Place on greased baking tray and flatten with fork. Bake for 20 minutes at 180°C.

Shortbread

Shortbreads are fun for children to make because they enjoy cutting out shapes.

225 g butter or failsafe margarine (p. 203)
½ cup caster sugar
3 cups plain or gluten-free flour
¼ cup cornflour
¼ tsp salt

Cream butter and sugar well, add sifted flour, cornflour and salt. Knead well, roll out 12 to 18 mm thick. Cut into shapes (diamonds, squares, rounds, animals). Place on cold greased tray and prick with fork. Bake about 30 minutes at 180°C.

Wheat and gluten-free cooking

Being gluten-free is much easier in Australia now than it was ten years ago due to the availability of good commercial gluten-free products. However, it is difficult socially because so much of our food is wheat-based compared to the traditional rice-based diets eaten by millions in countries such as China and India.

Most of the recipes in this book are gluten-free or have gluten-free options. All of the following recipes are gluten-free.

My gluten-free mainstays are:

- puffed rice/buckwheat/millet cereals and contamination-free oats
- gluten-free pancakes: homemade or commercial premix
- rice, rice cakes, potatoes including mashed, wedges, hash browns
- gluten-free flours in homemade rolled oat bars, cakes, muffins
- gluten-free bread: homemade, bread mix or commercial
- psyllium as a good gluten-free source of fibre (p. 204).

Rice is not as nutritious as wheat. Your dietitian can assist with nutrition and may recommend two serves of meat per day to contribute extra protein, iron and thiamine. Chickpeas, failsafe hummus, chickpea flour and cashews can be useful if tolerated. However, families with allergies will need to avoid cashews for young children and to consider cross reactivity problems with chickpeas due to nut, legume or soy allergies.

Ethan's nutritious menu

As eaten by three-year-old Ethan during his elimination diet, this dairy-free, gluten-free failsafe menu met or exceeded nutritional requirements for essential minerals and vitamins including folates (p. 191):

- **Breakfast:** soy smoothie with soymilk, carob powder, pear and egg, or gluten-free toasted bread or riceflake porridge with pear puree and soymilk.
- **lunch at preschool:** 4 rice cakes, homemade hummus or gluten-free sandwich with rissoles.
- **Morning/afternoon tea:** soy yoghurt or pear muffin or rolled oat bar or pureed pear icypole or packet plain crisps (only on treat days).
- **Dinner:** Darani's amazing chicken noodle stew (cooked in bulk, frozen, and eaten nearly every day for lunch or dinner, see p. 231) or spaghetti with failsafe topping or roast dinner or rice-crumbed chicken nuggets and chips or mince and potato casserole with hidden green vegetables.

Ingredients to avoid:

• wheat in breakfast cereals • rolled oats unless contamination-free • bran and wheatgerm (in breakfast cereals, muffins and other health foods) • flour (in bread, cakes, biscuits, pizza bases, wraps, tortillas and many others) • battered or crumbed foods such as fried fish • bread crumbs (use rice crumbs instead) • pasta except for gluten-free pasta • semolina, couscous, bulgur (pre-cooked cracked wheat), tabouli (Lebanese salad) • rye, barley, triticale, spelt, kamut • cornflour from wheat (cornflour from corn or maize is good) e.g. in marshmallows • icing sugar mixture with cornflour (pure icing sugar is good) • baking powder unless gluten-free • malt made from barley in cereals, malted milk, whisky (rice malt is good) • maltodextrin and thickeners (1400–1450) may contain tiny amounts of gluten if made from wheat, check labels.

Sensitivity to gluten varies. You may not have to avoid the small amounts of gluten in cornflour and malt unless you are a coeliac or extremely sensitive. If you are a coeliac there may be other ingredients to avoid (see www.coeliac.org.au). See the Shopping List, especially the Health Foods section, for gluten-free products and flours.

Gluten-free pancakes

There is an excellent gluten-free pancake mix available in Australian supermarkets. It's better than wheat-based versions because there's no added flavour (see Shopping List). Or you can make your own. I often eat pancakes instead of gluten-free bread.

1 cup gluten-free self-raising flour OR a mixture of any
    gluten-free flours, e.g. ½ cup rice flour, ½ cup buckwheat
    flour and 1 tsp gluten-free baking powder
1 egg or egg replacer
1 cup water, milk, soymilk or ricemilk

Beat together until smooth. Mixture will improve if left standing for 30 minutes. Cook pancakes in a medium to hot oiled pan. Serve with butter and maple syrup; yoghurt and stewed fruit; or a savoury topping such as chicken and chickpeas.

Gluten-free loaf

Gluten-free bread will never be as good as wheat-based bread, but there are some reasonable gluten-free premixes and breads (see Shopping List). This loaf can be made in a breadmaker or by hand.

450 ml warm water
2 tsp dry yeast
2 tsp sugar
1 cup brown rice flour
2 cups white rice flour
1 cup besan (chickpea) flour
1 tbsp xanthan gum

1 tsp salt (or less)
2 tbsp failsafe oil (p. 203)
2 eggs

In the oven: Combine water with yeast and 2 tsp sugar. Let
stand in a warm place for 10 to 15 minutes or until it froths
on top. Sift dry ingredients and make a well in the center.
Add oil and yeast mixture, add egg, beat with wooden
spoon. Pour into well-oiled loaf tin. Stand in warm place for
20 minutes. Bake at 200°C for 35 to 40 minutes.
Breadmaker: Follow directions for your machine. About ten
minutes after you start the machine, lift the lid without
stopping the machine and scrape sides of pan carefully
with a spatula. Test dough by lifting some on spatula (avoid
mixing blade). Dough should fall slowly from spatula. If too
thin, add 1–3 tbsp of rice flour, if too thick add 1–3 tbsp
water (it should look like a thick cake mix or stiff mashed
potato).

Gluten-free pastry
There are suitable gluten-free pastry mixes available in stores,
or make your own. This pastry can be used either for sausage
rolls or as the pastry for automatic pie and pasty makers, filled
with failsafe mince (p. 234) or chicken stir-fry (p. 243).

1½ cups mashed potato
2 tbsp failsafe oil (p. 203)
1 cup gluten-free cornflour
½ cup potato flour
2 tsp baking powder
1 tsp salt
1 egg, lightly beaten

Place warm potato in a large mixing bowl. Stir in oil. Add
sifted dry ingredients. Knead into a smooth ball, adding
enough egg to combine. Place on a lightly cornfloured
board and knead again lightly.

Quick pizza dough
Use a commercial premix or see p. 262.

Sticky gingerbread cake
I usually have some of this in my freezer. It's great for guests, travels well in lunchboxes and you'd never know it was gluten-free – although you can make it with wheat-based flour if you want. The 'gingerbread' flavour comes from the golden syrup.

125 g butter or failsafe margarine (p. 203)
¾ cup golden syrup
¾–1 cup caster sugar
2 cups of gluten-free flour
2 eggs
1 cup of milk, soymilk or ricemilk
2 tsp gluten-free baking powder

Combine butter and syrup in a large pan and stir over low heat without boiling until butter has melted. Add all other ingredients and beat until smooth. Pour into a lined 20 × 30 cm pan and bake until done, about 50–60 minutes at 160°C. Test for readiness with a skewer. Allow to cool before icing or dust with icing sugar.

Carob fudge cake
1 cup cornflour
½ cup soy flour
½ cup rice flour
⅔ cup carob powder
1½ tsp sodium bicarbonate
¾ tsp salt
1 cup sugar
1½ cups soymilk
125 g butter or failsafe margarine (p. 203)
2 eggs

Sift together flours, carob powder, bicarbonate and salt.
Add sugar, then combine. Add milk, margarine and eggs.
Beat for 3 minutes. Pour into a greased and cornfloured tin
and bake at 180°C – for two 20 cm round tins, bake for
25 minutes; for a slab or square tin (23 cm) bake for
45 minutes, or you can use patty pans, and bake
for 15 minutes. Ice with carob icing.

Cornflour sponge

This is a handy recipe when you need to take a plate and don't
want to seem gluten-free. Compared to other cakes, sponges
are low in fats and sugars. The secret of a good sponge is a
good mixer.

1 cup gluten-free cornflour
½ tsp sodium bicarbonate
1 tsp cream of tartar
¾ cup caster sugar
4 eggs

Preheat oven to 180°C. Grease and dust two 20 cm round
tins with cornflour. Sift together cornflour and bicarbonate
and tartar, twice. Separate eggs. Beat egg whites on high
speed in clean, dry bowl until quite stiff. Add sugar
gradually, keeping mixer speed constant. Add egg yolks
one at a time on slower speed, beating well after each
addition. Sift cornflour mixture all at once onto top of egg
mixture. Stir in gently but thoroughly with spoon. Divide
mixture between tins and bake for approximately
20 minutes. Sandwich together with mock cream (p. 288)
and sprinkle top with icing sugar. Or spread pear jam
(p. 271) and top with whipped cream.

Cupcakes (gluten free)

1 cup gluten-free cornflour
½ tsp sodium bicarbonate
½ tsp cream of tartar

pinch of salt
90 g butter or failsafe margarine (p. 203)
60 g caster sugar
1 egg, beaten
few drops vanilla essence (optional)

Cream butter and sugar. Beat in egg and vanilla. Sift
together cornflour, bicarbonate, tartar and salt, and
gradually beat this into the mixture. When combined, beat at
medium–high speed for 2 minutes. Bake in patty pans at
180°C for 10 minutes. Ice with white icing.

Gluten-free shortbread
120 g butter or failsafe margarine (p. 203)
⅓ cup sugar
1 cup rice flour
½ cup gluten-free cornflour
½ cup soy flour
½ tsp cream of tartar
pinch of salt

Cream butter and sugar well. Add sifted flours, cream of
tartar and salt. Form dough into a ball (you will not be able
to roll this out). Cut into 4 equal pieces and pat into large
flat circles on 2 baking trays. Cut into triangles and bake at
190°C for 8 minutes, until just turning golden brown.

Cashew balls
2 cups ground rice
2 cups ground cashews
½ cup golden syrup
190 g butter or failsafe margarine (p. 203)

Mix all ingredients together, roll into balls. Bake on oiled
oven tray at 170°C for 10 minutes.

Rolled oat bars

(See p. 289.)

Oat biscuits

For gluten-free, use oats free of wheat contamination. The biscuits are not intended to rise – they have a texture like a muesli bar.

100 g butter
1 egg
⅓ cup sugar
1½ cups oats
⅓ cup gluten-free cornflour or rice flour
3 tsp gluten-free baking powder

Put butter, egg and sugar in a large bowl, then mix well with an electric mixer. Work oats, flour and baking powder into mix. Form biscuits. Bake at 180°C for 15–18 minutes.

Gluten- and dairy-free carob oat squares

For gluten-free, use oats free of wheat contamination. These biscuits are especially quick to prepare.

1 cup sugar
2 cups rolled oats
50 g butter
2 eggs
1 tbsp carob powder
½ cup cashew nuts, chopped
2 tbsp soymilk
1 tsp baking powder

Put half of the sugar and all the oats in a pan, heat until golden brown, wait until cool. Beat remaining sugar, butter and eggs in a bowl. Add the rest of the ingredients, mix and pour into pan. Bake at 180°C for 15–18 minutes. When cool, cut into squares.

Sweet treats

No one is pretending these are healthy, but children need treats. For school holidays and parties, these are fun to make and delicious to eat.

Marshmallows

4 tbsp gelatine
1 cup warm water
4 cups sugar
2 cups boiling water
2 pinches citric acid
icing sugar
cornflour (gluten-free if necessary)

Sprinkle gelatine over warm water and stir to dissolve. Put sugar and boiling water into a large saucepan. Stir in gelatine mixture and boil gently, uncovered, for 20 minutes. Allow to cool until lukewarm. Pour mixture into the large bowl of an electric mixer, add citric acid. Beat fast until very thick and white. Pour mixture into two deep 20 cm square wetted cake tins. Refrigerate until set. When cold, cut into squares with a wet knife and toss in a mixture of icing sugar and cornflour. Store separated with greaseproof paper.

Carob crackles

4 cups Rice Bubbles
1½ cups icing sugar, sifted
5 tbsp carob powder, sifted
250 g butter or failsafe margarine (p. 203)

Combine the Rice Bubbles with the icing sugar and carob powder in a large mixing bowl. Stir in the butter and mix well. Using 2 tsp of the mixture per patty case, divide the mixture between 24 patty case papers placed on a scone tray and refrigerate.

Mega-bites

2 cups sugar
1 cup water
3 tbsp gelatine
¼ tsp citric acid
sifted icing sugar for coating

Place the sugar, water and gelatine in a saucepan over low
heat and stir until dissolved. Bring to the boil and boil
without stirring for 20 minutes. Add the citric acid and pour
into a lightly greased tin. Allow to cool and set. Cut into
bite-sized squares and roll in icing sugar.

Honeycomb

5 tbsp sugar
2 tbsp golden syrup
1 tsp sodium bicarbonate

Bring sugar and golden syrup to the boil, slowly stirring all
the time. Boil 4 minutes, stirring occasionally. Remove from
heat and add sodium bicarbonate. Stir in quickly until it
froths and pour at once into a greased tin. Break up when
cold. Store in airtight jars.

Easy butterscotch

125 g butter
2 cups sugar
1 cup cold water
1 tsp cream of tartar

Put butter, sugar and water into a saucepan. Heat slowly
and when butter is melted add the cream of tartar and boil
until a small amount poured into cold water will crack. Pour
into a buttered slice-tin.

Toffee

3 cups sugar
1 cup water
1 tsp citric acid

Put sugar, water and citric acid in a heavy saucepan. Stir
over low heat until sugar is dissolved. Increase heat and
boil rapidly uncovered for about 15 minutes until a small
amount poured into cold water will crack. Remove from
heat, then reduce heat by standing saucepan in cold water
for one minute. Wait until toffee stops bubbling and pour
into paper patty cases.

Toffee apples

These are fun if apples are tolerated, but not suitable for your
supervised elimination diet.

3 cups sugar
½ tsp citric acid dissolved in
    1 tbsp water or 1 tbsp malt
    vinegar (amines)
1 tbsp butter or failsafe margarine
    (p. 203)
¼ cup cold water
½ tsp cream of tartar
6 Golden or Red Delicious apples, peeled
    (salicylates)

Boil all ingredients except for apples together without stirring
until a drop snaps in cold water. Remove from heat, stand
saucepan in a basin of hot water and dip skewered apples
in the toffee. Stand apples on greaseproof paper until dry.

Lollipops

1 cup sugar
⅔ cup water

cochineal colouring (optional)
wooden sticks

Heat sugar and water in heavy-based saucepan over low
heat and stir with wooden spoon until sugar dissolves. Then
bring to the boil and simmer without stirring until a drop
snaps in cold water. Arrange rows of small sticks on oiled
trays. Drop one teaspoonful of the mixture onto the pointed
end of each stick. Allow to set firmly.

Caramel fudge

A favourite holiday recipe from New Zealand. Organise
people in shifts with a timer to help with the stirring.

3 cups sugar
½ cup milk
200 g (half a tin) sweetened condensed milk
125 g butter or failsafe margarine (p. 203)
¼ tsp salt
1 tbsp golden syrup

Put sugar and milk into a saucepan and bring to the boil.
Add condensed milk, butter, salt and golden syrup. Boil for
30 minutes, stirring frequently. Pour into a mixing bowl
quickly before it sets and beat for a few minutes. Pour into
greased tins. Mark into squares and cut when set. Store in
the refrigerator.

Toffee fudge

2 cups sugar
2 tbsp butter or failsafe margarine (p. 203)
2 tbsp milk
1 pinch citric acid dissolved in 1 tbsp of warm water
Combine ingredients in a saucepan, bring to the boil,
stirring, and boil while stirring for 5–10 minutes. Pour into a
greased slice tin, mark into squares when nearly set. Store
in an airtight container. Softer than toffee, easier than fudge.

Salicylate and amine recipes

This section is for people who are doing challenges or have passed their salicylate or amine challenge.

The aim of challenges is to concentrate on one food chemical at a time and to eat lots of it so you can observe reactions. So for the salicylate challenge, for example, you can't use tomato sauce, broccoli, oranges, your favourite lasagne recipe or any other foods that are very high in salicylates because they contain amines as well. Here is how one family managed their challenge:

> For a week we ate tinned apricots on our rice bubbles, preservative-free apple juice, curries or pumpkin soup for dinner, and large quantities of carrots, Granny Smith apples, kumara, corn, capsicum, cucumber, cinnamon and tea. We went for about the first three days with no reaction. My 8-year-old son became fractious and difficult and seemingly continuously involved in conflict with his brothers and sisters, pretty well back to pre-elimination behaviour. Yuk! The youngest two had wet beds and seemed a bit anxious and grumpy. I was tired and grumpy. I had bloating and tummy aches and alternating constipation and loose stools. My flesh felt like it was crawling, my eyes were stingy and I got restless legs very badly.

Keep a daily diary of foods and symptoms and review it at the end of the week. See an example of a challenge diary on the 'Challenges' factsheet on www.fedup.com.au.

Some salicylate suggestions

- Add pumpkin or carrots and 1 tsp of cinnamon to Margie's lunchbox muffins (p. 216), but not walnuts which contain amines.

- Turn the Irish stew (p. 238) into an Indian curry by adding 2 tbsp of curry powder. You can't use tandoori with artificial colours or pastes with unlisted synthetic antioxidant (320).
- Pear crumble (p. 274) can be made with apples, apricots, peaches or cherries but not with plums which contain amines.
- Make a Berry Smoothie from the recipe on p. 213 with strawberries, honey or other berries, except raspberries which contain amines.
- Make your own fresh juice and icypoles – watermelon or apple but not citrus which contains amines.
- Add zucchini, capsicums and corn to stir-fries and salads. but you can't use eggplant or broccoli.
- Add cucumber and alfalfa sprouts to sandwiches but not avocado or tomato.

Cinnamon toast (contains salicylates)

2 slices white bread or gluten-free bread
failsafe butter or margarine (p. 203) for spreading
2 tbsp sugar
1 tbsp cinnamon (salicylates)

Preheat grill to medium. Toast the bread on both sides.
Spread with butter and sprinkle sugar and cinnamon
mixture generously over both slices and toast until the sugar
melts and bubbles.

Some amine suggestions

- Double choc muffins (p. 217).
- Dried bananas for lunchboxes (but not banana chips that are deep-fried in coconut oil).
- Tuna or salmon rolls and sandwiches.
- Additive-free ham and bacon, usually available only from organic specialists
- Homemade mud cake (see *Failsafe Cookbook*).
- Homemade banana cake (see *Failsafe cookbook*).

Papaya smoothie (p. 213)

Choc chip banana ice-cream (contains amines)

Children who won't eat dark chocolate and ripe bananas will probably eat this delicious recipe.

Bananas, very ripe
Chocolate, dark choc bits, cooking chocolate or dark
    chocolate bars

Peel bananas, wrap in foil and leave in freezer until frozen, then whiz in food processor for a creamy banana ice-cream. Sprinkle with choc bits or melt chocolate in a double boiler (small saucepan in a larger saucepan of boiling water) and pour over.

The elimination diet on holiday
A mother's report

During the school holidays we travelled 3000 km through the Kimberley on roads like the Gibb River Road – lots of dust, rocks and dirt. The elimination diet went with us and we enjoyed cereal, toast and eggs for breakfast. Lunch consisted of sandwiches, rice cakes with fillings of homemade pear jam, golden syrup, cream cheese, maple syrup, or left-over noodles. Dinners were steak (one night only), stir-fried chicken thighs with noodles or rice and a combination of green beans, red beans, cabbage, leeks, chives, shallots, cream cheese and white potatoes. Dessert was fresh pears; canned pears; fresh and canned cream; fresh, powdered and canned milk; damper; golden dumplings and caramel dumplings. Snacks during the day consisted of the allowed biscuits, sweets and pears. Drinks consisted of 500 ml bottles of cold water, refilled many times over, and the most important item for the two-week camping trip was the car fridge, which made the whole trip very pleasant. John and I enjoyed gin and tonic at the end of the day. Everything worked out well as far as the food was concerned. The trip was interesting and, best of all, fun.

Notes

Most of the abstracts and some of the full text of cited articles are available from www.pubmed.com.

Introduction

p. xiv The British survey of additive consumption, commissioned by food manufacturer Birds Eye, found that many people do not understand which foods are most likely to contain additives – 'Additives lurk in everyday diets', http://news.bbc.co.uk/2/hi/health/6233395.stm.

p. xv **'changes in behaviour and learning ability are early signs of chemical toxicity'.**
Neurobehavioural reactions have been observed during the early stages of many toxic episodes and serve as early warning signals, according to Professor Bernard Weiss in 'Behavioural toxicity of food additives' in Weininger J. and Briggs, G.M., editors, *Nutrition Update Vol 1*, J. Wiley and Sons, New York (1983), pp. 21–38; and see Koger et al, 'Environmental toxicants and developmental disabilities', *Am Psychol* (2005) 60(3), pp. 243–55, abstract at http://content.apa.org/journals/amp/60/3/243.

Chapter 1: Sleeping Beauty

p. 7 Diet and IQ: Rebecca's IQ was measured on the WISC-R by different psychologists 12 months apart, before and after diet. 'E numbers and identical twins',

University of Southampton Bulletin (2004) vol 9 no. 27, http://www.bulletin.soton.ac.uk/0927/index.htm.

p. 8 **'. . . the marshmallow test was found to be twice as useful as IQ test scores'.** Goleman, Daniel, *Emotional Intelligence*, Bloomsbury, London, 1996, www.danielgoleman.info.

p. 9 **'CFS, mycoplasma and flu-like illness'** in Sairenji, .T, Nagata, K., 'Viral infections in chronic fatigue syndrome', *Nippon Rinsho* (2007) 65(6), pp. 991–6.

p. 11 **'during the time she had CFS she became more sensitive'.** Researchers observe that 'of all patients with food intolerance, those with fatigue and other constitutional symptoms are the most sensitive, reacting to a broader range of challenge substances, with lower dose thresholds and more prolonged symptoms' in a chapter by Loblay, R.H. and Swain, A.R. entitled 'The role of food intolerance in chronic fatigue syndrome', in Hyde, B., Goldstein, J. and Levine, P., editors, *The clinical and scientific basis of myalgic encephalomyelitis/chronic fatigue syndrome*, The Nightingale Research Foundation, Ottawa, (1992), pp. 521–559.

p. 11 CFS management strategies: sleep management such as not sleeping after 3 pm to prevent turning night into day as happens with many CFS sufferers, see principles of sleep hygiene at http://www.stanford.edu/~dement/howto.html; graded exercise (tiny amounts of increasing exercise) was useful during recovery periods but not during bad days and the worst months, see Wallman, K.E. et al, 'Randomised controlled trial of graded exercise in chronic fatigue syndrome', *Medical Journal of Australia* (2004) 180, pp. 444–448, and see http://www.abc.net.au/rn/talks/8.30/helthrpt/stories/s1103322.htm; regular brief exposure to sunshine (because people with CFS can end up with no sun exposure, see http://www.abc.net.au/catalyst/stories/s1048944.htm); a protein powder supplement (dried egg-white powder for bodybuilders). See the 'Chronic Fatigue' factsheet on www.fedup.com.au.

Chapter 2: Landing on their feet

p. 15 Hayfever: technically called allergic rhinitis, possible symptoms include runny or blocked nose, sneezing, impaired sense of smell, itching of the ears, nose or palate, itchy or watering eyes, associated cough, throat clearing, sinus headache, glue ear, fatigue. It is often possible 'to satisfactorily manage pollen allergies by giving attention to diet during the pollen season' (Bass, D.J., 'Clinically important pollens of NSW and the ACT', *Medical Journal of Australia* (1984) 141(5), pp. 13–14). Milk is the most commonly implicated food, however benzoates, other additives and/or salicylates may also be involved. See Pacor et al, 'Monosodium benzoate hypersensitivity in subjects with persistent rhinitis', *Allergy* (2004) 59(2), pp. 192–7; also see 'Hayfever and Allergic Rhinitis' factsheet on www.fedup.com.au.

p. 16 '**even babies and young children can have migraines**': see 'Migraine' factsheet on www.fedup.com.au.

p. 18 '**Ability to do homework is important**': Income throughout life is strongly related to reading ability according to the 1993 US National Adult Literacy Survey, http://nces.ed.gov/pubs93/93275.pdf.

p. 21 '**functionally illiterate**': a 1995 NSW survey of 14-year-olds found 35 per cent were functionally illiterate; the 1996 National School English Literacy Survey of more than 7,500 students, the most comprehensive in 16 years, found that 27 per cent of students in Year Three and 29 per cent of Year Five did not reach a set standard on reading, with writing performance marginally worse. In 1997, an Australian Bureau of Statistics survey of more than 9000 adults found that half the adult population had significant literacy problems. About one in five experienced significant difficulty in using printed material such as bus timetables encountered in everyday life, another one in three had some difficulty. American statistics are similar, see above and the Notes for p. 40.

Chapter 3: Adults too
p. 28 **'Food, behaviour and the brain . . .'**: Uhlig, T., and others, 'Topographic mapping of brain electrical activity in children with food-induced attention deficit hyperkinetic disorder', *Eur J Pediatr* (1997) 156(7), pp. 557–61.

p. 31 **'. . . family background of migraine. . .'**: Against the food–migraine connection is Dr Oliver Sacks in *Migraine*, Faber and Faber, London, 1991. For the food–migraine connection are Egger, J., and others in 'Is Migraine Allergy?', *Lancet* (1983) 2, pp. 865–868. Children with food-related behaviour often have relatives with migraines in Rowe, K.S. and Rowe, K.L., 'Synthetic food colouring and behaviour: a dose response effect in a double-blind, placebo-controlled, repeated-measures study', *Journal of Pediatrics* (1994) 125, pp. 691–8.

p. 37 **'Parents of children with propionic acidemia regard propionic acid as a toxic chemical . . . .'**: http://www.paresearch.org/; laboratory studies, Brusque, A.M., and others, 'Effect of chemically induced propionic acidemia on neurobehavioral development of rats', *Pharmacol Biochem Behav* (1999) 64(3), pp. 529–34.

p. 37 Dengate, S., and Ruben, A., 'Controlled trial of cumulative behavioural effects of a common bread preservative, Behavioural effects of calcium propionate,' *J Paediatr Child Health* (2002) 38(4), pp. 373–6.

p. 40 **'If a child hasn't learned to read well by the age of nine they are likely to remain poor readers for the rest of their lives'**. 'With that failure often comes a lifetime of disappointment and privation – and burdens for society,' according to reading researchers. An estimated 40 per cent of American children were found to be poor readers and half of those have severe problems (1997). Children's illiteracy has been declared 'a major health problem' by the US Public Health Service. Marego Athans, 'Young readers left to struggle', *Baltimore Sun*, 2 November 1997, pp. 1A, 10A, 11A. Figures are similar in Australia, see Notes for p. 21.

p. 40 Aboriginal children – during our time in the Northern Territory I was appalled by the highly processed, additive-laden food in remote Aboriginal community stores – there was virtually nothing I was prepared to feed our children. Yet a small change in nutrition can make a big change in health, see Jones, R., and Smith, F., 'Are there health benefits from improving basic nutrition in a remote Aboriginal community?' *Australian Family Physician* (2006) 35(6), pp. 453–4.

p. 40 Mothers need correct information – in a book about ADHD, doctors Green and Chee (*Understanding ADHD*, Doubleday, Sydney, 1997) described the RPAH elimination diet as 'placing the child and their family on a diet of water, pear juice, preservative-free bread and unseasoned meats' (p. 132). Many other nutritious and palatable foods are permitted, but not pear juice. This information is misleading because pear juice contains pear peel, is thus moderate in salicylates and one glass a day can be enough to negate the diet.

Chapter 4: Lives half-lived
p. 44 '. . . **bedwetting stopping completely in more than half** . . .': a finding in the Egger and co-workers study on migraine, see Notes for p. 31.

p. 45 '. . . **seniors need to know** . . .': Weiss, B., 'Vulnerability to pesticide neurotoxicity is a lifetime issue', *Neurotoxicology* (2000) 21(1–2), pp. 67–73.

p. 46 '. . . **a big study of juvenile offenders showed that changing their diet reduced more than half their behaviour problems** . . .': Schoenthaler, S.J., 'Diet and delinquency: empirical testing of seven theories', *International Journal of Biosocial Research* (1985) 7(2), pp. 108–131.

p. 46 '**Autism is a disorder of social interaction** . . .': for a fascinating account of autism, see *An Anthropologist on Mars* by Dr Oliver Sacks, Picador, Sydney, 1995.

p. 48 '. . . **an elimination diet with epileptic children** . . .': Egger, J. and others, 'Oligoantigenic diet treatment of children with epilepsy and migraine', *Journal of Pediatrics* (1989) 114, pp. 51–8. (See the 'Epilepsy' factsheet on www.fedup.com.au.)

Chapter 5: How many people are affected?
p. 55 '**Only a small percentage**': the figure of about 5 per cent of ADHD children is often quoted, see Conners, C.K., *Food Additives and Hyperactive Children*, Plenum, New York, 1980, which is a review of now outdated studies. Ironically, Conners himself later changed his mind.

p. 55 '. . . **practically any one of us may be [affected by additives] if we consume enough** . . .': in Weiss, B., 'Colour me hyperactive', *American Health* (May/June 1982), pp. 68–73.

p. 56 Nearly 60 per cent of parents from the Dingley school in Cheshire reported an improvement in their child, with Professor Jim Stevenson from the University of Southampton. See Martin, Nicole, 'Food additives affect concentration', *The Daily Telegraph*, 1 May 2003. http://www.spcottawa.on.ca/ofsc/food_additives.html.

p. 56 **'There can be feelings of incomplete evacuation (sticky poos) after passing a bowel motion'**: in Francis, C.Y., and Whorwelk, P.J., 'The irritable bowel syndrome', *Postgraduate Medicine* (1997) 73, pp. 1–7 and see http://www.emedicine.com/med/topic1190.htm for the Rome III criteria (2006) for the diagnosis of IBS.

p. 57 **'. . . an additive-free diet by itself would be of little benefit'** (for ADHD children): Carter, C.M. and others, 'Effects of a few food diet in attention deficit disorder', *Arch Dis Child* (1993) 69(5), pp. 564–8.

p. 57 The Few Foods diet from Britain is restricted and difficult, see study above and Pelsser, L.M., Buitelaar, J.K., 'Favourable effect of a standard elimination diet on the behavior of young children with attention deficit hyperactivity disorder (ADHD): a pilot study', *Ned Tijdschr Geneeskd* (2002) 146 (52), pp. 2543–7.

p. 58 **'. . . a prison probation officer named Barbara Reed . . .'**: described in Conners, C.K., *Feeding the Brain: How Foods Affect Children*, Plenum, New York, 1989.

p. 58 Feingold, B.F., *Why your child is hyperactive*, Random House, New York 1974

p. 58 **'. . . refined by Australian researchers'**: Swain, A.S. and others, 'Salicylates, oligoantigenic diets, and behaviour', *Lancet* (1985) 2(8445), pp. 41–2.

p. 59 Feingold, B.F., 'Dietary management of nystagmus', *J Neural Transmission* (1979) 45, pp. 107–115; Feingold, B.F., 'Recognition of food additives as a cause of symptoms of allergy', *Ann Allergy* (1968) 26, pp. 309–13, www.feingold.org.

p. 59 Developmental disorders, see the 'PDD-NOS' factsheet on www.fedup.com.au.

p. 59 **'. . . the Feingold diet achieved mixed results . . .'**: Harley, J.P., and others, 'Hyperkinesis and food additives: testing the Feingold hypothesis', *Pediatrics* (1978) 61(6), pp. 818–28.

p. 59 **'. . . new salicylate lists . . .'**: Swain, A.R., and others, 'Salicylates in foods', *Journal of the American Dietetic Association* (1985) 85, pp. 950–960.

p. 59 The problems with early research, see the ADHD factsheet on www.fedup.com.au.

p. 60 Additive-free school trials, see the 'Eating for Success' factsheet on www.fedup.com.au.

p. 61 '. . . **ADHD medication** . . .': Berbatis, G., et al, 'Licit psychostimulant consumption in Australia, 1984–2000: international and jurisdictional comparison', *MJA* (2002) 177 (10), pp. 539–543: http://www.mja.com.au/public/issues/177_10_181102/ber10505_fm.html.

p. 61 Independent scientists at the Washington-based Center for Science in the Public Interest issued a quarter-century review entitled 'Diet, ADHD and behaviour', http://www.cspinet.org/diet.html.

p. 61 Judge Conlon – 'Judge anger at Ritalin' by Janet Fife-Yeomans, *Daily Telegraph*, 26 April 2007. http://www.news.com.au/dailytelegraph/story/0,22049,21620629-5007132,00.html

p. 61 National Health and Medical Research Council guidelines regarding diet – in the report on *Attention Deficit Hyperactivity Disorder*, Australian Government Printing Service, 1997.

p. 62 Diet and avoidance of VOCs for autism – Slimak, K., 'Reduction of autistic traits following dietary intervention and elimination of exposure to environmental substances', in *Proceedings of 2003 International Symposium on Indoor Air Quality and Health Hazards*, National Institute of Environmental Health Science, USA, and *Architectural Institute of Japan*, 8–11 January 2003, Tokyo, Japan, vol 2, pp. 206–216, see http://www.immuneweb.org/articles/slimak.html. See the 'Autism' factsheet on www.fedup.com.au.

p. 63 Not only ADHD children who improve – Rowe, K.S., Rowe, K.J., 'Synthetic food coloring and behavior: a dose response effect in a double-blind, placebo-controlled, repeated-measures study', *J Pediatr* (1994) 125(5 Pt 1), pp. 691–8; McCann, D. and others, 'Food additives and hyperactive behaviour in 3-year-old and 8/9-year-old children in the community: a randomised, double-blinded, placebo-controlled trial', *The Lancet* (2007) 370(9598), pp 1560-1567. http://www.precaution.org/lib/food_additives_and_hyperactivity.070906.pdf.

p. 64 '**Contrary to the prevailing wisdom, parents were found to be reliable observers and raters of their children's behaviour** . . .': in the study by Rowe and Rowe (see Notes above).

p. 65 The Shipley Project used the Few Foods diet but failsafe eating is easier and can get the same results – Bennett, C.P.W. and others, 'The Shipley Project: Treating Food Allergy to Prevent Criminal Behaviour in Community Settings', *Journal of Nutritional & Environmental Medicine* (1998) 8(1), pp. 77–83.

p. 67 '. . . **40 per cent of children . . . could be doing much better in their schoolwork . . .**': in Bernard, M., 'International epidemic in search of solutions', *Score* (1996) 3(6), pp. 6–7.

p. 67 Low additive policy in schools – Schoenthaler, S.J., and others, 'The impact of a low food additive and sucrose diet on academic performance in 803 New York City public schools', *International Journal of Biosocial Research* (1986) (8)2, pp.185–195.

p. 67 Wolney Junior school and others, see the 'Schools Go Low Additive' factsheet on www.fedup.com.au.

p. 70 Jamie Oliver: *Jamie's School Dinners* DVD, www.jamieoliver.com.

p. 71 '. . . **decreases in attention span . . .**': attributed to declining attention spans, the sound bite – the length of time a person receives airplay on radio or television – was reduced in Australia by half in the five years to 1997, from 35 seconds to 18. In the USA sound bites were reduced from 30 seconds to 8 seconds. 'Sound nibble', *The Australian*, 13 September 1997, Focus, p. 36.

Chapter 6: Are you affected by foods?

p. 72 Allergy and intolerance – in Clarke, L., McQueen, J., Samild, A. and Swain, A., 'The dietary management of food allergy and

food intolerance in children and adults', *Australian Journal of Nutrition and Dietetics* (1996) 53(3), pp. 89–94.

p. 73 True allergy – for medical information about IgE-mediated allergy and anaphylaxis, including comprehensive allergen cards, go to www.allergyfacts.org.au.

p. 74 Laboratory tests for allergy see http://www.allergy.org.au/ aer/infobulletins/allergy_testing.htm.

p. 74 Peanut allergy and nappy rash cream – Lack, G., and others, 'Factors associated with the development of peanut allergy in childhood', *N Engl J Med* (2003) 348(11), pp. 977–85; http://sciencenewsmagazine.org/ articles/20030315/food.asp.

p. 74 Allergy and the 'Teflon chemical' – in Fairley, K.J., 'Exposure to the immuno–suppressant, perfluorooctanoic acid, enhances the murine IgE and airway hyperreactivity response to ovalbumin', *Toxicol Sci* (2007) 97(2), pp. 375–83, http://www. environmentalhealthnews.org/ newscience/2007/2007-0529 fairleyetal.html.

p. 75 Gluten sensitivity – Duggan, J.M., 'Coeliac disease: the great imitator', *Med J Aust* (2004) 180(10), pp. 524–6, free full text at http://www.mja.com.au/public/ issues/180_10_170504/dug10818_ fm.html.

p. 78 The 30 minute rule – in McDonald, J.R. and others, 'Aspirin intolerance in asthma: detection by oral challenge', *Journal of Allergy and Clinical Immunology* (1972) 50(4), pp. 198–207.

p. 79 Reaction to artificial colours on TV: *A Current Affair*, 1 June 2004.

Chapter 7: And the asthma went away

p. 88 Diet and asthma – Hodge, L. and others, 'Assessment of food chemical intolerance in adult asthmatic subjects', *Thorax* (1996) 51(8), pp. 805–9.

p. 88 Jamie Oliver in *Jamie's School Dinners*, see Notes for p. 70.

p. 89 Sulphites are most likely to affect asthmatics. This study found more than 65 per cent of asthmatic children were sulphite sensitive – Towns, S.J. and Mellis, C.M., 'Role of acetyl salicylic acid and sodium metabisulfite in chronic childhood asthma', *Pediatrics* (1984) 73(5), pp. 631–7.

p. 89 The 30-minute rule applies – see Notes for p. 78.

p. 90 **'For the majority of sulphite-sensitive asthmatics . . .'**: Corder, E. H. and Buckley, C.E., 3rd, 'Aspirin, salicylate, sulfite and tartrazine induced bronchoconstriction', *J Clin Epidemiol* (1995) 48(10), pp. 1269–75.

p. 91 Illegal sulphites in mince – NSW Food Authority 'Authority cracks down on illegal use of food preservative', *Food Safety Bytes*, Issue 3, August 2004, http://www.foodauthority.nsw.gov.au/pdf/Food-S@fety-Bytes-Issue-3-August-2004.pdf#search="MINCE".

p. 91 Possible sulphite intakes – based on maximum permitted levels according to the Food Standards Code, www.foodstandards.gov.au.

p. 91 Sulphites in meat – Bell, S., 'Social networks and innovation in the South American meat industry during the pre-refrigeration era: Southern Brazil and Uruguay in comparison', *Revista Electronica de Geographia y Ciencias Sociales*, Universidad de Barcelona, 2000, 69(84), www.ub.es/geocrit/bell_eng.htm

p. 91 Use of sulphites in meats was banned in the USA because sulphites can cause thiamine deficiency – Taylor, S.L. and others, 'Sulfites in foods', *Adv Food Res* (1986) 30, pp. 1–76; more details on p.130 and p. 320.

p. 91 Top ten asthma countries – in The International Study of Asthma and Allergies in Childhood (ISAAC) Steering Committee, 'Worldwide variation in prevalence of symptoms of asthma, allergic rhinoconjunctivitis, and atopic eczema', *Lancet* (1998) 351(9111), pp. 1225–32.

p. 92 Restaurant salad deaths – in Tollefson, L., 'Monitoring adverse reactions to food additives in the U.S. Food and Drug Administation', *Regul Toxicol Pharmacol* (1988) 8(4), pp. 438–46.

p. 92 WHO recommended reducing sulphites and revised upwards their estimate of the number of sulphite-sensitive asthmatic children from 4 per cent to 20–30 per cent – in Fifty-first meeting of the Joint FAO/WHO Expert Committee on Food Additives. 'Safety Evaluation of sulfur dioxide and sulfites' addendum, Geneva: World Health Organisation, 1999, http://www.inchem.org/documents/jecfa/jecmono/v042je06.htm.

p. 92 Food regulators working to reduce sulphites – ACT Government Health Services Food Survey Report: Rigg, A., 'Sulphur Dioxide in sausages and other products', July 1996 – March 1997: http://health.act.gov.au/c/health?a=da&did=10017393&pid=1053855655.

p. 92 The decline in asthma rates – Pearce N and others, 'Worldwide trends in the prevalence of asthma symptoms', *Thorax* (2007) 62(9), pp. 758–66.

p. 92 FDA website (note that WHO estimates for the number of children affected by sulphites has substantially increased since then) – Papazian, R., 'Sulfites: safe for most, dangerous for some', *FDA Consumer Magazine*, December 1996, http://www.fda.gov/fdac/features/096_sulf.html.

p. 92 Asthma and benzoates – in Petrus, M. and others, 'Asthmé et intolérance aux benzoates' *Arch Pédiatr* (1996) 3(10), pp. 984–7; Freedman, B. J., 'Asthma induced by sulphur dioxide, benzoate and tartrazine contained in orange drinks', *Clin Allergy* (1977) 7(5), pp. 407–15.

p. 93 Asthma and colours in the 1960s and 1970s – Speer, 1958, reported in Feingold, 1968 (see Notes for p. 59), and Chaffee, F.H. and Settipane, G.A., 'Asthma caused by FD&C approved dyes', *J Allergy* (1967) 40(2), pp. 65–72; see also Freedman on Notes for p. 92.

p. 94 CSPI (Center for Science in the Public Interest) report, see Notes for p. 60.

p. 94 Asthma and MSG – Allen, D.H. and others, 'Monosodium L-glutamate-induced asthma', *J Allergy Clin Immunol* (1987) 80(4), pp. 530–7; David Livingston, Plaintiff, versus Marie Callender's Inc., Defendant, from caselaw.findlaw.com or www.truthinlabeling.org/scripps-1.html.

p. 95 Asthma and salicylates – Jenkins, C. and others, 'Systematic review of prevalence of aspirin induced asthma and its implications for clinical practice', *BMJ* (2004) 328(7437), p. 434, http://www.bmj.com/cgi/content/full/328/7437/434;

for hospital-run trial, see Towns and Mellis, Notes for p. 89.

p. 96 Asthma and salicylates in flavours – see Feingold, 1968, Notes for p. 59.

p. 96 Asthma and laughter – Liangas, G. and others, 'Mirth-triggered asthma', *Pediatr Pulmonol* (2003) 36(2), pp. 107-12; for popcorn workers lung, http://www.defendingscience.org/case_studies/A-Case-of-Regulatory-Failure-Popcorn-Workers-Lung.cfm.

p. 97 Other additives such as sorbates, nitrate/nitrites and antioxidants are rarely mentioned in the medical literature and are less frequently a problem, but for asthmatics who are sensitive they are important: see references in the 'Asthma' factsheet on www.fedup.com.au.

p. 97 Food allergies and asthma, Beasley, R. and others, 'Has the role of atopy in the development of asthma been over-emphasized?', *Pediatr Pulmonol* (2001) Suppl 23, pp. 149–50; Turkish researchers found 4 per cent of asthmatic children affected by milk or egg allergy and commented that food challenges were more effective than laboratory tests: Yazicioğlu, M. and others, 'Egg and milk allergy in asthmatic children', *Allergol Immunopathol* (Madr) (1999) 27(6), pp. 287–93. If you have a true allergy, see individual allergen cards e.g. – 'Milk' – with all

dairy products to avoid listed at www.allergyfacts.org.au.

Chapter 8: How to eat fast food
p. 103 The five per cent labelling loophole goes on to say that additives can be unlisted if they 'no longer perform a technological function'. We lobbied for years to have this loophole closed with regard to antioxidants but had to withdraw our submission when FSANZ said they would defeat it unless we could provide proof in the form of a double-blind placebo-controlled study that antioxidants really affected our children (see lobbying letters on www.fedup.com.au).

p. 105 '. . . all the meat topping on Pizza Hut pizzas contained MSG, as did KFC chicken batter mix . . .': in 'Fast Food', *Choice*, July 1990, p. 8.

p. 105 'McDonald's provide a useful product ingredient list . . .': http://www.mcdonalds.com.au/PDFs/IngredientListing.pdf.

p. 106 'The college is very much opposed . . . to the use of aniline dyes': in Webster, Jean, *Daddy Long Legs*, Cornstalk, 1992, first published in 1912.

p. 108 Annatto and urticaria: Mikkelsen, H. and others, 'Hyper-sensitivity reactions to food colours with special reference to the natural colour annatto extract (butter colour)', *Arch Toxicol Suppl* (1978) 1, pp. 141–3.

p. 109 **'Preservatives found to cause problems . . .'**: in the Clarke paper, see Notes for p. 72; also Hanssen, M., *The New Additive Code Breaker*, Lothian, Sydney, 1991. European Union guidelines for additive health warnings in medication: http://www.foodcomm.org.uk/PDF%20files/EU_guidelines.pdf.

p. 110 **'. . . additives are on the increase . . .'**: see applications in *The Food Standard*, registered bulletin of the National Food Authority, issue 19, March 1996.

p. 111 Developmental toxicity of antioxidant BHA (320) – Vorhees, C.V. and others, 'Developmental neurobehavioral toxicity of butylated hydroxyanisole (BHA) in rats', *Neurobehav Toxicol Teratol* (1981) 3(3), pp. 321–9; Jeong, S. H. and others, 'Effects of butylated hydroxyanisole on the development and functions of reproductive system in rats', *Toxicology* (2005) 1: 208(1), pp. 49–62.

p. 112 Introduction of MSG – see a chilling account in Samuels, A., 'The toxicity/safety of processed free glutamic acid (MSG): a study in suppression of information', *Accountability in Research* (1999) 6, pp. 259–310, full text at http://truthinlabeling.org/l-manuscript.html, including 'the structure of the industry organization; an overview of their research; suppression of information; dissemination of misinformation; dirty tricks; and the special role of agencies of the United States government'. Dr Samuels started researching after she found her husband's Alzheimer symptoms were MSG-related.

p. 112 Chinese restaurant syndrome – Schaumburg, H.H. and others, 'Monosodium L-Glutamate: its pharmacology and role in the Chinese restaurant syndrome', *Science* (1969) 163, pp. 826–828.

p. 113 **"the banner 'no artificial colours or flavours'"**: see http://www.dailydave.net/viewarticle.php?postid=772.

p. 113 New flavour enhancers: the impact of glutamates on taste is intensified by a factor of 10 to 15 when used in combination with ribonucleotides 635 (a combination of disodium guanylate 627 also called GMP and disodium inosinate 631 IMP), Sommer, R., 'Yeast Extracts: production, properties and components', paper given at the 9th International Symposium on Yeasts, Sydney, August 1996.

p. 114 Caffeine per serve – from Bunker, M. L. , and McWilliams, M., 'Caffeine content of common beverages', *Journal of American Dietetic Association* (1979) 74(1), pp. 28–32.

p. 115 **'. . . teachers rated the high caffeine consumers nearly three times higher . . .'**: in Rapoport, J.L. and others, 'Behavioural effects of caffeine in children: relationship between dietary choice and effects of caffeine challenge', *Archives of General Psychiatry* (1984) 41, pp. 1073–1076.

p. 117 **'How aspartame was approved'**: described in Chapter Two of Dr C. Keith Conners (1990), see Notes above for p. 58. Italian aspartame studies, see Ramazzini Foundation, http://www.ramazzini. it/fondazione/blogDetail.asp?id=22.

p. 118 **'Americans are leading the way in the obnoxious children stakes . . .'**: In 1996 in the USA, more than 2900 juveniles were arrested for murder or manslaughter, about double the number from a decade earlier – US Department of Justice statistics.

p. 119 Scottish diet one of the world's worst – in a 2004 World Health Organization survey, Scottish children were in the top ranks in Europe for consumption of fizzy drinks and sweets. http://news.bbc. co.uk/1/hi/scotland/3774081.stm.

p. 119 First University of Southampton study – Bateman, B., and others, 'The effects of a double blind, placebo controlled, artificial food colourings and benzoate preservative challenge on hyperactivity in a general population sample of preschool children', *Arch Dis Child* (2004) 89(6), pp. 506–11.

p. 119 EU health warnings, which must appear on package leaflets when additives are used in medication, is applied to artificial colours and the following preservatives: sorbates, benzoates, sulphites, BHA (320) and BHT (321): http://www.foodcomm.org. uk/PDF%20files/EU_guidelines.pdf

p. 119 Second University of Southampton study – McCann D., and others, see Notes for p. 63.

Chapter 9: What's wrong with fruit and other healthy foods?

p. 121 Fruit eating increased from 70–90 kg per person per year during the 1930s to 1960s, to nearly 130 kg in the 1990s, according to data from the Apparent Consumption of Foodstuffs and Nutrients 1993/94, Australian Bureau of Statistics.

p. 123 **'People have died from a single 300 mg dose of aspirin . . .'**: in Rainsford, K.D., *Aspirin and the Salicylates*, Butterworths, London, 1984.

p. 123 Salicylates and children: Fitzsimon, M. and others, 'Salicylate sensitivity in children reported to respond to salicylate exclusion', *Med J Aust* (1978) 2(12), pp. 570–2.

p. 123 Effects of natural and artificial flavours – Feingold, B.F., (1968), see Notes for p. 59.

p. 124 **'Salicylates generally affect the majority of those with irritable bowel symptoms, headaches and rashes . . .'**: in Loblay, R.H. and Swain, A.R., 'Food intolerance', in Wahlqvist, M.L. and Truswell, A.S., editors, *Recent Advances in Clinical Nutrition*, John Libbey, London, 1986, pp. 169–177.

'although only about 20 per cent of asthmatics' – higher when determined by oral challenges rather than asking asthmatics, lower in children – in Jenkins, C. and others, 'Systematic review of prevalence of aspirin induced asthma and its implications for clinical practice', *BMJ* (2004) 328(7437), pp. 434–40, http://www.bmj.com/cgi/content/full/328/7437/434.

p. 125 Salicylate contents in foods – there are many salicylate lists on the internet, e.g. http://www.purr.demon.co.uk/Food/Salicylate.html. Most contain mistakes (e.g. fresh green peas should be 0.04) and don't list amines and glutamates. For an up-to-date chart of salicylates, amines and glutamates in foods see *Friendly Food: The Essential Guide to Avoiding Allergies, Additives and Problem Chemicals* by Swain, Anne R., Soutter, Velencia L., Loblay, Robert H., Royal Prince Alfred Hospital Allergy Unit, Murdoch Books, Sydney, 2004 (www.cs.nsw.gov.au/rpa/allergy). See also the 'Salicylate' factsheet on www.fedup.com.au.

p. 127 '. . . children of **Mediterranean families are five times more likely than others to be born with a "difficult temperament"** . . .': and parallel data collected on Greek infants living in Greece showed a similarly raised incidence of difficult temperament, reported in Prior, M.A., Sanson, A. and Oberklaid, F., 'The Australian Temperament Project', in Kohnstamn, G.A. and others, editors, *Temperament in Childhood*, Wiley, Chichester UK, 1989, pp. 537–554.

p. 130 Sulphites and thiamine deficiency – use of sulphites in meats was banned in the USA in 1959 because sulphites can cause thiamine deficiency. A dose of 1000 ppm (parts per million) of sulphites will inactivate 95 per cent of thiamine not only in the sulphited food but also in other foods or vitamin supplements taken at the same time. Dried fruit can contain the highest doses of sulphites, with up to 3000 ppm. Australian veterinarians say 'It could be effectively argued that sulphite preservatives are actually "drugs" . . . the implications of thiamine deficiency are sufficiently severe that they should be considered a life-threatening adverse drug reaction'. Malik, R. and Sibra, D., 'Thiamine deficiency due to sulphur dioxide in "pet meat" – a case of déjà vu', *Australian Veterinary Journal* (2005) 83(7), pp. 408–411, http://www.catvet.com.au/articles/thiamine_deficiency_pdf.pdf.

Chapter 10: How do you get difficult children to eat failsafe?
p. 133 '. . . the most entertaining and useful introduction to behaviour management . . .': for details of *1-2-3 Magic* see p. 328.

p. 134 '**Children who are unhappy at school** . . .': see Irvine, J., *Who'd be a Parent?*, MacMillan, Sydney,

1998. See also the ten rules of effective punishment without raising your hand or your voice at http://www.parentlink.act.gov.au/parenting_guides/dr_john/punishment.

p. 135 **'Diet detectives'**: in Breakey, J.M. and others, 'A report on a trial of the low additive, low salicylate diet in the treatment of behaviour and learning problems in children', *Aust J Nutr Diet* (1991) 48(3), pp. 89-94, http://www.ozemail.com.au/~breakey.

p. 138 **'Psychologist Steve Biddulph recommends . . .'**: in *Raising Boys*, (Finch, 1997), http://www.stevebiddulph.com/raising-boys.htm.

p. 139 **'McDonald's is "exploiting children" through its advertising . . .'**: for more details of the McLibel trial see Vidal, J., *McLibel: Burger Culture on Trial*, Pan, London, 1997 and the website http://www.mcspotlight.org/.

p. 139 Coughlan, A., 'Junk Food Ads target the young', *New Scientist* (1996) 2058:8.

p. 142 **'Families who see results with diet will stick to it . . .'**: follow-up on families using diet in Egger J. and others, 'Controlled trial of oligoantigenic treatment in the hyperkinetic syndrome', *The Lancet* (1985) 1(8428), pp 540-5 and in Conners (1980), see Notes for p. 55.

Chapter 11: Non-food factors

p. 144 Adverse effects of healthcare – Starfield, B., 'Is US health really the best in the world?', *JAMA* (2000) 284(4), pp. 483–5, http://www.health-care-reform.net/causedeath.htm; and see the 'Medication' factsheet on www.fedup.com.au.

p. 145 Drugs and autism – Miller, M.T. and others, 'Autism with ophthalmologic malformation', *Trans Am Ophthalmol Soc.* (2004) 102, pp. 107–20, http://www.pubmedcentral.nih.gov/articlerender.fcgi?tool=pubmed&pubmedid=15747750.

p. 145 Probiotics – Kajander, K., 'Korpela Clinical studies on alleviating the symptoms of irritable bowel syndrome', *Asia Pac J Clin Nutr* (2006) 15(4), pp. 576–80. Flatulence: LeBlanc, J.G. and others, 'Reduction of alpha-galactooligosaccharides in soymilk', *J Appl Microbiol* (2004) 97(4), pp. 876–81. Probiotics and eczema – Rosenfeldt, V. and others, 'Effect of probiotic Lactobacillus strains in children with atopic dermatitis', *Allergy Clin Immunol* (2003) 111(2), pp. 389–95. Kefir and allergies – Je-Ruei Liu and others, 'The anti-allergenic properties of milk kefir and soymilk kefir and their beneficial effects on the intestinal microflora', *J Sci Food Agric* (2006) 86(15), pp. 2527–2533: http://www.sciencedaily.com/releases/2006/10/061015213714.htm. Also see the 'Probiotics' factsheet at www.fedup.com.au.

p. 146 Vaccination – a survey showed a 22-fold increased risk of measles and six-fold increased risk of whooping cough (pertussis) for an individual unvaccinated child – in McIntyre, P. and others, 'Refusal of parents to vaccinate: dereliction of duty or legitimate personal choice?', *MJA* (2003) 178 (4), pp. 150–151, http://www.mja.com.au/public/issues/178_04_170203/mci10747_fm.html.

p. 147 Sunlight – van der Mei, I.A. and others, 'Past exposure to sun, skin phenotype, and risk of multiple sclerosis: case-control study', *BMJ* (2003) 327(7410):316, http://www.abc.net.au/catalyst/stories/s1048944.htm.

p. 148 Breastfeeding – http://www.breastfeeding.asn.au/bfinfo/general.html.

p. 148 Vulnerability of the elderly – see Weiss (2000) in Notes for p. 311.

p. 150 *1-2-3 Magic* from American psychologist Thomas Phelan. DVD or book available from www.parentmagic.com or www.parentshop.com.au and the course is offered by many community centers.

p. 150 The gift of time – Judy Radich's stay-at-home quote from Eccleson, Roy, 'The dumb country' *The Bulletin*, 3 April 2007, p. 43; Ruth Schmidt Neven is director of Melbourne's Center for Child and Family Development; Mrs Kennedy's quote from http://www.whitehouse.gov/history/firstladies/jk35.html; Rebuilding a positive relationship with your child – Dr Russell Barkley in *Managing Life with ADHD*, Guilford Press, New York, 1995.

p. 151 Home schooling – school teacher and Pulitzer prize-winning author David Guterson suggests that home schooling allows children to develop a more balanced set of relationships – 'my students' parents have often expressed dismay at how school has shaped their children', referring to the alienation of children from parents and the unnatural massing of children with their own age group – in his book *Family Matters,* published in 1993, but still considered by many to be the finest book ever on home schooling. 'If I had read this book before my eldest entered kindergarten, we would have started home schooling years ago' said one mother – Guterson, David, *Family Matters: Why Home Schooling Makes Sense*, Harvest, 1993. For how to home school see 'Getting Started' articles on the Home Education Association website: www.hea.asn.au.

p. 153 Sensitivity to perfumes: Caress, S.M., Steinemann, A.C., 'A national population study of the prevalence of multiple chemical sensitivity', *Arch Environ Health* (2004) 59(6), pp. 300–5.

p. 153 Don't clean! – Farrow, A. and others, 'Symptoms of mothers and infants related to total volatile organic compounds in household products', *Arch Environ Health* (2003) 58(10), pp. 633–41; Sherriff, A. and others, 'Frequent use of chemical household products is associated with persistent wheezing in pre-school age children', *Thorax* (2005) 60(1), pp. 45-9; also Anderson, R.C. and Anderson, P.J., 'Acute toxic effects of fragrances,' *Arch Environ Health* (1998) 53(2), pp. 138–46.

p. 153. Chemicals as sensitisers – some scientists think that acute or chronic exposure to manmade industrial chemicals can result in loss of tolerance and consequent triggering of symptoms such as migraine, headaches, depression, chronic fatigue syndrome and fibromyalgia by small quantities of previously tolerated chemicals (traffic exhaust, fragrances, gasoline), foods and drugs: Miller, C.S., 'The compelling anomaly of chemical intolerance', *Ann N Y Acad Sci* (2001) 933, pp. 1–23; Ziem, G. and McTamney, J., 'Profile of patients with chemical injury and sensitivity', *Environ Health Perspect* (1997) 105 Suppl 2, pp. 417–36; http://www.pubmedcentral.nih.gov/articlerender.fcgi?tool=pubmed&pubmedid=9167975.

p. 153 Jonathan Wilson-Fuller's story appears in the book, *Will You Please Listen: I Have Something To Say*, ABC, Sydney, 1990 and on the website www.jwff.zip.com.au.

p. 154 VOCs in blankets, houses, cars – Burke, K., 'Carcinogenic blanket recall', *Sydney Morning Herald*, 8 June 2007, http://www.smh.com.au/news/national/carcinogenic-blanket-recall/2007/06/07/1181089242127.html; Edwards, R., 'When a new house is positively sickening', *New Scientist*, 10 March 2001, p. 20; 'Sick auto syndrome', *New Scientist*, 12 January 2002, p. 11.

p. 154 VOCs in computers – triphenyl phosphate emissions from the plastic of your computer's video monitor may be affecting your health: http://www.sciencedaily.com/releases/2000/09/000919080653.htm.

p. 155 The NSW adult health survey 2002, NSW Public Health, p.82: http://www.health.nsw.gov.au/public-health/phbsup/adult_health_survey.pdf.

p. 156 'Chemical sensitivity can result . . .': Center for Children's Health and the Environment (CCHE) of the Mount Sinai School of Medicine, www.childenvironment.org.

p. 156 White, R.F. and Proctor, S.P., 'Solvents and Neurotoxicity', *Lancet* (1997), 349, pp. 1239–1242.

p. 158 Nitrates and cancer: 'the risk of colorectal cancer increases by 21 per cent for every 50 grams of processed meat eaten every day on average' according to the 2007 report from the World Cancer Research Fund, www.wcrf-uk.org.

p. 158 Chemicals to avoid in the longer term – the friendliest site I have found on this topic is the Body of Evidence project in Maine, see introduction at www.cleanand healthyme.org or go straight to the chemicals to avoid; also, Collin and Michelle are building a non-toxic sustainable home in Canberra, http://members.pcug.org.au/~chowell/buildsust.htm.

p. 159 Phthalates in beauty products: http://www.cleanand healthyme.org/BodyBurdenReport/TheChemicals/Phthlates/tabid/96/Default.aspx.

p. 159 Some good news – blood lead levels are dropping, see the heartwarming graph at http://amwac.health.nsw.gov.au/public-health/chorep02/env/env_bloodpb.pdf; and the PCB story *Our Stolen Future* by Theo Colborn and others, Abacus, London, 1996, p. 187; also http://www.oregon.gov/DHS/ph/envtox/pcbs.shtml. See how pregnant women can avoid these effects on their children in Myers, P., *Good genes gone bad*, *American Prospect*, April 2006, http://www.ourstolenfuture.org/Commentary/JPM/2006-0401goodgenesgonebad.html.

Chapter 12: Failsafe eating

p. 180 Don't take drugs unless necessary – see the Public Citizen health research group – http://www.citizen.org/hrg/ – and for healthcare providers who 'dare to say no to drug company reps' go to www.nofreelunch.org. Also see the

'Medication' factsheet on www.fedup.com.au.

p. 183 **'Our bodies have their own defences . . .'** See Werner, D., *Where There is No Doctor*, Herperian, 2007, claimed to be 'perhaps the most widely used health care manual in the world', Chapter 5: Healing without Medicines, http://hesperian.info/assets/WTND/WTND_Chapter_5.pdf.

p. 184 Food-induced constipation – Carroccio, A. Iacono, G., 'Review article: Chronic constipation and food hypersensitivity – an intriguing relationship', *Aliment Pharmacol Ther* (2006) 24(9), pp. 1295–304.

p. 186 losing weight – Raynor and others, 'Television Viewing and Long-Term Weight Maintenance: Results from the National Weight Control Registry', *Obesity Research* (2006) 14(10), pp. 1816–1824; Klem, M.L. and others, 'A descriptive study of individuals successful at long-term maintenance of substantial weight-loss', *American Journal of Clinical Nutrition* (1997) 66 pp. 239–246, http://www.nwcr.ws/Research/published%20research.htm.

p. 190 Antinutritional effects of food additives – Stammati, A. and others, 'In vitro model for the evaluation of toxicity and antinutritional effects of sulphites', *Food Addit Contam* (1992) 9(5), pp. 551–60; also Steel, R.J.S., 'Thiamine deficiency in a cat associated with the preservation of "pet meat" with sulphur dioxide', *Aust Vet J* (1997) 75, pp. 719–721; Koutsogeorgopoulou and others, 'Immunological aspects of the common food colorants, amaranth and tartrazine', *Vet Hum Toxicol* (1998) 40(1) pp. 1–4. Propionic acid causes in vitro immuno-suppression, Wajner, M. and others, 'Inhibition of mitogen-activated proliferation of human peripheral lymphocytes in vitro by propionic acid', *Clin Sci* (Lond) (1999) 96(1), pp. 99–103.

p. 190 Salicylates and Vitamin C compete for excretion in the kidney – Basu, T.K., 'Vitamin C-aspirin interactions', *Int J Vitam Nutr Res Suppl* (1982) 23, pp. 83–90.

p. 192 'changes in essential nutrients' – Lobstein, T., 'Plants lose their value', *Food Magazine* (Jan/Mar 2004) 64, pp. 12–13, www.foodcomm.org.uk/PDF%20file s/plants_lose_value.pdf; 'Meat and dairy: where have the minerals gone?', *Food Magazine* (Jan/Mar 2006) 72, www.foodcomm.org. uk/PDF%20files/meat_dairy2.pdf; 'Vegetables without Vitamins', *Life Extension Magazine*, March 2001, www.lef.org/LEFCMS/aspx/Print VersionMagic.aspx?CmsID=34628; bagged salads, Serafini and others, *Br J Nutr* (2002) 88(6), pp. 615–23.

p. 192 Folate (also called folic acid) is probably the most common vitamin deficiency according to nutritionist Dr Rosemary Stanton in *Eating for Peak Performance*, HarperCollins, Sydney, 1998. For more about folate and pregnancy, ask your doctor, dietitian or see the Folate report at www.choice.com.au.

p. 192 Organic gardening more nutritious, higher in salicylates – see Nutritional Considerations by the Organic Trade Association, 2006, http://www.ota.com/ organic/benefits/nutrition.html.

p. 193 Introducing food to babies – Australasian Society of Clinical Immunology and Allergy, http:// www.allergy.org.au/aer/infobulletins/ food_allergy.htm; for gluten introduction while breastfeeding: Guandalini, S., 'The influence of gluten: weaning recommendations for healthy children and children at risk for coeliac disease', *Nestlé Nutr Workshop Ser Pediatr Program* (2007) 60, pp. 139–55, see http:// content.karger.com/ProdukteDB/ produkte.asp?Doi=106366; salicylate contents from Swain and others, 1984, see Notes for p. 59.

p. 194 failsafebaby group/dietitian – email 'subscribe' to failsafebaby-subscribe@yahoogroups.com. Write for our list of supportive dietitians to confoodnet@ozemail.com.au.

Chapter 13: Failsafe recipes

p. 196 'The food industry has worked hard to turn you into a flavour junkie . . .': see McBride, R., *The Bliss Point Factor*, Sun MacMillan, Melbourne, 1990 for an explanation of the cynical food industry viewpoint by an insider. You don't have to be manipulated. You can reset your bliss point!

p. 206 Chemicals in canned food –
http://www.cleanandhealthyme.org/
BodyBurdenReport/TheChemicals/
BisphenolA/tabid/99/Default.aspx.

p. 293 Gluten intolerance and
coeliac disease, see p. 75.

p. 293 Some varieties of oats
previously thought to contain gluten
are suitable for coeliacs if free of
wheat contamination during
growing and processing, see
Shopping List for contamination-
free oats, Garsed, K., and Scott
B.B., 'Can oats be taken in a
gluten-free diet?' *Scand J
Gastroenterol* (2007) 42(2),
pp. 171-8.

Support and further information

The Food Intolerance Network at www.fedup.com.au provides:
- independent information about the effects of food on behaviour, health and learning ability in both children and adults
- support for families using a low-chemical approach, free of additives, low in salicylates, amines and flavour enhancers (failsafe) for health, behaviour and learning problems.

Quarterly **Failsafe Newsletters** are available free (email with 'subscribe' in the subject line to failsafe_newsletter-subscribe@yahoogroups.com) or can be seen on the website.

You can join one of several free failsafe support groups, where experienced people can provide information and assistance. Special groups include failsafebaby, failsafeadult and failsafeasthma. See **email support groups** on www.fedup.com.au for up-to-date information.

There are many local contacts and regional email groups that can provide information about local foods and dietitians. See **local contacts** and **email support groups** on www.fedup.com.au.

For our list of supportive dietitians, email confoodnet@ozemail.com.au. Also see the DAA (Dietitians Association of Australia) website and look for those who have listed Allergy and Intolerance as an area of practice: http://www.daa. asn.au/find_a_dietitian/index.asp?pageID=2145835649. Hospital and community dietitians can sometimes be supportive.

Books

General information about food intolerances, along with comprehensive charts showing the content of natural salicylates, amines and glutamate in most common foods is available in *Friendly Food* by Anne Swain, Velencia Soutter and Robert Loblay, Murdoch Books, Australia, 2004. *Friendly Food* and additional information about the RPAH Elimination Diet and challenge protocols can be obtained online via the RPAH Allergy Unit website (www.cs.nsw.gov.au/rpa/allergy).

Sue Dengate, *The Failsafe Cookbook: reducing food chemicals for calm, happy families*, Random House, Australia, 2007, ISBN 9781741668766.

Bill Statham, *The Chemical Maze: Shopping Companion*, Griffin Press, 2005, ISBN 9780957853539 (available at www.thechemicalmaze.com and through bookstores).

Julie Eady, *Additive Alert: Your guide to safer shopping*, Additive Alert Pty Ltd, 2004, ISBN 9780977517619 (available at www.additivealert.com.au and through bookstores).

Sue Dengate's earlier books are now out of print but may be found in many public libraries. They are: *Different Kids: Growing Up with Attention Deficit Disorder*, Random House, Australia, 1994, ISBN 9780091830519; *Fed Up with Asthma: How food affects asthma and what you can do about it*, Random House, Australia, 2003, ISBN 9781740510561. *Fed Up with ADHD: How food affects children and what you can do about it*, Random House, Australia, 2004, ISBN 9781740512305.

DVDs

Fed Up with Children's Behaviour: How food and additives affect behaviour, Sue Dengate, 2006, ISBN 9780646459257 (available through www.fedup.com.au, Australia Online Bookstore www.bookworm.com.au, Capers Bookstore www.capersbookstore.com.au, or by ordering at any Angus & Robertson bookstore).

1-2-3 Magic: managing difficult behaviour in children 2–12, Dr Thomas Phelan, 2004, ISBN 9781889140162 (available from www.parentmagic.com or in Australia from www.parentshop.com.au).

Scientific references

There is a detailed list of current scientific references on www.fedup.com.au.

What can I do to help?

- Become a food warrior – email food and drug manufacturers, tell them you refuse to buy any products that contain harmful additives.
- Join our email newsletter and be counted as a supporter: email 'subscribe' to failsafe_newsletter-subscribe@yahoogroups.com.
- Help make food safety a political issue – write and talk to your local parliamentary representative using the policy guidelines below.

Policy issues and responses

Education: cutting down food additives has been shown to improve children's behaviour and learning and to improve school functioning
- All schools should phase out harmful additives so as to improve education outcomes.

Health: cutting down on food additives has been shown to improve a very wide range of children's and adult's health problems, including major health budget items like asthma.
- Harmful food additives should be systematically removed from the Australian food system to benefit the nation's health.

Regulatory processes: food additives are not tested for their effects on children's behaviour or learning before approval, despite overwhelming evidence of effects, nor are they tested on children before approval.
- Food additives should be publicly assessed for their effects on children's health, behaviour and learning before approval, and withdrawn or not approved if shown to be harmful during approval or in systematic monitoring afterwards.

In the EU, drugs containing many additives used in food have to carry warning labels. In Australia/New Zealand the five per cent labelling loophole means that many additives are hidden.
- All food additives should be shown on food and drug labels so that consumers can make an informed choice.

Research funding: responsibility for research on the impact of food and food additives is not accepted by either regulators or the food industry.
- Independent research funding from a new food industry levy should be applied to food issues in consultation with regulators and consumers.

Index

Food additives to avoid (see also p. 166)

COLOURS
Natural colour annatto (bixin, norbixin) 160b
Artificial colours 102, 104, 107, 110, 122, 123, 124, 127, 128, 129, 132, 133, 142, 143, 151, 155

Allura red 129 (red 40 in USA)
Amaranth 123 (red 2 in USA)
Azorubine red, carmoisine 122
Brilliant Black 151
Brilliant Blue 133 (blue 1 in USA)
Brown 155
Erythrosine 127 (red 3 in USA)
Fast Green 143
Green S 142 (green 3 in USA)
Indigotine 132 (blue 2 in USA)
Ponceau 4R 124 (red 4 in USA)
Quinoline yellow 104
Sunset yellow 110 (yellow 6 in USA)
Tartrazine 102 (yellow 5 in USA)
Yellow 2G 107

USED IN a wide range of sweet and savoury foods, drinks, confectionery, medicines, USA breakfast cereals. Rarely used in Europe.

PRESERVATIVES
Sorbates 200–203
Calcium sorbate 203
Potassium sorbate 202
Sodium sorbate 201
Sorbic acid 200

USED IN
processed fruit and vegetables products, drinks, cheese, ice-cream, breads and pasta, processed meats, dips, sauces, wine.

Benzoates 210–219, especially 211 in soft drinks
Benzoic acid 210
Calcium benzoate 213
Potassium benzoate 212
Sodium benzoate 211
Ethyl 4-hydroxy-benzoate 214,
Sodium ethyl 4-hydroxy-benzoate 215,
Propylparaben 216,
Sodium propylparaben 217,
Methyl paraben 218,
Sodium methylparaben 219, permitted in food colours, ointments and medicines in Australia and New Zealand

USED IN most soft drinks, diet drinks, cordials, juice drinks. Also in semi-preserved fish products, desserts, dips and snacks.

Sulphites 220–228
Calcium hydrogen sulphite 227
Calcium sulphite 226
Potassium bisulphite 228
Potassium metabisulphite 224
Potassium sulphite 225
Sodium bisulphite 222
Sodium metabisulphite 223
Sodium sulphite 221
Sulphur dioxide 220

USED IN wine, beer, bread, processed meat like sausages, seafood like prawns, prepared salads, fruit salads, fruit and vegetable products like drinks. Very high in most dried fruits.

Nitrates and nitrites 249–252
Potassium nitrate 252
Potassium nitrite 249
Sodium nitrate 251
Sodium nitrite 250

USED IN processed meats like ham, salami, devon, and in cheese.

Propionates 280–283, especially 282 in bread
Calcium propionate 282
Potassium propionate 283
Propionic acid 280
Sodium propionate 281

USED IN many breads in Australia and the USA, and in cheese, jam, fruit and vegetable products. Very rare in Europe. Also added as fermented whey powder.

SYNTHETIC ANTIOXIDANTS
Antioxidants 310–321
BHA 320
BHT 321
Dodecyl gallate 312
Octyl gallate 311
Propyl gallate 310
TBHQ 319

USED IN oils and margarines to prevent rancidity, chips, fried snack foods, fast foods. Not necessarily listed on labels where vegetable oil is a component.

FLAVOUR ENHANCERS
Glutamates 620–637, 640, 641 (MSG is 621)
Calcium dihydrogen diglutamate 623
Disodium guanylate 627
Disodium inosinate 631
Ethyl maltol 637
Glycine 640
L-Glutamic acid 620
L-leucine 641

Magnesium diglutamate 625

Dodecyl gallate 312

Maltol 636

Monoammonium glutamate 624

Monopotassium glutamate 622

Monosodium glutamate 621

Ribonucleotides 635

USED IN tasty foods like flavoured noodles, snack foods, chips, crackers, sauces and fast foods. Glutamates are in hydrolysed vegetable (HVP) and plant protein, yeast extract, caseinate, broth, stock, soy sauce and 'natural flavourings'.

ARTIFICIAL FLAVOURS

No numbers since they are trade secrets

USED IN many foods, particularly where flavour has been damaged by processing.

Names and numbers from Australia New Zealand Food Standards Code (to Amendment 87, 2006). The letter E preceding a number (e.g. E102) stands for European regulations, but the numbers are the same.

If you have found *Fed Up* helpful, see over
for information about *The Failsafe Cookbook*
and the DVD *Fed Up with Children's Behaviour*,
both by Sue Dengate

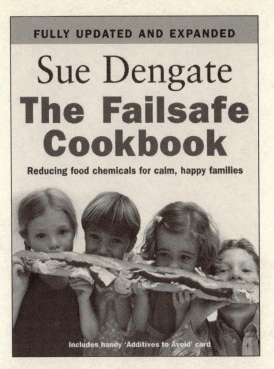

FULLY UPDATED AND EXPANDED

Sue Dengate
The Failsafe Cookbook

Reducing food chemicals for calm, happy families

Includes handy 'Additives to Avoid' card

In this long-awaited, fully revised and expanded edition of *The Failsafe Cookbook*, Sue Dengate has compiled hundreds of new and improved recipes for all kinds of occasions, as well as up to the minute information about food intolerance and elimination diets.

With the help of these tasty, healthy and easy-to-follow recipes for breakfasts, lunches, main meals and desserts, through to food for special occasions, vegetarian cooking and gluten-free food, you and your family can be free of a wide range of health and behavioural problems.

An essential tool for parents wanting a calmer, happier – and healthier – family.

'Thank you for writing your fantastic cookbook, I'm SO grateful for the simple, family friendly recipes.' – Kirsty, South Australia

Available from all good bookshops

ISBN 978 1 74166 876 6

This lively DVD is Sue Dengate's famous presentation about the effects of food on children's health, learning and behaviour, released in 2006. Families throughout Australia and New Zealand, from young children to grandmothers, were interviewed about their surprises, pitfalls, horror stories, cute kids, laughs, determination and triumph through tears in finding which foods affect their children.

More than 10,000 people have attended Sue's talks over the past three years. Mothers who have seen this DVD say it really helped them to manage their diet successfully.

'Wow!!! Hearing Sue speak was probably the most enlightening experience I have had this year, if not this decade.' – Eleanor, Australian Capital Territory

Available from www.fedup.com.au.
ISBN 978 0646 459257

Nasty additives
wallet list

Cut out along lines as shown, laminate the card, and keep in your wallet or purse. Alternatively, photocopy pages, cut out cards and stick together. For more copies of this card, please see www.fedup.com.au.

Nasty additives
www.fedup.com.au

COLOURS

Artificial

102 tartrazine	129 allura red
104 quinoline yellow	132 indigotine, indigo carmine
107 yellow 2G	133 brilliant blue
110 sunset yellow	142 green S, food green, acid brilliant green
122 azorubine, carmoisine	151 brilliant black
123 amaranth	155 brown, chocolate brown
124 ponceau, brilliant scarlet	
127 erythrosine	**Natural**
128 red 2G	160b annatto, bixin, norbixin

PRESERVATIVES

200–203 sorbic acid, all sorbates
210–219 benzoic acid, all benzoates
220–228 sulphur dioxide,
        all sulphites, bisulphites,
        metabisulphites
249–252 all nitrates and nitrites
280–283 propionic acid,
        all propionates

SYNTHETIC ANTIOXIDANTS

310–312 all gallates
319–321 TBHQ, BHA (butylated
        hydroxyanisole), BHT (butylated
        hydroxytoluene)

FLAVOUR ENHANCERS

620–625 glutamic acid and all
        glutamates, MSG
        (monosodium glutamate)
627 disodium guanylate
631 disodium inosinate
635 ribonucleotides
Yeast extract, HVP HPP
        (hydrolysed vegetable or
        plant protein)

FLAVOURS

No numbers since they are
        trade secrets